AN
UNEXPLAINED
DEATH

AN
UNEXPLAINED
DEATH

The True Story of a Body at the Belvedere

MIKITA BROTTMAN

CANONGATE

First published in Great Britain in 2018 by Canongate Books Ltd,
14 High Street, Edinburgh EH1 1TE

canongate.co.uk

1

First published by Henry Holt and Company, 175 Fifth Avenue,
New York, NY 10010

British Library Cataloguing-in-Publication Data
A catalogue record for this book is available on
request from the British Library

ISBN 978 1 78689 263 8
Export ISBN 978 1 78689 265 2

Designed by Kelly S. Too

Printed and bound in Great Britain by Clays Ltd, Elcograf S.p.A.

Author's Note

In order to maintain privacy, I have changed the names and identifying characteristics of certain people. Conversations have been reconstructed to the best of my recollection, some from notes and recorded interviews, and others from court transcripts and legal documents.

Then I turned like a man, intent
on making out what he must run from
undone by sudden fear,
who does not slow his flight
for all his looking back:
just so I caught a glimpse of some dark devil
running toward us up the ledge.

Dante, *Inferno*, XXI, 25–31

I

MY BULLDOG IS only ten months old. He still needs to go out early in the morning, while it is dark. I get out of bed, put on my sandals, pick him up, and, in my nightdress, quietly leave my apartment and press the button for the elevator. In the lobby, we slip silently past the concierge, asleep in his chair behind the desk, and out into the morning. Although the sun has not yet risen, the air is already warm.

I see strange things at this hour. Once I saw five rats walking toward me, one in front of the other, right in the middle of the street.

The poster is new. I notice it right away, taped to a utility pole. Beneath the word "Missing," printed in a bold, high-impact font, are two sepia-toned photographs of a man dressed in a bow tie and tux. One shows a close-up of his face; the other is shot from medium distance, showing his head and shoulders. He looks like an old-fashioned movie idol. Under the images are the details.

Name: Rey O. Rivera. Age: 32. Description: 6′5″, brown hair, brown eyes, 260 lbs. Last Seen: Tuesday, May 16, six p.m. Leaving home (Northwood neighborhood) to run errands in his wife's car. Wearing pullover jacket, shorts, and flip-flops. Carrying $20 in cash, no bank cards. There's the name of a detective in the missing persons division, a phone number to call, and a $1,000 reward for information leading to Rey Rivera's safe return.

The poster intrigues me. Rey Rivera parts his hair on the left. He has a slightly bashful smile. In the medium close-up photo, you can just see the trace of a flower in his buttonhole. Not a rose or a carnation; something less traditional—a sprig of jasmine, perhaps. He's so tall and handsome I find it difficult to believe he's gone missing. But then I realize I've rarely seen a "Missing" poster for an unappealing or angry-looking person. People on "Missing" posters generally look happy and beautiful because whoever makes the posters chooses the best pictures they can find. Often, they're professional portraits taken at a prom, graduation, or wedding. To grab your attention, missing people have to possess a certain allure. They have to mesmerize you.

A student, Rachel, went missing when I was at college. I didn't even know she had gone until I noticed the posters. The last person to see her was her boyfriend, John. He told the police that after visiting Rachel, he went to the train station, and Rachel went with him. Waiting for his train, they ran into someone Rachel knew—a friendly, long-haired young man who offered her a ride home.

It didn't escape notice that John had long hair himself.

The next time I saw my tutor, I asked whether there had been any news about Rachel. It seemed the polite thing to do, the way you might ask about someone's sick mother. I was expecting a friendly platitude. *Fingers crossed!* But my tutor's answer made me catch my breath.

"They won't find her alive," she said.

My tutor was the kindest person I've ever known. When I missed my tutorial because I had strep throat, she came to my dormitory, sat down on the bed beside me, and placed her hand on my hot brow.

"The police gave us all the facts about missing people," she explained. "They said it's extremely rare that responsible people disappear the way Rachel did, without even taking their purse. But when they do, if they're not found the same day, they have almost no chance of being found alive. The police said now it's just a matter of finding her body. They're about to trawl the river."

She was right. Rachel's body was found eighteen days after she first went missing. John, it appeared, had strangled her in a fit of jealous passion. He'd spent hours looking around her house for a place to hide the body. Eventually, he'd found an eight-inch gap at the back of a closet under the stairs crammed with household junk. After emptying the cupboard of its contents, he'd pushed Rachel's body through the gap into the recess and under the floor.

He'd then stretched out on his belly, pushed the dead body in front of him, and pulled himself along through the cavity until he was all the way under the floorboards of Rachel's bedroom. After eighteen days in this small, hot space, Rachel's body had partially mummified.

Full urban mummification is not as common as you might think. It requires a particular set of circumstances. Not only does the environment have to be either extremely hot or extremely cold, with low humidity and good ventilation, but also these conditions have to remain stable during the several years it takes for mummification to occur. Urban mummies are formed only when a person dies in a home with the right kind of atmospheric conditions, and only if the death goes undetected for a long time. In one recent case, the mummified bodies of a sixty-three-year-old German woman, her neurologically impaired thirty-four-year-old son, and their German shepherd dog were found preserved in their home in Florida. The cause of death was determined to be an overdose of benzodiazepines. The mother had administered the drugs, dissolved in liquid, first to her son and then to their dog, laying the pair out to die on twin beds beside each other. She left a handwritten note in German, which translated as "God's perfection now finds expression through my body." The trio's mummified cadavers were found four years later. Mother was lying on the kitchen floor, clad in a dressing gown surrounded by insect larva cases, her eyeglasses adjacent to her head, a full brown wig resting gently on her bare skull.

The posters of Rey Rivera multiply. The reward has now been increased to $5,000. Walking down Charles Street in the morning, I point one out to D., who recalls how, as a young boy, he used to hear about men who went out to buy a packet of cigarettes and never came back. They usually turned out to be supporting another family in another town, he tells me. Either that, or they had just walked away from their wife and kids and gone to start life over again in another state. D. says you never hear about men doing that anymore.

I wonder: Why was it always a packet of cigarettes? What if they didn't smoke?

As soon as you go missing, according to the FBI's National Crime Information Center, the chances of your survival start to diminish rapidly. Still, there are miraculous exceptions. A small percentage of people who have been missing for years manage to reach out from whatever dark world they now inhabit and leave signs for friends and family to decipher: a garbled, untraceable phone call, a scrawled message on a dollar bill, a note scratched in red nail polish in the restroom of a public eatery. Kidnap victims have been recovered as long as eighteen years after their abduction. Often, they've been both here and not here all along, living among us in a locked basement, a converted bomb shelter, a box under someone's bed.

High-profile missing people are almost always young white women, and on the rare occasions when they're found, an uneasy feeling seems to be generated around the question of their return. It is almost as if, once people enter the liminal realm of the missing-and-presumed-dead, there's an unspoken assumption—you might even call it a faith—that they are no longer one of us. Some follow every development in such cases, vowing they'll never give up hope that missing girls will one day be safely back home with their loved ones. But the same people often express disquiet if, after begging for the public's help in finding their daughter, sister, or wife, family members suddenly go mute, or request privacy, when the missing woman returns.

When no explanation is offered for a person's absence, those who have been following the story in the media or online will sometimes feel they have been cheated. In the comments section of newspaper articles and in threads devoted to the case online, there will often be grumbles that the story does not add up, that we are not being given the full picture, that the missing girl might not have been "really" missing but off on a jaunt or drug binge. You will hear the complaint that, since taxpayers' money has been spent on the search, then we have a right to find out what "really happened."

In the case of missing women who escape their abductors after having been kept captive for many years, people sometimes believe that anyone who remains so long with her kidnapper must be complicit in her situation, at least to some degree. This incredulity is compounded if it is revealed that, as sometimes happens, the kidnap victim had eventually been allowed to go outside her captor's house, to do yardwork or accompany him to the grocery store. Our unease and mistrust around the stories of missing people are a defense mechanism that lets us keep the horror at bay; we can reassure ourselves that many missing people aren't "really" missing, and as for kidnap victims, they must have been weak and gullible enough to fall in love with their captors, something a stable, rational person would surely never do.

Rey Rivera, a freelance video director, is last seen on Tuesday, May 16, 2006, when he's on a tight deadline. He is working from home, on a quiet street in a middle-class neighborhood. His wife, Allison, a sales executive, is in Richmond, Virginia, on business when Rey goes missing. A work colleague of Allison's, Claudia, is staying over for a few days.

Around four p.m., according to Claudia, Rey goes into the kitchen and gets himself a snack: a bag of sour cream potato chips and a bottle of sparkling grapefruit juice. Normally, Rey enjoys cooking and is health-conscious, but today he is pressed for time and grabs whatever comes to hand.

Rey is back in his office when Claudia hears his cell phone ring. A very brief conversation follows. She hears him say, "Oh, shit," and sees him run out the back door as if he is late for an appointment. His office light is still on and his computer running. Then a couple of minutes later he comes back—but just for a moment, as if he has forgotten something. Then he leaves again. He drives off in Allison's black 2001 Mitsubishi Montero.

At five thirty p.m., Allison calls Rey from Richmond. His phone rings for a while then goes to voicemail. Allison asks him to call back when he has a chance. Before going to bed, around ten p.m., she tries again. Still Rey doesn't pick up. She calls Claudia, who's sleeping when the phone rings, to ask whether Rey is home. Claudia says she isn't sure. "He went out earlier," she says. She goes to see if he's back, calling his name, looking in his office and in his bedroom, but there's no sign of him. Allison apologizes for waking her up and says she'll try again later.

Rey and Allison Rivera

At five the following morning, Wednesday, May 17, Allison is woken by a call from Claudia. Rey still hasn't come home. Claudia sounds concerned, but Allison tells her not to worry. At this point, Allison assumes Rey has drunk too much and stayed out all night. After all, she thinks, while the cat's away . . .

She calls Rey's phone again. There's no answer, so she leaves another message asking him to call, then showers, gets dressed, and packs her suitcase. When she calls her husband again and there's still no response, she starts to realize something must be wrong. Normally, she and Rey talk to each other five or six times a day. It's not like him to ignore so many calls. But then, Allison does not worry easily. She's experienced, worldly, and used to dealing with unpredictable situations. At first, she thinks Rey must have left his phone somewhere. She keeps calling. Eventually, her calls go directly to voicemail, which means Rey's phone battery is dead.

During the drive back to Baltimore, Allison calls as many of Rey's friends and family members as she can get hold of, but she can find no one who has spoken to him in the last two days. At home, she searches the house for anything that might give her a clue. She notices that Rey left his toothbrush behind, and the retainer he wore to straighten his teeth, which makes Allison think he wasn't originally planning to stay out all night.

After spending Tuesday looking for Rey, talking to his friends, and calling the local hospitals, Allison realizes she needs to file a missing persons report. This report, filed on Wednesday, May 17, 2006, at three p.m., states that Rey Rivera is a thirty-two-year-old Hispanic male, six feet five inches tall, weighing two hundred and sixty pounds. He has a scar on the right side of his face, his teeth are crooked, and he is believed to be wearing thick-rimmed black glasses. He's taking no medications, has no medical or psychological problems, and has never gone missing before. He's lived in the city for two years and two months, and he's registered with a dentist but not with a doctor. Allison doesn't know his blood type.

If the FBI gets involved with a missing persons case, it's because the individual is obviously endangered, and the disappearance clearly involuntary. The majority of these "severe and urgent" cases involve young children. But in ordinary busy police departments, where budgets are limited and resources spread thin, missing persons cases are a low priority. This is because the vast majority of such cases turn out to have nothing to do with law enforcement.

The missing people turn out to be travelers who return home later than planned, or seniors with dementia who've wandered off; they may have stormed out after an argument, or not returned home after a drink or drug binge. And, of course, a number of people "go missing" by choice, skipping town deliberately to escape bad debts, an unhappy marriage, or a web of lies that's starting to come undone. Perhaps the police assume Rivera is someone like this. No crime has been committed; somebody's husband hasn't come home. No doubt the cops assume the couple are involved in some kind of domestic dispute, especially since Rey's wife is out of town and there is another woman staying in their home.

When I first read about the case, I have to confess, I, too, blithely assumed that "female houseguest" implied "cheating husband." But after Tuesday, May 16, Claudia exits stage left, leaving an empty space where she once stood. She is merely an extra in the plot.

The days pass. There is no sign of either Rey Rivera or his wife's SUV. There's been no new activity on his cell phone. As word of his disappearance spreads, friends and family members arrive to help with the search. His brother, mother, and sister come to town from Florida; Allison's parents arrive from Colorado. Everybody says that for Rey to disappear without a word is completely out of character. They all say he's the kind of man who will tell you not only where he's going, but why, and for how long, and exactly when he'll be back.

The case is still not high priority, but it is not low priority, either. The fact that so many people turn up to help gives it significance. The subjects of low-priority missing persons cases have no friends or family to put the pressure on: they may be transients, shut-ins, or senile elders with no living relatives. They may be people with high-risk lifestyles—drug addicts, alcoholics, illegal immigrants, ex-inmates, sex workers, heavy gamblers—or who have disappeared before, especially if they suffer from mental illness.

Sometimes, when people go missing, friends and family discover they have a secret life. They may turn out to have been involved in complicated relationships or to have been hiding addictions, debts, diseases, pregnancies, or problems with the law. But nothing like this seems to be true of Rey Rivera. Everything points to the fact that he is exactly what he appears to be: an upstanding citizen. He is a married homeowner with a steady job, a stable mind, a substantial income, and a close network of supportive friends. No skeletons emerge from any closets. Still, this is not enough to spur the police into action. For that, the case has to involve concrete evidence of foul play.

I hear nothing more about Rivera until the following Tuesday, May 23, 2006, when, suddenly, his name is all over the news. His wife's car has been found. That afternoon, Rey's in-laws had decided to recheck some of the parking lots close to his former place of employment. The first lot they visit is on St. Paul Street, four or five blocks from the brownstone in the Mount Vernon neighborhood where Rivera used to work. Here, they find their daughter's black Montero, undamaged. The lot attendant, who'd gone home at six the evening before, did not recall the Montero entering the lot, but he'd seen the car—had given it a parking ticket, in fact—on the morning of Wednesday, May 17, almost a week ago.

Has the Montero been parked there for six days, right in the middle of the very neighborhood that is being searched so carefully by Rey's friends and family? On either side of the parking lot, the streets are still plastered with missing posters. But the posters show a photograph of Rey Rivera, not of a Mitsubishi Montero. The vehicle could easily have been overlooked while in plain sight, like the purloined letter in Edgar Allan Poe's story of the same name. Poe's detective, Auguste Dupin, the connoisseur of the obvious, sees what the police have overlooked precisely because it is right in front of their eyes.

As soon as she recognizes the vehicle, Allison's mother calls her daughter; then she phones the police, who say they'll have to impound the car and then bring Allison and her parents in to headquarters for questioning. When Allison gets the call from her mother, she's just gotten out of the shower and goes into a state of panic, grabbing the first items of clothing she sees. She asks a friend to take her to the parking lot, as she is in no state to drive, and gets into her friend's car wearing a tank top, cutoff jean shorts, and no shoes. Her hair is still wet. At police headquarters, Detective James Mingle of the Missing Persons Unit interviews her for more than eight hours. Television trucks are on hand to cover the story. Now that the car has been found, the case has become high priority.

When it comes to missing people, the first day or two after they have gone, it is as though they have left a door open behind them, and they can still turn around and come back. But after five or six days, you get the sense they have crossed all the way over. All that remains, if you're lucky, is a vague glimpse, caught on tape somewhere, of a pixelated ghost.

When I was at college, I answered an advertisement on a university notice board placed by a retired psychoanalyst offering treatment free of charge. Dr. B. was a tall, elderly, white-haired gentleman with time on his hands. He always wore sweaters or cardigans with house slippers. He'd decided to continue to treat one or two students who would not normally be able to afford his fees. I saw him twice a week for two years.

I sought help from Dr. B. because I'd started to feel invisible. Other people didn't seem to notice me, or, if they did, they didn't remember me when they saw me again. I'd talk to someone in a bar or coffee shop, eat lunch with them on the library steps; then a week later they'd sit next to me in a lecture and ignore me, or walk past me in the street without a glimmer of recognition. I didn't seem to be even slightly familiar to them. I appeared to be completely forgettable. To make matters worse, I've been cursed with an infallible memory for faces and names. For someone so easily forgotten, this is not an enviable gift. It makes me feel even more invisible.

One day, during our session, Dr. B. seemed to suddenly grow impatient. He told me that my analysis was going nowhere. I was too inhibited, he said.

He told me I was like a snail whose antennae were attuned to pick up the interest and attention of others, and when I sensed none, I immediately withdrew. I could tell at once when people didn't register my presence. Dr. B. said that I suffered from "paranoia with a minus sign." Instead of believing that everyone was plotting against me, I felt that nobody ever paid the least bit of attention to me at all.

He told me I had to overcome this problem. Fortunately, he said, he knew a technique that often worked in such cases.

"Close your eyes," he said, cracking his knuckles.

I heard him moving his chair closer to the head of the couch. Then he placed one finger gently between my eyebrows and began slowly running his fingertip down the length of my nose. I could feel his hot breath on my face. He repeated the action five times before I asked him to stop. I told him it was not working. I felt even worse.

"On the contrary," he said. "You have just insisted on something very firmly. You've never expressed yourself to me so openly before."

The nose stroking, when it happened, came out of the blue and took me completely by surprise. I searched long and hard, but never found it in any book of psychoanalytic, therapeutic, or mesmeric techniques.

It is, however, the only reliable method of hypnotizing a shark.

Thirty years later, I am still invisible. Returning with my bulldog from his lunchtime walk, I step out of the elevator in our building and notice a musty smell in the hall. The carpet is covered with plastic. Two contractors emerge from a doorway, pulling a cart loaded with trash bags.

"Does somebody have a leak?" I ask.

"A leak? No," the younger guy replies. "We're just putting the plastic down to protect the carpet."

"Oh. Did somebody die?"

The older guy laughs.

"Don't worry. If he did, it wasn't here," says the younger guy.

They're cleaning out Mr. Becker's apartment.

I spoke to Mr. Becker only once. He'd introduced himself to me in the elevator about a year ago. I remember thinking that he looked like Martin Luther. Or at least, he looked like the image that came to mind when I thought of Martin Luther—a Flemish portrait of a thin-lipped, ruddy-cheeked man in black robes and a black hat. Mr. Becker had the same thin lips and suspicious feline eyes.

A week after meeting Mr. Becker, I was about to step into the elevator when I saw him again, walking through the lobby. I held the elevator doors open, smiled at him, said hello, and pressed the button for the fifth floor. Unsmiling, not meeting my eyes, he went to press it again right after me, even though, when he'd introduced himself to me just a week earlier, we'd discussed the fact that we both lived on the fifth floor. It was not that he was politely ignoring me, I realized, the way people will sometimes do when your presence is inconvenient to them. He seemed too young to have dementia. No. Mr. Becker had forgotten me already. Even the presence of my dog did not remind him. My cloak of invisibility had made everything around me vanish, even the bulldog at my feet.

It is a kind of contagion.

On the fifth floor, the musty smell lingers in the hallway for about a week after the contractors have left. When it has finally disappeared, I walk down to Mr. Becker's apartment. The door is slightly ajar. I don't knock; I just push it a little. It swings open, and I can tell at once the apartment is empty. It's a corner apartment, like the one D. and I share, with windows facing the back and the side of the building. It's been stripped to the bone. Even the carpet has been pulled up, exposing the bare concrete floor. Not a sign of life remains.

Well, Mr. Becker, I think. Who's invisible now?

II

THE YEAR BEFORE Rey Rivera went missing, D. and I took possession of our newly purchased apartment on the fifth floor of Baltimore's Belvedere Hotel. This grand building, whose doors opened in 1903, is one of the city's oldest and best-known landmarks. It is 188 feet high, configured in a shallow "U" shape, with the opening to the south, and it stands at the corner of North Charles and Chase Streets, on the top of a hill overlooking the city.

Its architects designed the hotel in the grand style of the French Beaux Arts. The exterior, built of a beige-pink brick, has a two-story-high rusticated base and two cornices: one at the third floor and one at the eleventh. Graceful embellishments in terra-cotta—quoins, balustrades, a row of carved lion heads—adorn all four façades. At the top, elegant dormer windows project from a thirty-five-foot-high slate-covered mansard roof.

In its early days, this once-stately establishment hosted gala dinners for five hundred, grand balls, fireworks, symphony performances, dancing girls, kangaroos. Prominent jewelers, society dames, company presidents, traveling salesmen, bank chiefs, and clubmen all used the Belvedere as their Baltimore pied-à-terre.

Postcard from the Belvedere Hotel, 1906

In 1905, on a tour of the East Coast, Henry James stepped off a train at the city's old Union Station and took a horse-drawn taxi up Charles Street to the Belvedere, which he described as "a large fresh peaceful hostelry, imposingly modern yet quietly affable . . ."

At a cost of $1.75 million, this spectacular edifice was designed for wealthy tourists and socialites rather than the commercial travelers who make up the majority of the hotel trade, and while the restaurant and banquet rooms were always busy, most of the hotel's three hundred luxury suites stood empty even as early as 1905. The Belvedere struggled financially from the beginning, with frequent changes in management and five different owners

Crowd outside the Belvedere during the
Democratic National Convention, June 1912

between 1903 and 1917. Only four years after it was built, it went into receivership and was purchased by the Union Trust Company for $1 million, including furniture and supplies.

In 1917, a popular and sociable fellow from Virginia named Colonel Charles Consolvo bought the Belvedere, still sinking in value, for $450,000. The rank was honorary—in 1913, Consolvo had been made a "colonial" on the staff of the governor of Minnesota—but he was a genuine hotel baron; among his other properties were the Monticello Hotel in Norfolk and the Jefferson Hotel in Richmond. A former circus clown, the colonel stayed in touch with his pals from the big top, and was known to impress the ladies by walking on his hands in the Belvedere lobby.

Consolvo owned the building for the next fifteen years; under his ownership and with the guidance of managers John F. Letton and William J. Quinn, the place finally started to turn a profit. This was also due to the war. Celebrities like Mary Pickford would come to the Belvedere to help sell war bonds, and after the opening of Fort Meade a contingent of dashing British and French officers, sent to instruct Americans in the art of modern warfare, would drink in the hotel bar in their off hours, attracting a steady stream of female attention.

Consolvo spent most of the year traveling on business; nonetheless, he took over the entire second floor of the Belvedere and stayed there whenever he was in town, along with his second wife, the former Blanche Hardy Hecht, an opera singer thirteen years her husband's junior. When she was in town, this bohemian lady had the habit of walking around her rooms in the buff while singing the "Habanera" from *Carmen* (her mezzo-soprano voice was, according to the *Virginian-Pilot,* "smooth, and of good quality and range"). Accompanying this interesting pair was the colonel's "mentally subnormal" "adopted" son (who may have been Consolvo's natural child).

In Italy in early 1922, Mrs. Consolvo, thirty-seven, drew the admiration of Count Manfredi Cariaggi, thirty-two, a major in the Italian army. On May 8 of that year, she obtained a quickie divorce in Reno, Nevada, and was married in Fredericksburg, Virginia, five days later, thus progressing from an honorary American colonel to a real Italian count. She left with her new husband for Italy, sailing on May 23.

All ties between Colonel Consolvo and the Belvedere ended in 1936, and although it continued to operate under the able management of Albert Fox, ownership was turned over to the bank. In 1946, the financially troubled Belvedere was offered up in an arranged marriage to the Sheraton Hotel Corporation, making her the Sheraton-Belvedere. It was a match made for money, not love—nobody liked to see the grande dame becoming part of a corporate chain—but, like many arranged marriages, it worked surprisingly well. For the next twenty-two years, business was good and finances stable. The week before Christmas 1954, Albert Fox opened the doors to African-American guests. His decision was a bold one, but it was felt to be the right time, and business increased—despite pressure from the conservative Baltimore Hotel Association. Two months later, after media scrutiny, the hotel association changed its restrictive guest policies, and other hotels in the city gradually began to accept African-American clients.

Thanks to the proximity of Johns Hopkins University, the Belvedere has hosted some prestigious intellectual guests. The poet Marianne Moore arrived in Baltimore on a summer afternoon in June 1960. "Never felt such oven heat as in the taxi to the Belvedere," she wrote to a friend. "I had waited in the sun but the hotel is *very cool* even with no air conditioner, which I turned off

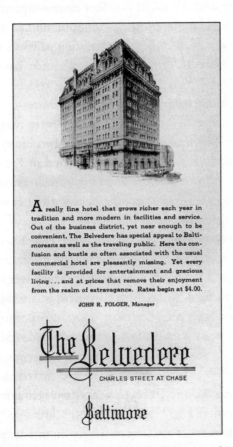

A really fine hotel that grows richer each year in tradition and more modern in facilities and service. Out of the business district, yet near enough to be convenient, The Belvedere has special appeal to Baltimoreans as well as the traveling public. Here the confusion and bustle so often associated with the usual commercial hotel are pleasantly missing. Yet every facility is provided for entertainment and gracious living . . . and at prices that remove their enjoyment from the realm of extravagance. Rates begin at $4.00.

JOHN R. FOLGER, Manager

The Belvedere

CHARLES STREET AT CHASE

Baltimore

Magazine advertisement for the Belvedere Hotel, 1936

immediately. A better hotel than the Ritz in this respect; the coat hangers are not locked to the rod and the bathroom would satisfy Nero—either scented or unscented soap—huge towel racks peopled with bath towels—and on another wall, linen—well it is crucial." Staying with Moore at the hotel were Margaret Mead and Hannah Arendt; the three women had come to receive honorary degrees from Johns Hopkins. (Afterward, Arendt described it as "an idiotic affair," calling Moore "an angel" and Mead "a monster.")

Six years later, over the weekend of October 18–21, 1966, Johns Hopkins again relied on the Belvedere to accommodate various academic luminaries, this time those attending the inaugural conference of the Johns Hopkins Humanities Center. Guests at the hotel that weekend included Roland Barthes, Jacques Lacan, Paul de Man, and Jacques Derrida, who, at age thirty-six, was just beginning to make a name for himself.

Upon his arrival at the Belvedere, then, Derrida was surprised to learn that the charismatic and far more famous Lacan had already taken the liberty of requesting a deluxe room for the younger man. Over a buffet dinner in the hotel restaurant that evening, the two Frenchmen finally got the chance to discuss their ideas, but quickly found themselves at odds. Their argument remained unresolved. Lacan, who still had not written his conference paper, went to bed, then got up very early and wrote as he sat at his window watching dawn break over the city. Those who attended the conference recalled that, while all the other speakers spoke in elegant French and relied on the talented translators provided by the university, Lacan insisted on using his terrible English.

"When I prepared this little talk for you, it was early in the morning," the eccentric Frenchman began. "I could see Baltimore through the window, and it was a very interesting moment because it was not quite daylight, and a neon sign indicated to me every minute the change of time, and naturally there was heavy traffic."

He then declared, in a startling and bizarre insight, that "the best image to sum up the unconscious is Baltimore in the early morning."

This gathering of luminaries provided a last moment of glory for the hotel; in 1968, Sheraton sold it to Gotham Hotels, Inc., which in turn leased it to a shady corporation that rented it out, in September 1971, as a dormitory for students at all the colleges and universities in Baltimore.

It was a stroke of genius that became a nightmare. Each university that sent students to the Belvedere assumed that the company would provide appropriate supervision for the hundreds of young men and women living in the old hotel, many of whom had arrived from small towns and were away from home for the first time. Their parents, who may have stayed at the hotel ten or fifteen years earlier, no doubt imagined their sons and daughters sipping tea in the John Eager Howard Room. But the truth could hardly have been more different.

It was the tail end of the 1960s, and the hotel dorms were coed and unregulated. There were all kinds of drugs and plenty of sex. Every weekend, all-night parties took place in the ballrooms, at which drag queens would mix with locals who had walked in off the street in hopes of picking up a shy young student. These festivities would attract local underground celebrities like the movie star Divine, as well as street hustlers and drug dealers who came to prey on fresh meat.

Those who lived through the four-month experiment all remember their majestic dorm rooms, the chandeliers, and the fancy furniture (although the meals, served in a cafeteria in the basement, were anything but fancy). The atmosphere was recalled as being pleasantly communal during the day, but it could get threatening at night. On the eighth floor, shy art students from the nearby Maryland Institute lived in uneasy harmony with the Morgan State University football team—a group of burly guys with little interest in abstract painting. The only supervisor anyone can remember seeing was a creepy guy with an artificial leg who was always hanging around at the parties, trying to pick up girls.

By the time the first semester was drawing to a close, things had started to get seriously out of hand. Fights broke out in the hallways. Two rapes were reported. The trash went uncollected. Police raids became regular events. By January 1972, the city had announced that the building would be closed because of extensive code violations, and everyone had to get out. Some of the students, angry at their sudden eviction, retaliated with vandalism, destroying their rooms and the hallways; others took along a few fancy lamps and end tables with them when they moved, mementos of the hotel's former majesty.

Today, the Belvedere is a condominium complex. We live in an apartment that was originally two hotel suites, 501 and 502. The moment I laid eyes on the space, I fell in love with its shabby grandeur, the Swarovski chandeliers, the bare concrete floor, and the peeling paint. We've lived here for over ten years now, and our love is still strong. But as we soon discovered, there are drawbacks to living in a building constructed over a hundred years ago and designed as a hotel. The original kitchens are tiny, the windows almost impossible to clean; the air-conditioning system leaks, and until they were recently replaced, the elevators would regularly break down.

Thanks to its location and lack of outdoor space, the Belvedere is a quiet building, unsuited for families. Most of its inhabitants are older single people. Hardworking, quiet medical students at Johns Hopkins rent a number of the one-bedroom units, and there are a few older couples, like the two elderly ladies on our floor whom we see only on Sundays, when, dressed in matching wigs and hats, they make their way shakily to church. The grand ballrooms are owned by an events company, Belvedere & Co., which rents them out for weddings, rehearsal dinners, and other social functions. Enter the lobby through the revolving doors and you can still sense the old grandeur, but go upstairs to the residential floors and you will notice the carpets are worn, the light fixtures coated in dust.

In 1912, the *Washington Post* reported that an "Esthetic Nobleman" named Count August Seymore had planned to construct a "hotel for suicides" in the nation's capital. This building, according to the count, would be a "haven for the depressed and weary of life." Once the disillusioned guest had checked into his "eternal rest room," taken the complimentary sedative, and pressed a bedside button to indicate his readiness, the desk clerk would discreetly turn on a gas tap in his room (thereby ensuring none of the furniture or carpets will be "spoiled by grewsome gore"). A crematorium on the roof would assist in disposing of the guests' bodies, its furnace providing the hotel with a cheap and handy source of power.

Unsurprisingly, this imaginative scheme came to nothing, and the next time Count Seymore appeared in the newspapers, he was spending an hour a day in the window of a department store in Pittsburgh "demonstrating the correct method of wearing clothes." Within a year he had moved on to a new obsession—the reanimation of the dead. Yet the count's "suicide hotel" does make a certain kind of sense, if only in its acknowledgment of the fact that it's much easier for people who want to commit suicide to do so in a private place away from home. And what place could be more private than a hotel?

This conceit forms the basis of *The Suicide Club,* Robert Louis Stevenson's 1878 trilogy of short stories involving a secret society for those who "have grown heartily sick of the performance in which they are expected to join daily and all their lives long." As one of the society's members explains, "We have affairs in different places; and hence railways were invented. Railways separated us infallibly from our friends; and so telegraphs were made that we might communicate speedier at great distances. Even in hotels we have lifts to spare us a climb of some hundred steps." The ulti-mate convenience—a key to "Death's private door"—is provided to all members of the Suicide Club.

Outside of fiction, those seeking a key to "Death's private door" will often register, with brave equanimity, at a hotel. There are various reasons for this, some emotional and others practical, but, to put it bluntly, at home people get suspicious. They want to know why you're not sleeping, why you're drinking so much, why you suddenly need a gun. Away from home, there's far less chance of being interrupted. And even if they're the reason for your suicide, do you really want your family cleaning up the mess?

According to a 2006 study by a pair of psychiatrists, the risk of suicide among hotel guests is much higher if they're local resi-dents. In some cases, suicide notes explain the choice of location. One man mentioned the desire to conceal the act from his daughter; another hoped to avert exposure in local media. In cases where no note is left, the authors assume the choice of a hotel is a way of "diminishing the chances of rescue and treatment." Their study found that hotel suicides were slightly younger than average, but "maintained the male preponderance of suicide in the general population." (The researchers also noted that suicidal men who are widowed or have never been married have less use for hotels, because "this population tends to live alone more frequently and could be less likely to need to implement strategies to reduce chance of rescue.")

For hotel managers, dealing with suicide has always been an occupational hazard, though the cleaning staff usually bears its immediate impact. Casino hotels in particular have a higher than average suicide rate. More people kill themselves every year in Las Vegas than in any other place in America. The big Vegas hotels are suicide magnets—partly, though not exclusively, for those who've lost their life savings at the gaming tables. For this rea-son, most Las Vegas hotel rooms have neither balconies nor windows that open more than the inch or two that will permit the minimum required ventilation.

The suicidal leap has many advantages: you cannot change your mind, nor can you be interrupted halfway through; and, as long as the building is high enough, the jump is reliably fatal. In effect, however, the result of "plunge-proofing" Las Vegas hotel rooms has mostly been to drive would-be jumpers to a more public location, such as an interior atrium. In consequence, employees are instructed to be alert for guests who appear agitated and distraught, or for anyone lingering suspiciously in an elevated place. Such vigilance may appear altruistic, but human kindness is often simply a side effect of liability prevention. Suicides are bad for business, and in many cases, hotel proprietors can be held responsible for the damages.

According to an article entitled "How to Properly Respond to a Guest Death in Your Hotel," published in a journal for hotel managers, one of the major problems of a hotel suicide is what the article's author refers to candidly as "the gore factor." "Think of a guest jumping from a balcony and landing in the atrium-style lobby or on the hotel's sidewalk and I am sure you understand what I mean," the author explains. "It will be messy and guests will be sickened if they witness the impact or see the impact site." He goes on to suggest that hotel managers keep "very large dark-colored tarps made of impermeable material" readily available in case such a situation should arise, and advises that "management and security must uphold the utmost discretion in order to maintain some semblance of dignity for the decedent, the decedent's family, and the reputation of the hotel."

Today, people commit suicide in hotels for the same reasons they always did. While hotel managers rarely forget suicides on their premises, for obvious reasons they're reluctant to release or even discuss statistics. However, Neal Smither, owner of the San Francisco–based company Crime Scene Cleaners, says that hotel and motel chains are his company's biggest clients, and suicide cleanups provide most of his business. After Las Vegas, according to Smither, the region of the country with the most hotel suicides is the I-85 corridor between Alabama and the Virginias.

These days, it is companies like Crime Scene Cleaners, rather than the hotel's housekeeping staff, that deal with the aftermath of suicides. Today, if a member of the staff encounters what appears to be a dead body in a hotel room, they are usually instructed to back out immediately and alert security. In most of the larger corporate establishments, staff members are given strict instructions not to speak about the incident. Once the coroner has arrived, the body has been removed (through the rear exit when possible), and the police have completed any necessary investigation, the room will be sealed and a professional crime-scene cleanup service brought in, with protective gear and special equipment, to make the room hygienic and presentable.

How long this takes depends on the method of death and the size of the room. Unfortunately for hotel owners, suicidal guests—since they know they will not be paying their bill—tend to choose large and luxurious rooms for their last night on earth. Most hotels err on the side of caution when such incidents occur, replacing the entire bed rather than just the linen and blankets, the whole carpet rather than just a stained rug; they may even replace drywall. Potentially hazardous material needs to be properly disposed of and the smell dissipated. Some hotels will bring in a priest to bless the room, not just for the sake of future guests but also for the benefit of housekeeping staff.

Unfortunately, small, independent hotels that don't have the financial resources or moral accountability of the larger chains continue to rely on their own staff to clean up after such events. I learned this from a Reddit forum called "Tales from the Front Desk," where hotel employees share their tales of pitiless managers, indignant guests, and grueling shifts at minimum wage. "A guy committed suicide on my shift," recalls a hotel maid. "Once the owner found out about how much it cost for professionals to clean up deaths like that, he just had the maintenance guy flip the mattress." A housekeeper describes how, in her first days on the job, a guest committed suicide using a gun placed under his chin while he was lying in bed. After the body had been removed, her boss asked for a volunteer to clean the room; wanting to make a good impression, she took the job. Before she went inside, she writes, a detective handed her two bags: one for any pieces of body matter she came across, and the other for the bullet, which was still missing. She did as she was asked, placing small scraps of flesh in a plastic bag while searching for the bullet (which turned up during the autopsy inside the corpse). "I still wake up from dreams where I am back in that room with those two bags," she admits.

Even though larger hotel chains bring in professional cleaning teams to deal with the situation, coming unexpectedly upon a body is still a nasty shock. A desk clerk writes that he, his coworker, and his boss have all walked into guest rooms only to find "brains and blood everywhere." A porter who works in a Washington, D.C., hotel recalls "a guy who broke down the roof door one night, jumped off, and landed on the second story, smashing into the window. In a room full of kids at 1AM." Another desk clerk remembers how he "watched a jumper hit the ground from 20 stories up . . . I was traumatized." And yet business must go on as usual: "Still I am expected to smile all night, preen like a peacock, and try not to cringe when some guy tries to dispute his adult movie charges that he clicked on 'by accident.' "

In his well-known essay "The Jumping-Off Place," first published in the *New Republic* in 1931, the writer Edmund Wilson described the Coronado Beach Hotel in San Diego as "the ultimate triumph of the dreams of the architects of the eighties," contrasting its fabulous façade with the grim truth that San Diego had, for a time, become the suicide capital of the United States. The coroner's reports, Wilson wrote, made melancholy reading, for they contained "the last futile effervescence of the burst of the American adventure." In San Diego,

> they stuff up the cracks of their doors and quietly turn on the gas; they go into their back sheds or back kitchens and eat ant-paste or swallow Lysol; they drive their cars into dark alleys, get into the back seat and shoot themselves; they hang themselves in hotel bedrooms, take overdoses of sulphonal or barbital; they slip off to the municipal golf-links and there stab themselves with carving-knives, or they throw themselves into the bay . . .

Those who come to the city to escape from "ill-health and poverty, maladjustment and industrial oppression" discover that "having come West, their problems and diseases remain," and that "the ocean bars further flight." These lonely visitors soon realize that the "dignity and brilliance" of exclusive hotels like the Coronado are intended for out-of-towners and convention-goers, not locals with little left to live for. For such people, the hotels' cruel opulence is often the final insult.

I have tried to learn all I can about the suicides that took place in the former Belvedere Hotel. The brief accounts in early newspapers are compellingly suggestive. These vignettes of private tragedy are windows on the changing century; they refer to the introduction of automobiles, the telegraph, and the telephone; to the Great Depression, Prohibition, segregation, and revolutions in the hotel trade. Their casts of characters include alienated parents, sons with too much money, the lonely wives of railway tycoons, and businessmen suffering from existential angst. They evoke the genteel and bohemian Baltimore of F. Scott Fitzgerald and Gertrude Stein, a prosperous city whose kings were Confederate generals, tobacco lords, and bootleg emperors. They reveal private crises and intimate tragedies that are even today rarely discussed outside the family, except in strained and awkward whispers. I find the suicide notes left by hotel guests especially touching, with their polite, self-deprecating apologies, their regrets to hotel staff for the necessary cleanup job.

Most of the Belvedere's reported suicides occurred before 1946, when the hotel was sold to the Sheraton corporation. After that, it isn't clear whether there were actually fewer suicides (this is certainly possible, since the Belvedere was no longer Baltimore's highest building nor its fanciest hotel), or whether changes in reporting made it appear that way (suicides no longer made the papers unless they involved unusual circumstances or well-known individuals, or occurred in public places). It is possible that for a while, the Belvedere may have seen more than its share of suicides because it was often the first port of call for those who arrived in Baltimore to register as patients at the Henry Phipps Psychiatric Clinic at the Johns Hopkins University School of Medicine, one of the country's earliest and most sophisticated psychiatric hospitals. With its marble floors, its rose gardens, its private rooms with porches and fireplaces, and its spacious auditorium containing a pipe organ, the Phipps Clinic was considered the height of luxury for the nervously ill. It was where F. Scott Fitzgerald installed his wife, Zelda, in 1934, after her second breakdown (her doctor infuriated Fitzgerald by suggesting that he, too, could benefit from a course of psychoanalysis). The Phipps patients who took their lives at the Belvedere were mostly women; some did so before checking in to the clinic, some after checking out, and others while on a break from treatment.

Freddie Howard, currently the evening concierge, has worked at the Belvedere for over twenty years and has seen almost everything. This is a place where things happen, he tells me. Although there are rumors of ghosts, Freddie has spent hundreds of nights in the lobby and never seen or felt anything supernatural. There have certainly been plenty of deaths, including suicides, since the hotel became a condominium complex, but Freddie mentions only the two most recent examples he can think of. A gentleman hanged himself on the eighth floor last year. Freddie is not sure whether anyone ever knew the reason. A few years before that, Freddie recalls, another gentleman, on the third floor, cut his wrists over a failed love affair. He survived, but a few days later, he put a pillow over his head and shot himself.

The second time, he got it right.

III

IT IS LUNCHTIME on Wednesday, May 24, 2006. Rey Rivera has now been missing for eight days. Mark Whistler and Steven King leave their office in Mount Vernon and walk down Charles Street to get lunch. King and Whistler both work for the Oxford Club, a financial company for which Rivera has recently been doing some freelance video production work. Steven has known Rey for about a year, but Mark, who's only recently moved to Baltimore, has met him once, and then just briefly.

Steven and Mark go to pick up some lunch from Eddie's, a nearby grocery store. On the way back, they see Steven's friend George Rayburn. He seems to be hanging around outside the gay bar across the street. Steven has known George for a long time; in fact, it was George who first brought him into the company, though they currently work for different subsidiaries.

For a joke, Steven calls George on his cell phone. "Hey, George," he says. "What are you doing hanging around outside a gay bar?"

George isn't in a mood to joke around. Steven and Mark cross the street to find out what's going on. George says he's been looking for Rey. He's visibly upset.

For eight days now, George, Mark, and Steven have been canvassing the streets, handing out missing-person flyers at bars and restaurants, putting up posters, asking business owners whether they've seen anyone matching Rey's description. On Wednesday morning, George returns to work but finds himself unable to sit still in his office, unable to concentrate on ordinary business affairs. He tells Mark and Steven he's been walking around the block where Rey's car was found, looking for clues. Anything might help, he reasons.

"If Rey's been abducted or killed, there must be some kind of evidence," says George. Rey is a really big guy, an athlete. "He'd never go down without a fight." George wants to check out the Belvedere's parking garage.

"That place is creepy," says Steven. "We'll go with you."

The three men cross the street and walk a block north to the seven-floor indoor parking garage on Charles Street next to the Belvedere and adjacent to the outdoor garage on St. Paul, where the Montero was found.

To the east, this garage is attached to an extension of the first three floors of the old hotel. This extension, the parking lot, and a cocktail lounge on the thirteenth floor were all added in 1964, when the Belvedere underwent renovation. The basement level of the extension contains retail space. A Japanese hibachi restaurant occupies the storefront level on Charles Street, which is accessed through a glass-and-steel entrance to the hotel, built along with the extension. There's a glass roof above this entrance; behind the glass roof is the flat roof of a retail office. Above this is a second flat roof, one side of which abuts a row of windows. These look down on the hotel's indoor swimming pool, which was made into offices when the Belvedere was turned into a condominium complex. Above these windows, there is a third roof, which would once have been the top of the pool, from which protrude two half-barrel-shaped glass skylights.

The three men walk through the parking garage, searching for anything that might be a clue—Rey's wallet, maybe, or his phone, or his money clip. They get all the way up to the top level of the parking garage, but find nothing out of the ordinary. Mark decides to search the stairwell. A few minutes later, his phone rings. It's Steven, telling him to come back up to the roof. He and George have found something, says Steven, though they're not sure what.

Mark goes back up to the top of the garage. Looking over the lower roof toward the Belvedere, all he sees are the kinds of things you might expect to see on a roof—rocks, plastic planters, cans, other kinds of trash.

But then he sees something else.

It is a very large brown flip-flop.

Steven touches his shoulder and points out a second flip-flop, along with a cell phone and what could be a wallet and a bunch of keys. Also, there is a hole in the lower roof.

Not a huge hole. Bigger than a Frisbee, but smaller than a hula hoop. Steven leans over and tries to see inside it, but the glare of

The hole in the roof

the midday sun is too bright. When the men look up to the top of the building, they see an old banquet chair dangling off the edge of the building, caught by one of its metal legs. Steven starts to feel a sense of dread.

George calls James Mingle, the detective in the missing persons unit assigned to Rey's case. He describes the scene, the hole, and the chair to Mingle. The men feel very uncomfortable. Mingle asks them to stay where they are—he'll be right there, he says. But ten minutes later, he calls back: he can't work out how to get into the Belvedere's parking garage. George tells him just to pull his car into the Charles Street entrance to the west. "If you show your badge," says George, "surely the attendant will let you in?"

Detective Mingle tells the three men to go downstairs and wait for him in the Belvedere's lobby. They find an elevator that takes them to the back quarters of the hotel, and from there, they find their way to the reception desk. A security guard shows them to an area by the wall where they can wait. There are no chairs, so the men sit down on the floor. Here, they wait in awkward silence.

They've been sitting there for what seems like forever when suddenly everything starts happening at once. There are cops everywhere—a big crowd of cadets. There is a man in uniform, wearing rubber gloves, with a stethoscope around his neck. Realizing he must be the coroner, Steven almost loses consciousness. Later, when the cops come back, Mark goes over to one of them and asks whether the body is Rey's, but the officer won't tell him. A few moments later, a policeman approaches the three friends, introduces himself as a detective from the Baltimore police's Central District, and tells them they need to come downtown with him. Steven, Mark, and George get shakily to their feet, and the detective leads them through the crowds in the lobby, into the street, and into an unmarked vehicle. Through the wing mirror, as they drive away, Steven glimpses a local news anchorman straightening his tie.

The concierge on duty at the Belvedere that day is a capable, heavyset gentleman in his fifties named Gary Shivers. At the request of a man who introduces himself as a police detective, Shivers goes into the room behind the front desk to find the keys to the offices on the second floor, then leads the police and the pack of cadets up two long, steep flights of stairs, through a double set of doors, and down the hallway toward the annex. Taking a right turn, he leads the parade past the second-floor freight elevators and pushes open a door at the top of three steps. This door opens onto a narrow hallway leading to the hotel's former swimming pool. When the Belvedere was turned into a condominium complex in 1991, this space was divided into two offices, each with a half-barrel skylight and a row of windows at the top of its eastern wall.

One of these offices belongs to the Belvedere's in-house catering company, which at that time was a business called Truffles. The other is empty, although its opaque glass door announces it as the headquarters of the Army of God Church in Christ and the Elijah School of the Prophet Institute. This Pentecostal congregation was using the space when D. and I first moved into the building in March 2005. It took us a while to locate the source of the praying and chanting on Sunday mornings, and when we realized it was coming from the old swimming pool below our apartment window, we were worried that it might become annoying. But the Army of God Church in Christ soon found a new home, and by early April 2006, the Sunday-morning hallelujahs had ceased.

The Truffles staff have been complaining about a bad smell for the last few days. They think there might be a dead rat in the wall. When they hear Gary and the police arriving, they stick their heads out of their office to see what all the fuss is about.

Gary is fumbling among all the keys on his big key ring, trying to work out which one fits the door of the vacant office. He isn't thinking about how the hole got in the office roof. When he finally locates the right key, he opens the door and lumbers into the room. He's taken three or four steps across the floor before the smell hits him and he realizes he's looking at a dead body.

Gary Shivers turns and runs. He runs past the lead detective, who's casually taking out a stick of Vicks VapoRub. He runs past the girls from Truffles, who later tell me that Gary, who is black, had "turned white." He runs all the way downstairs to the basement, runs down the hallway and past Antiques at the Belvedere, then bursts out through the side door into the heat of the afternoon. He runs west across Charles Street and up the steps into Zena's salon. Zena is in the middle of a manicure when Gary bursts through the door, shaking and sweating. He tells Zena he has had a shock and he needs a drink. Zena asks one of the girls to take over her client's manicure. She leads Gary to the back room where he can sit down, and fetches a shot glass and a bottle.

Gary closes his eyes and swallows. He takes three shots. By the third he is no longer shaking. But he knows it's too late. He'll never forget what he has just seen.

Zena asks him what happened.

"A dead man fell out of the ceiling," says Gary.

When the Truffles girls realize that what they thought was a dead rat in the wall was, in fact, a dead person, they can't avoid thinking about the wedding reception held at the Belvedere four days ago. The bride and groom were photographed in rooms on the second floor. Violets Are Blue, a wedding photography website, still features images from the reception. In one of the photographs, the loving couple can be glimpsed looking down romantically from a window in the old hotel. In another room on the same floor, at the very time this photo was shot, Rey Rivera's dead body was decaying in the summer heat.

Half an hour after the body has been removed from the Belvedere, I come down to take my dog for his afternoon walk. The building is still swarming with police. Charles Street has been closed to traffic and pedestrians. Crime scene tape is tied from one side of the road to the other. I ask one of the officers what's going on. He tells me they're "conducting an investigation." He refuses to say anything else. Turning away, I see a neighbor walking his elderly dachshund, and ask if he has any idea what's happening.

He's heard they found a body. "They think it's that missing guy."

I finish my walk and return to our apartment. Upstairs, I open the living room window and wedge myself tightly into the frame, which gives me an almost perfect view of cops climbing around on the annex roof. A small group of people is also observing the scene from the top floor of the parking garage directly opposite.

We all watch as two policemen use a ladder to get from the second to the third level of the annex roof, then from the third to the fourth. One of the cops goes to retrieve the flip-flops and cell phone, almost indiscernible against the dark membrane of the roof. I can see the hole. It is just within my line of vision, and seems remarkably small for someone of Rivera's height and weight. It's almost circular, not one of those people-shaped holes you see in cartoons.

Even though they can see we're watching them, the cops are surprisingly casual about the whole thing. The first cop is on the pool roof. The second cop stays on the lower level, holding the ladder. The first cop picks up a flip-flop and throws it down to his colleague on the lower level. He then throws the second flip-flop, which almost hits the other guy on the head. The second cop yells something at the first cop, who laughs and yells something back. I do not see them putting anything in an evidence bag, taking photographs, or checking for fingerprints. Neither that day nor at any time afterward does anybody knock on our door to ask questions about anything we might have seen; nor, as far as we know, do the police interview any of our neighbors.

Some accounts, confusing the mystery further, report that Rivera's corpse was found in an "old church adjoining the Belvedere hotel."

At the Central District police station downtown, George Rayburn, Steven King, and Mark Whistler are sent to wait in a room painted in bright colors, with children's toys and games scattered around the floor. It's completely wrong. A television is tuned to WJZ-TV, a local channel. When the news comes on, the men see images of the Belvedere, and a long line of police cadets entering the hotel. The news announcer, Richard Sher, reports that a body found in "a conference room of the Belvedere Hotel" has been identified as that of "the missing financial writer Rey Rivera." The three men sit in silence again, this time for hours. Eventually, they're brought out one by one to be interviewed separately by detectives, one of whom is either so tired, so bored, or so hungover that he actually falls asleep while interviewing George. The questions they ask are strange and inappropriate—for instance, "Where are your parents?"

After this comes more silence. None of the three friends are interested in speaking to the press, so whenever anyone contacts them, they forward the inquiries to their company's public relations officer. Jayne Miller, an investigative reporter, tries repeatedly to contact George. He talks to her once, very briefly. Among the three men, there is little discussion of the incident. Steven King enters therapy to deal with it. George Rayburn continues working for the same subsidiary until 2013, when he joins King at the Oxford Club. The year after Rey's death, Mark Whistler is let go from his job.

Once the corpse has been removed, the police have left, and all the commotion is over, I find my way down to the former swimming pool. I assume the door will have been sealed by police tape and I'm surprised to find it propped open—to get rid of the smell, I imagine. There is nothing to prevent me from entering the room.

From beneath, the hole is substantially bigger than it appears from above. The ceiling is half collapsed; some of the rafters and roof beams have fallen in, and the musty carpet is covered in big chunks of plaster. The main area of damage is in the back right-

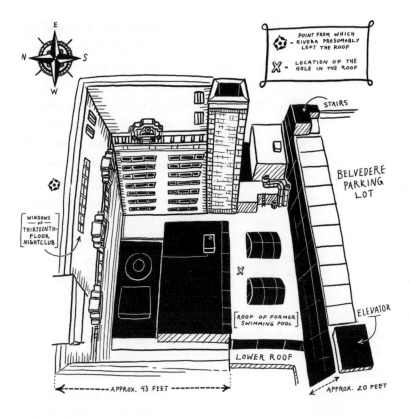

hand corner of the room, where the carpet is stained almost black and scattered with what look like grains of rice, which, when I get down on the floor to study them more closely, turn out to be dried insect larvae.

While I'm inspecting the scene, two girls who work in the nightclub at the top of the building come by to take a look before their shift begins.

This nightclub is called the 13th Floor.

The majority of hotels, in deference to superstition, don't list a thirteenth floor on their elevators. Most commonly, the number 13 is simply skipped, so the floors listed on the console go from

12 to 14. In some hotels, the thirteenth floor may be called 12A or 14A; in others, it may have a special name such as the Marble Floor or the Magnolia Floor, or it may be used to house offices, storerooms, or mechanical equipment. Some hotels don't even have rooms numbered 13. Even progressive modern psychiatry pays homage to this ancient superstition. Although the formal dedication of the Phipps Clinic at Johns Hopkins took place on April 16, 1913, the date engraved on the plaque above the main entrance says 1912.

In this regard, the Belvedere is remarkably progressive—or dangerously hubristic, depending on your point of view. But perhaps the curse doesn't count: the top floor is not actually the thirteenth floor but the fourteenth, the fifteenth, or something in between, since the ballrooms on the first and twelfth floors are two stories high, and the Belvedere is built on the slope of a hill.

As soon as the two girls enter the room, they hold their noses and make theatrical gagging noises. I don't find the smell to be so bad. Something has obviously been sprayed around the room to cover up the worst of it: a sweet, floral scent. Plus, the door has been propped open for hours. Still, the girls act as though they can hardly stand it. One of them says that, unlike me, she's smelled a dead body before. She repeats the well-worn cliché: "You never forget the smell of death."

If this is the smell of death, I think, it's been well concealed. The room smells no worse than a bag of trash that has been left out for couple of days in the sun.

Apart from being surprised that the door to the former swimming pool was left open and that I was able to get inside with no problem, D. expresses little interest in Rey Rivera's death, and although he is happy to listen to and even indulge my speculations, they don't seem to spark any curiosity.

He is not uninterested in death, but his concerns are different from mine. For example, not long ago he asked me whether I had

heard anything about a man who had committed suicide by jumping from a roof at Lincoln Center onto a New York street. He
didn't want to know the name of the man or the reasons for his
suicide, but the particular structure at Lincoln Center that he
jumped from. D. knows Lincoln Center well, or he used to, and
he couldn't picture a building whose roof abuts the street. "There's
been a lot of rebuilding going on there," he tells me. He can just
about still recognize Alice Tully Hall, but most of the other structures are unfamiliar to him. "It must have been one of the new
buildings," he decides, stoically, as if living outside New York for
ten years is a form of suicide in itself.

The night the body is found, I go to visit a new friend, C. Although
her apartment is small and cramped, she's arranged things nicely
for the two of us. She's put sparkling wine on ice and set out little
plates of strawberries dipped in powdered sugar. I don't tell her
about the dead body right away. It's not appropriate, partly
because C.'s boyfriend, a poet twice her age, has been undergoing
treatment for brain cancer. When I finally tell her about Rey
Rivera, she doesn't seem as interested as I thought she'd be. I was
hoping that C. might be the friend I was longing to find, who
shares my "love of all that is bizarre and outside the conventions
and humdrum routine of everyday life," as Sherlock Holmes says
of the deep bond between himself and Dr. Watson. I am disappointed, but given her boyfriend's brain cancer, I imagine that C.
wants relief from depressing subjects.

The next time we see C.'s boyfriend, he is in front of a large
audience and reading a poem about his erectile dysfunction, an
unanticipated side effect of chemotherapy. After the reading, he
announces that not only is he in remission, but he has just been
declared 100 percent cancer free. This earns him a standing ova-
tion. Three years later, he is discovered alone in his apartment,
dead at sixty-two. C. had broken up with him by then. She stopped
calling me around the same time. Apparently, she had lost interest

in me, too. Or perhaps I had become invisible to her. Even among those who see me at first, I gradually fade out of sight.

Sometimes I wonder whether I am perfectly visible but people simply don't like me. Perhaps I am just a thoroughly unpleasant person, stubborn and morbid, saturnine and antisocial, like the writer Patricia Highsmith, who thrived on lies and deceit, loved busting up couples, and preferred snails to people, bringing them to dinner parties in her handbag, attached to a head of lettuce.

When I get home the night the body is found, the air is still warm, and the moon is almost full. Before entering the Belvedere, I go up to the roof of the parking garage to get a look at the hole from above. There is a much better view from the garage roof than from our apartment window, and at midnight, I think, no one will wonder why I'm standing gazing over the edge of the parking lot for so long. Or so I assume. But as I stand there, I hear voices above me, and look up. On the Belvedere roof are the two bar girls from the 13th Floor. They have gone up to smoke cigarettes. When they see me, they cling together in mock terror, laugh, and wave, the tips of their cigarettes glowing like fireflies in the summer night.

Later that night, lying in bed, I suddenly remember something. About a week ago, around ten at night, while we were reading in bed, D. and I heard a loud noise outside. It was loud enough to make the windows shake in their frames, loud enough to make me get out of bed, go over, and look down into the street to see if there had been a car crash. The Belvedere stands on the intersection of two busy streets in the middle of an area with plenty of bars and restaurants. It can be noisy at weekends, but this was a weeknight and the streets were quiet. Seeing nothing, and hearing nothing more, we quickly dismissed the crash as just another of those inexplicable noises in the night.

I'd made a note of the mysterious noise in my journal. It had occurred on the previous Tuesday, May 16, the day Rey Rivera went missing.

The police report of the incident describes how officers from the Central District were dispatched to the Belvedere Hotel to deal with a questionable death. "Upon arrival," the report continues, "the area was searched and located in a vacant room under the damaged roof . . . a decomposed body of a male was discovered." On the "Missing" poster, Rey was described as wearing a "black pull-over jacket, shorts and flip-flops" and carrying $20 in cash, no bank cards. Allison Rivera, who must have given this description, was right about the black jacket and flip-flops, but Rey was actually wearing a yellow shirt, and long green pants (not shorts), in the pocket of which were an American Express card and his Maryland driver's license.

"A decomposed body of a male." This is what the handsome Rey Rivera has become. The body is taken to the forty-one-year-old building at Pratt and Penn Streets that houses the Office of the Chief Medical Examiner; here, an autopsy is performed. The building is part of the University of Maryland School of Medicine, which opened in 1807 and was immediately closed again for almost seven years because of riots protesting the dissection of human corpses, many of which, rumor had it, were stolen from St. Paul's churchyard adjoining the medical school. So great was the public outrage that dissection wasn't a part of the curriculum until 1832, and even then, it had to be carried out in secrecy; human dissection was not permitted in Maryland until 1882.

It seems right to be unhappy about cutting up corpses. There is something nightmarishly inevitable about the autopsy, with its photographs and final report. I'm already the kind of person who cringes at any business that involves putting my living flesh in the hands of another, be that a hairdresser, dentist, or gynecologist. It's not that I'm afraid of what they will do to me, but rather that I dread their unspoken criticism, and the idea of being judged by my body alone: my weight; the condition of my skin, my teeth, my hair. An autopsy, should we be subject to one, is the ultimate impersonal procedure to which our bodies will have to submit: our final, official summing-up.

Cora Crippen, the wife of the famous murderer Dr. Hawley Harvey Crippen, was identified by a piece of her belly that clearly showed an old abdominal scar. Escaping the quicklime in which the rest of Mrs. Crippen's body was destroyed, this fragment of flesh was later exhibited at Crippen's trial, where it was passed around among members of the jury on a soup plate.

If, when leaving the Belvedere, you turn right and walk four blocks, you come to a bridge over the highway. I think of this bridge as the gateway to the Other City. Cross the bridge, and you are in a ghost world. Street after street lies empty. The houses are boarded up. Perhaps one in every twenty houses in the Other City is inhabited. Some are fully vacant, some semi-abandoned, some you just never know. A house with planks nailed over the doors and windows and trash piled ankle deep outside might turn out to have a pit bull on a leash that rouses up to bark and lunge at you as you hurry by.

There is something sublime about this ghost city, with its forbidding tracts of emptiness, derelict yards, and cul-de-sacs, its homes that could be crime scenes and perhaps are. I love the bright graffiti, the old brick, the flaking paint, the cracks and holes exposing the innards of buildings, the rusting fire escapes overgrown with ivy. Here in the mists and barrens of this shadow city, I've seen a man walking a fox on a leash, a thick black snake coiled up inside an abandoned baby buggy, a mural of crocodiles and Egyptian goddesses painted on the inside wall of a vacant garage. I have found bullet casings, human teeth, a dead cat, an intelligence scale for children, a rusting unicycle, a string of seed pearls, a Mexican silver-and-abalone letter opener, a typewriter, a collection of old tobacco pipes, and four cans of tinned mackerel from times gone by.

IV

AT FIRST, LIKE everyone else, I assume Rey Rivera has taken his own life. When you learn that a man has plunged to his death from the top of a high building, you generally assume he has jumped, not that he has been pushed.

But those who knew Rivera say the idea of suicide makes no sense at all. They say he never showed the least sign of depression, and is the very last person they can imagine wanting to die. He was young, good-looking, newlywed, and excited about the future. He and Allison had put their house on the market, and were making plans to move back to Los Angeles to start a family. After her husband's death, Allison looked through all Rey's private journals, notebooks, computer files and caches, but she found nothing conspicuous or unusual, certainly nothing to suggest he was unhappy in secret.

What's more, Rey had been particularly busy the week he died. Earlier on the day he went missing, he made a call to a company that rented out video editing equipment, and he booked an editing suite for the coming weekend to finish a project. He spoke to a man named Mark Gold, who'd rented equipment to him before.

Gold said Rey sounded under a lot of pressure to get the project finished on time, but that "it sounded like a fairly average editing task." Other than that, said Gold, it was an ordinary, everyday conversation.

Rey's colleague, Steven King, confirmed that Rey's editing project was due the following week. In March 2006, Rey had filmed the Oxford Club's annual conference in Delray Beach, Florida. "We needed the video to send out to those subscribers who hadn't been able to make it to the conference," King told me. "Rey had been working on the video along with our advertising team. Our advertising manager spoke to him about it the day he went missing. She asked him if he had any idea when the video would be ready, and he'd said he'd have it to her by Monday."

Rey booked the edit suite for Saturday, May 20, but he never showed up. After learning about his death, Mark Gold said that, in conversation, Rivera sounded "totally not like someone who would throw himself off a building. It was too banal. He sounded like he was under a crunch for work." Steven King said he never got hold of the videotape Rey had been working on. All Rey's computers and video equipment were confiscated by the police, and the company had to reimburse the subscribers who had already paid for the video.

The phone call on Tuesday, May 16, that caused Rivera to leave home in a hurry was from somebody at Agora, the umbrella organization of which the Oxford Club was a subsidiary. At the time, Agora used a business line that diverted all its connections to a single number, so it is impossible to know who placed the call. No one at Agora admits to calling or meeting with Rivera that day, although the company's phone records for that day show five calls to Rivera's number. To all appearances, Rey rushed off because he was late to a meeting. If so, it must have been pretty informal, or a meeting with someone he knew well, since he was wearing a T-shirt and flip-flops.

After Rey's death, employees at Agora were instructed not

to speak about the matter to the police. They were protected by the company's lawyers. Allison never learned who placed that final call.

According to NAMI (the National Alliance on Mental Illness), 90 percent of suicide "completers" display evidence of a diagnosable mental disorder. I am constitutionally skeptical of statistics, and I would certainly not trust any claims made on behalf of suicide "completers." Since the questions must have been asked after the suicides were "completed," who is being consulted about "displays of evidence"—the suicide's family and friends? To me, the conclusions drawn from this "data" are indicative of the paradox at the heart of the issue: the fact that a person commits suicide has come to be regarded, retroactively, as a symptom of mental illness—rather than, for example, an expression of personal will.

In contrast, people in some cultures consider suicide to be a morally responsible act when the alternative will bring shame or suffering to others. Such cultures do not consider individuals as beings with an existence separate from those of their families, as we do in the West. Japan is perhaps the best-known example of a culture in which even today, people are, for the most part, deeply tied to either their family or their business—and men, Japan's most common suicide victims, are often joined tightly to both. In Japan, what happens to you happens to your family and the organization you work for, and so if you have done something that causes public shame—if you have stolen company money to cover gambling debts, for example, or paid money to prostitutes— suicide may be considered preferable to inflicting your shame on your family and your business. In such situations, suicide would not be regarded as a sin; on the contrary, it is often seen as a way to restore and make restitution to the family and the company. In some cases, it may even be considered the natural and morally responsible action, just as we in the West expect that someone who has experienced the death of a close relative will want to take time off from work to grieve their loss.

Although things are slowly changing, large Japanese cities still have problems with public suicides, especially on the subway. In Tokyo, at least one person every day throws himself on the tracks. When this happens, the words that appear on the screen on the platform announcing the reason for the delay are *jinshin jiko,* which translates as "human accident." Such suicides are so common that they have become an inevitable part of the daily commute, hardly worth grumbling about.

Japan Rail has tried to discourage *jinshin jiko* in various ways, such as undermining the family honor rationale by introducing a rule that the suicide's family is charged an enormous fine to compensate for commuter delays—a sum that would be financially devastating if it had to be paid all at once (fortunately, it can be paid in installments). Other disincentives include platform barriers, telephone hotlines, emergency buttons by the tracks, soothing blue lights, even softly lit photographs of kittens; yet *jinshin jiko* goes on as before. People with a profound and constant desire to end their lives will manage to find a way, even in a closely guarded prison cell. Surely this shows us that suicide is not always an irrational act.

Even here in the United States, at least six states have now legalized physician-assisted suicide, confirming that death is an acceptable choice for anyone with a degenerative illness, in chronic pain, or otherwise unable to enjoy a decent quality of life—which cannot be measured only in terms of physical health. Those whose bodies are still robust and who seem fully engaged in the world may nevertheless be experiencing great psychological pain. Medication and therapy can go only so far.

Interestingly, when it comes to suicide, all the medical examiner needs to prove is that the person caused their own death; no motive need be established. The same is true in legal terms. A motive for suicide, while useful, is not necessary. It is not the job of medical examiners or attorneys to concern themselves with the psychological disposition of the decedent. If a motive is not obvious, they do not need to find one. It is, to put it crassly, none of their business. A 1947 article in the *Yale Law Journal* by Orville Richardson and Herbert S. Breyfogle reminds us that in distinguishing suicide from accident, motive is irrelevant. "The springs of human action are often hidden," conclude the authors, "and are of such obscure origin that not even a psychiatrist with the full and voluntary cooperation of his patient can find them."

Rey Rivera died in the middle of May. Most people assume the absence of sunshine triggers suicide risk. Winter can certainly be depressing, but it is indisputable that suicide rates worldwide increase significantly as soon as winter is over. From the cold depths of hibernation, it is common for the depressed to become so numb they cannot feel what Freud calls the "ordinary unhappiness" of daily life—they cannot mourn, grieve, or cry. They are on ice. When the winter comes to an end, however, the frozen depths begin, very slowly, to melt. Forgotten memories emerge. Old desires resurface. Movement and action are possible. "The bright day brings forth the adder."

Spring is the real suicide season.

If Rey Rivera killed himself, it means he went from rushing to finish editing a video and making plans for the weekend, to suddenly deciding to jump off a very high building.

Is there such a thing as impulsive suicide? Do people really kill themselves suddenly and spontaneously, out of the blue? Those who study the subject believe so; they call this type of death the Richard Cory suicide, after Edwin Arlington Robinson's famous poem. The Richard Cory suicide is considered to be the act of a supreme narcissist, a person who cannot admit, even to himself, that everything in his life has gone awry. The grandiose and mysterious final gesture thereby performs a kind of alchemy, transforming passive humiliation into an active mastery of the situation.

On an Internet suicide grief support forum, I found accounts of some of these Richard Cory suicides. At least, they were reports of people who apparently committed suicide abruptly and unexpectedly, in the middle of what appeared to be an otherwise ordinary day. One man wrote that his partner woke up late, realized she'd missed an important meeting, called in sick to work, showered, had lunch, and then hanged herself. A woman described how her father put laundry in the dryer then lined the stairs with masking tape, as if making ready to paint them, then changed his mind and hanged himself instead. Some accounts, more specific, led me to newspaper articles, Facebook pages, and memorial websites, where I learned about these perplexing deaths in more detail.

On December 18, 2010, Miss P., a popular and successful twenty-seven-year-old investment banker and charity worker, left her apartment on the Upper West Side of Manhattan early in the morning and walked sixteen blocks north to 180 Riverside. Surveillance video showed her entering the building dressed in Ugg boots and a winter jacket. She got into the elevator along with a woman who'd just returned from walking her dog. Miss P., who seemed alert and aware, asked the woman how to get to the roof of the building. The woman told her. At 8:13 a.m., Miss P.'s body was found in an interior courtyard; she was pronounced dead at the scene. She left no note. Friends and family say Miss P. was bright, attractive, ambitious, and well loved, and that she always appeared to be in high spirits. The day of her suicide, she'd planned to meet a close friend for brunch. "It's like something just changed overnight," said the friend.

On Tuesday, July 1, 2014, around nine in the morning, a number of people saw a man jumping from the Tobin Bridge in Boston. The jumper was reported on various Twitter accounts, including that of the Boston EMS, where he was described as "non-viable." The Tobin Bridge is a two-level cantilevered structure, and the man, who was killed on impact, landed not in the water, but on the lower, northbound level of the bridge, which is an extension of the Charlestown neighborhood's Terminal Street. He was later identified as Dr. F., fifty, a brilliant, handsome, and talented MIT professor and scientist. Well loved as a teacher, mentor, and passionate community activist, he was described by friends, family, and colleagues as cheerful, extroverted, and successful. He was married with two young daughters, and according to reports, had never suffered from depression or any mental illness.

On October 19, 2014, a former BBC journalist, K., fifty, was found hanged by her own bootlaces in a toilet at Istanbul's Atatürk Airport. K., who had been working in Iraq as the interim director for the Institute for War and Peace Reporting, was also working on a Ph.D. at the University of Canberra, and had just submitted the first chapter of her thesis to her supervisor. CCTV footage shows her entering the women's bathroom alone. There was no sign of a struggle. She had two credit cards in her wallet, along with a large amount of cash. When her death was ruled a suicide, there was an outcry of disbelief. Those who knew her found it impossible to believe that K. would simply abandon her friends, loved ones, colleagues, and pets, and her important humanitarian work in the field of conflict.

On February 8, 2016, fifty-four-year-old Mrs. H. of Mountlake Terrace in the state of Washington, a systems analyst who worked at a center for HIV/AIDS research and prevention, took a piece of meat out of her freezer for dinner, drove to the overflow lot at the nearby park-and-ride as she did every workday, then texted the driver of her car pool that she had forgotten her workplace identification key, was running late, and would meet her in ten minutes. Then she left her car in the lot, walked a mile and a half, disposed of her work ID and cell phone so well they were never found, crawled into a ditch, taped a plastic bag over her head, and suffocated.

Friends, family, and coworkers describe Mrs. H. as "full of

life." At least five hundred people attended her funeral. She had been married for over thirty years, had a grown son, enjoyed her job, was active in the community, and had recently adopted a cat. Her car was found locked and secured, and nothing had been taken from it. Her clothes were intact and not in disarray. According to the autopsy report, the cause of death was "asphyxiation and fresh water drowning." There were no injuries or defensive wounds consistent with an assault, abduction, or struggle. Toxicology tests revealed no unusual substances in Mrs. H.'s system. There was nothing to suggest she had been robbed. All suspects, including her husband, were eliminated. Her death was ruled a suicide.

These apparently impulsive and spontaneous acts of self-destruction baffled the police and bewildered family and friends, many of whom, as in the cases of K. and Mrs. H., refused to accept the verdict of the medical examiner. And yet we do not know how long any of these people had been contemplating the act; neither, perhaps, did they.

Consider the case of K., for example: just prior to her death, she had fallen asleep at the airport in Istanbul and missed her flight by fifteen minutes. The next flight was not for another twelve hours. For a seasoned traveler used to working in war zones, this should have been a minor setback, but K.'s sister, who gave interviews with the British press, believes it was the breaking point. Friends and colleagues regarded K. as fearless and resilient, but her sister suspects this was a persona K. worked hard to project. In her sister's opinion, K. was fragile, vulnerable, and plagued by a sense of incompetence; she took on the problems of other people as a way to escape from her own. We assume that years of living and working in war zones makes a person tough, but K.'s sister thinks it had weakened K. to the breaking point, and that the accumulated trauma may have been just too much for her to bear.

On this particular night, her sister speculates, K. may have been simply "exhausted" and "emotionally raw." It was late, K. was tired, she'd missed her flight, and perhaps the person at the desk had been rude or short with her. When told by airline staff she had to buy a new ticket, K. apparently became "tearful." Surrounded by unfriendly strangers, she may have been feeling unbearably desolate and sad, and the thought of spending another twelve hours at the airport may have simply pushed her over the edge, leaving her unable to think about anything except extinguishing her pain. "I think she just took a snap decision to check out," said her sister.

In the case of Mrs. H., we have no idea what could have happened over the weekend that might have sent her into a state of despondency by Monday morning. Had she learned some bad news? Had she been diagnosed with an illness? Had her husband asked for a divorce? Had she discovered an act of betrayal? Had she somehow lost hold of the thread that drew together the fabric of her life? I picture her taking the meat out of the freezer in the morning to defrost for her husband's dinner, getting ready to go to work as usual, then suddenly realizing: There's no point.

In other words, the suicide that appears impulsive to outsiders is often the result of inner preparation that may have been going on for a long time—perhaps even, as Albert Camus suggests in his essay *The Myth of Sisyphus,* unconsciously: "An act like this is prepared within the silence of the heart, as is a great work of art. The man himself is ignorant of it. One evening he pulls the trigger or jumps." Survivors of suicide attempts that they themselves describe as "impulsive" may be unaware of how often and how deeply they may have been thinking about the act (which is not to say that such acts are necessarily preceded by any obvious warnings). We are generally unaware of our habitual ruminations, prior notions, and mental rehearsals, and the suicidal in particular often develop habits of secrecy and duplicity. If the survivor of a suicide attempt describes their unsuccessful effort as "impulsive," this may simply mean that they were not conscious of their motive at the time, or that they are ashamed to tell the truth. As

Douglas Kerr remarks in his book *Forensic Medicine,* "The most unlikely people sometimes take their own lives, and their behavior immediately before the act frequently gives no indication of their intentions."

In short, no one can know exactly what goes through the mind of a person who takes his or her own life. They may have been struggling with suicidal feelings for many years for unknown reasons. They may have barely been managing to maintain balance for weeks, perhaps months, before something finally tips them over the edge. It could be anything or nothing: a look, a gesture, a toothache, a headache, an unpleasant word, a fleeting, transient thought.

After the suicide of Dr. F. from the Tobin Bridge, local residents suggested that antisuicide barriers should be installed, as they have been on other bridges and landmarks known to attract suicidal jumpers. Such arguments are usually overruled on the grounds of expense, the fact that such barriers spoil the "life-enhancing" view (and may themselves even inspire thoughts of suicide), and the "common knowledge" that anybody wanting to kill him or herself will do so in the end, one way or another.

But every human mind is different, and each case is unique. Some people have a constant and profound desire to die that only grows more intense over time. Others may be genuinely suicidal, but if they have no opportunity to act, their feelings may gradually change. The suicidal impulse may manifest itself again when the chance to act arises, but it may not. It may appear in another form, or it may fade away altogether.

The idea that "anybody wanting to kill himself will do so in the end" was disproved at least thirty years ago by the British "gas suicide study," which found evidence that between 1963 and 1975, the annual number of suicides in England and Wales showed a sudden, unexpected drop at a time when suicide was on the rise in most other European countries. This abrupt decline in suicides, it turned out, correlated with the progressive removal of carbon monoxide from the domestic gas supply, as the government had discovered that natural gas was much cheaper to use. The reduced suicide rate was an unanticipated and accidental consequence of this conversion, proving that most of those unable to kill themselves in the kitchen did not, eventually, look for different keys to Death's private door.

Rey Rivera may have had good reason to be in the neighborhood of the Belvedere when he went missing, since the offices of Agora are in Mount Vernon, the historic district north of downtown where the former hotel is situated. He may even have been meeting someone in the Belvedere's Owl Bar, which is open to the public, although bar staff have no recollections of seeing the conspicuously tall, handsome man that day. Still, even if he went to the Owl Bar, there was no reason for him to be anywhere else in the building, especially not on the roof, which is out of bounds even to condominium owners, who are legally entitled to access all the residential floors. And those who knew Rivera describe him as reliable and responsible, not the kind of person who was prone to spontaneous acts, of which jumping off a fourteen-story building is perhaps the embodiment.

Among the ranks of suicides, those who leap to their deaths have a special place. They are widely agreed to be the most impulsive. All you need is somewhere high. There is no need for any preparation—the gun, the noose, the car in the garage, the plastic bag, the razor blades, the right amount of medication. Most suicide methods hold the promise of pain, but high places are dizzying, intoxicating; with the sight of sky comes the idea of flight and final deliverance. In this regard, gravity is your friend. "To the mouse and any smaller animal," writes J.B.S. Haldane in his essay "On Being the Right Size," "gravity presents practically no dangers. You can drop a mouse down a thousand-yard mine shaft; and, on arriving at the bottom, it gets a slight shock and walks away, provided that the ground is fairly soft." But as the saying goes, the

The Owl Bar, date unknown

bigger they come, the harder they fall. "A rat is killed, a man is broken, a horse splashes." Those who leap from high buildings into public places are, even if they are not conscious of it, angry with somebody, or perhaps everybody. They want to make an impact. They want to ruin your day.

In a 1914 article on the many causes of human fear, the psychologist G. Stanley Hall described those who are afraid they will suddenly jump from a high place with no reason:

Very common is the impulse, usually very sudden, to hurl oneself down from towers, windows, roofs, bridges, high galleries in church or theater, precipices, etc., and not a few grew rigid, livid, clenched their hands and teeth, clung almost convulsively to railings or bystanders, or had to be held by their friends from plunging off in order to escape the tension by "ending it all" or "to see how it would feel" to fall or get the "beautiful sensation" of it. . . . The pure suicide motive in these cases is often a sudden eruption, it is a good opportunity to die and have it all over in a moment. There is little doubt, however, that this jumping off instinct in the young and old may lead to death without any real plan of suicide.

For many years, the Belvedere was one of Baltimore's tallest buildings, and accessible to anyone with enough money to book a room for the night. Unsurprisingly, it has had its fair share of jumpers. For example, on February 22, 1954, thirty-three-year-old Dr. Marvin Alpert registered at the hotel with his twenty-seven-year-old wife, Lorraine. The couple had been married for just over five years, and had a young daughter. Normally, they lived at the Park Drive Manor, a large apartment-hotel in Philadelphia, but the previous October, Lorraine had been admitted to the Phipps Clinic at Johns Hopkins, suffering from depression.

Dr. Alpert, a respected ophthalmologist at the University of Pennsylvania Hospital, arrived in Baltimore that morning and went directly to the clinic to pick up his wife to spend the day with her. The weather was chilly, and Mrs. Alpert was in no mood for sightseeing, so it makes sense that the couple spent their conjugal visit at the Belvedere. Dr. Alpert was planning to stay overnight in Baltimore and to return to Philadelphia the following morning. Lorraine had to be back at the clinic by six p.m. About an hour before her curfew, Dr. Alpert left his wife in their fifth-floor room while he went to make a purchase at a nearby drugstore. When he returned, the room was cold, and his wife was nowhere in sight.

The window was standing open. Alpert ran to it, looked over the edge, and saw Lorraine lying unconscious on the roof of the hotel kitchen four stories (about fifty feet) below. An ambulance was called and a crowd gathered. Mrs. Alpert was barely conscious when medics retrieved her from the kitchen roof; they took her to Johns Hopkins Hospital, where she was found to have two broken legs and a fractured skull. She died two hours later.

Mrs. Alpert, with her history of depression, was clearly at risk, but on the whole, jumpers rarely show the usual warning signs associated with suicidal behavior. Compared to those who use other methods, jumpers are less likely to have known histories of mental illness. They have fewer previous suicide attempts. Jumping from a high place offers ease, speed, and the certainty of death, all of which encourage impulsive action. In general, however, perhaps because it is so resolutely final and demands a certain steely bravado, jumping accounts for only 2 percent of suicides worldwide. In the United States, firearms are the method of choice for men, and overdoses for women. In Europe, where firearms are more difficult to come by, the noose, for men, replaces the gun.

Another reason why the proportion of jumpers is so low is that the world's highest suicide rates are found in extremely poor countries—for example, Guyana, Sri Lanka, Suriname, and Mozambique—places in which it is very rare to find high buildings that are accessible to ordinary people. As a result, those in rural agricultural areas resort to the method used by around 30 percent of the suicides committed in the world every year, and one of the most painful: drinking pesticides.

As might be expected, jumpers are much more common in densely populated cities known for their skyscrapers. The cities with the most high-rise buildings are also the cities with the highest proportions of jumping suicides. In Singapore, for example, 72 percent of suicides are jumpers; in Hong Kong, the figure is 50 percent; in New York, 23 percent. If you live in a town with no buildings higher than five stories, you are advised to select an alternative method. Suicide guidelines from the Hemlock Society, a right-to-die advocacy group, suggest that if your town has few buildings higher than four or five floors, jumping might not be the best way of taking your own life, since such relatively low leaps are not always fatal. If you have no choice but to jump from a fourth or fifth floor, the guidelines suggest, you should try to land on your head in order to maximize the chances of brain hemorrhage—the most frequent cause of death for suicidal jumpers. Gruesome as this may sound, according to physicist and philosopher Sascha Vongehr, in a blog entry devoted to the science of suicide, the half-second delay between brain receptor activity and awareness of experience means that the jumper dies before the impact of the landing. This speculation, obviously, cannot be confirmed.

While six floors should be enough to kill you, a drop of at least ten floors is advisable. In such circumstances, you do not have to concern yourself about what part of your body hits the ground first, assuming you have an adult body weight and that you land on a solid surface. Of course, there have been bizarre and miraculous exceptions—people have survived falls from airplanes without parachutes, while others have died after tripping over their shoelaces.

Yet are not all individuals exceptions to the statistical average? The French sociologist Emile Durkheim believed so. In his famous book on the subject, he wrote that "each victim of suicide . . . gives his act a personal stamp which expresses his temperament, the special conditions in which he is involved, and which, consequently, cannot be explained by the social and general causes of the phenomenon." To make sense of the death of Rey Rivera, we must ask what the detective Auguste Dupin in "The Mystery of Marie Roget" describes as "the proper question in cases such as this," which is "not so much 'what has occurred?' as 'what has occurred that has never occurred before?'" For detailed particulars, the best place to begin is the autopsy report.

According to this document, Rivera hit the ground feet first. He had rather less external damage than one might expect after a fall of 118 feet, no doubt because his fall was broken around twenty feet from the ground, when he crashed through the roof of the former swimming pool. Still, the report makes nightmarish reading. These are the injuries found on Rivera's body: two cuts to the forehead, one of which is four inches long; fractures to the nose and jaw; four ejected teeth; fractures to the cheekbone; multiple fractures to the skull from the top of the spine to the eye sockets, resulting in a brain hemorrhage; torn neck muscles, leading to further hemorrhage; cuts and bruises to the chest; two fractures to the collarbone; twenty-four broken ribs, which have punctured the heart and lungs and damaged the liver; a broken pelvis; cuts and tears to the right groin and testicle; many cuts and bruises on the torso in addition to two enormous lacerations on either side, one nine by seven inches long, and the other nine by four; torn skin on the front and back of the arms; legs cut so badly that muscles and tendons can be seen; the right leg broken in two places, with bone protruding through the skin.

V

THE EVIDENCE SUGGESTS that Rivera died not long after he disappeared. The medical examiner told Allison that his stomach cavity contained a residue of brown matter, presumably the potato chips he ate before leaving home around four p.m. Since he did not pay the parking attendant, he must have arrived at the parking lot sometime after six that evening, which is when the attendant goes home. If the crash D. and I heard around ten was the sound of Rivera falling through the roof, that leaves six hours between the time he left home and the time of his fatal plunge.

At some point in those six hours, he found his way to the roof of the Belvedere without being seen. The roof is not easy to get to, even for those familiar with the building. Twice, when we first moved in, I went up there to sunbathe. In doing so, I was effectively trespassing, since the roof is definitely out of bounds. It's a dangerous place. A single thin iron railing immediately opposite the access door is the only barrier against the drop. When I lay down and closed my eyes, the edge of the building always felt much closer than it was, though it was never really very far away. It was too hot and scary and uncomfortable to stay up there for

Access to the Belvedere Roof

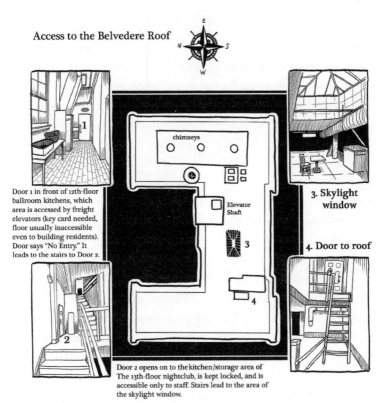

Door 1 in front of 12th-floor ballroom kitchens, which area is accessed by freight elevators (key card needed, floor usually inaccessible even to building residents). Door says "No Entry." It leads to the stairs to Door 2.

chimneys

Elevator Shaft

3. Skylight window

4. Door to roof

Door 2 opens on to the kitchen/storage area of The 13th-floor nightclub, is kept locked, and is accessible only to staff. Stairs lead to the area of the skylight window.

long. Both times, when I got up after lying in the sun, I found myself overwhelmed with dizziness, and had to sit down until I had recovered my balance.

The roof is reached via a ladder in the attic, but the attic is hard to find. There are two ways to get there. One is through a door, accessible only to staff, at the back of the 13th Floor nightclub. The other way is through a door in the service area next to the kitchens on the twelfth floor, which is also off-limits. This door is marked "No Entry." A resident's key card is needed in order to take any of the building's four elevators, but even the card will take you only to the tenth floor. To go any higher, the elevator must be unlocked by the concierge.

From the attic, however, the ladder that leads to the roof is not difficult to find. The rest of the attic space is taken up by the elevator mechanisms, heating and cooling ducts, insulated pipes, fuse boxes, storage areas, and a loft space lit by a dusty glass skylight. When I was up there, someone had put a table and two chairs in this space; on the table were a pack of cards and an ashtray full of stale butts. There was also a dead fern hanging from the rafters in a plastic pot. I wondered whether the bartenders or cleaning staff were using the loft as a place to relax or nap between shifts. Farther back was a narrow hallway leading to a series of small, low-ceilinged rooms where the hotel's staff once slept.

According to the police report, "it was determined that the roof was accessible." I do not know where this information came from or what it means, but it is true that in 2006, when Rivera found his way to the roof, the elevator was often left unlocked, many of the fire doors were not alarmed, the security cameras didn't always work, and the bartenders at the 13th Floor would go up to the roof to smoke, so the roof access door was usually left unlocked.

I think the question that needs to be asked is not whether the roof was accessible, but whether a man who looked like Rey Rivera could have found his way up there without being seen, stopped, and questioned. Even if he knew exactly where he was going and how to get there, this seems hard to fathom. With regard to this latter point, the police report contains another unsourced claim: "The victim had frequented the Belvedere on several occasions in the past."

The Belvedere has both a bar and a nightclub, and in 2006, the same bar staff worked in both the Owl Bar and the 13th Floor. Allison says she and Rey went to the Owl Bar twice at most—though it is possible Rey may have been there more often with his colleagues from work, since Agora's offices are close by—but she is certain that Rey never went to the 13th Floor. Allison works in sales, and is very careful with her accounts. During the time she lived in Baltimore, she kept all her credit card receipts (she and Rey rarely used cash) in the accounting program QuickBooks; after Rey's death, she went back over her records and found no receipts from the 13th Floor. More significantly, the 13th Floor is well known for the spectacular view of downtown Baltimore from its floor-to-ceiling windows, and according to his wife, Rey had such a terrible fear of heights that he was barely able to climb the ladder to put up their Christmas decorations.

Rivera's cell phone was a stylish, ultrathin model: the Sanyo Sprint SCP-6000, which weighed just 2.29 ounces. It landed on the annex roof next to his flip-flops, and according to police, it was still "functional." It seems unusual that after a fall of 118 feet onto the roof's solid surface, the shell of the phone could remain undamaged, with the LCD screen intact, and the circuit board in full working order.

The surface of the swimming pool roof is a common type of single-ply roofing used in commercial buildings. I ask two friends, one a physicist and the other an expert on the technology of electronic devices, for their opinions. They both say the same thing: that it is unlikely the phone would be intact after the fall, but not impossible. For example, it might have stayed in Rivera's trouser pocket, since his body appeared to have remained upright, and come out only when he hit the roof. What was not found on Rey's body, nor on the roof, was an antique money clip that, according to his wife, he always carried with him. It was a wedding gift from Allison, inscribed with his initials, and she had seen him put it in his pocket before she left Baltimore that morning. In fact, she had never seen Rey without it. The money clip has never been found.

Media reports of the case state that the security cameras at the Belvedere "malfunctioned" on the night of May 16—the evening, presumably, of Rivera's death. Still, the tape was given to the police, who kept it for weeks, which suggests it must have contained something of interest. When it was finally returned to the

Belvedere, Gary Shivers sat with Allison Rivera in the concierge booth and watched the footage with her. She was there for a long time. The tape covered a period until the night before Rey went missing; then it jumped to more current footage, as if someone had deleted the night of May 16.

An engineering study obtained by Stephen Janis for the *Washington Examiner* concluded that, to judge by the distance Rey Rivera's body landed from the wall of the Belvedere—an estimated forty-three feet—his velocity on takeoff would have had to be at least 11 mph. The Belvedere roof is narrow and studded with small ventilation ducts; still, there is enough room for someone to run in a straight line for some distance before jumping.

I also talked about the case with Dr. Charles Tumosa, who, before he took up his current position as director of the University of Baltimore's forensic studies program, ran the criminalistics laboratory at the Philadelphia Police Department. Tumosa agreed

The roof of the Belvedere

that Rivera could not have been pushed from the roof, nor could his fall have been accidental, given the horizontal velocity involved. "I've never heard or seen a suicide take a running jump, but there would have to be a certain amount of propulsion," he added. "That leaves me with the impression that he took a dive off the building."

When someone leaps from a height, they can travel a significant horizontal distance even without a running start, if their initial velocity is strong enough. This fact was observed in the early hours of Wednesday, May 29, 1929, about two hours before sunrise, when a motorist driving north on Charles Street saw a man dressed only in his underpants leap from an open window of the Belvedere and land on the far side of the trolley tracks. The motorist pulled over, ran into the hotel lobby, and told the night clerk what he had seen. The night clerk called an ambulance and summoned the hotel detective, who had the Nabokovian name of Harry Shade. The jumper was taken to Mercy Hospital, where he was pronounced dead on arrival. According to the coroner, he was killed instantly from the terrific impact. Almost every bone in his body was smashed.

The room with the open window was on the eighth floor. From the guest register, Shade learned that two Yale students, Leigh Marlow and Robert Phillips, had checked into the room two days earlier, on Monday, May 27. When the detective investigated further, he interrupted two young men packing in haste. One was Robert Phillips; the other gave his name as James Mayfield, and confessed he was not a registered guest. The two men were taken to the police station for questioning, and admitted that their companion, Leigh Marlow, had either jumped or fallen out of the window. They had no idea why he would have done such a thing, but, terrified they would be held responsible, Phillips and Mayfield had been rushing to leave the Belvedere before Marlow's body was found.

Leigh Miltz Marlow came from one of the most prominent families in Helena, Montana, and had been given the best of everything. He and Robert Phillips were seniors at Yale; as freshmen, they had both been students of high standing, fraternity members, and members of the university polo team. They had quickly become close friends and had both been doing well until their junior year, when things had started to change. To the surprise of their friends and families, neither Marlow nor Phillips had been elected to any of Yale's senior societies. Right before Christmas 1928, Marlow was placed on academic probation for skipping classes.

He was reinstated at Yale in the spring semester of 1929, but friends said his "spirit seemed broken, and he had lost all interest in his studies." That semester, he and Phillips had begun drinking heavily and cutting classes again. In the third week of May, he was summoned by the dean and warned that if he missed one more class he would be immediately dismissed. The following week, he missed another class, considered himself expelled, and rather than waiting at Yale for the official letter, decided to spend the weekend in Baltimore with Phillips, hoping to get together with two girls they knew at Goucher College, a private school on the outskirts of the city. Marlow was extremely upset about the situation at Yale, which he had not revealed to his parents. He was especially anxious about what his father would say. Thomas A. Marlow was president of the National Bank of Montana; until his retirement from politics several years earlier, he had been the oldest member of the Republican National Committee.

Marlow and Phillips checked into the Belvedere around six p.m. on Monday, May 27, 1929, and were given a room on the eighth floor that had twin beds and two windows, both overlooking Charles Street. Nobody knows what the boys did on Friday night, but on Saturday, around six p.m., they were turned away from the home of one of the Goucher girls by her father, who told the boys she would not be permitted to see them. Disappointed, they returned to the Mount Vernon neighborhood where, around seven thirty p.m., they ran into a Yale friend, James Mayfield, who joined them for the rest of the evening. Although it was the age of Prohibition, alcohol was not difficult to find in Baltimore, which was known to be a center of resistance; liquor continued to be sold, distributed, and consumed in the city, often even under the auspices of government.

At eleven p.m., Mayfield accompanied Marlow and Phillips to their room at the Belvedere, where they continued drinking heavily. A bellman was called at three a.m. to bring up ice water. He later described seeing three young men in the room; he said one of them was in "a highly nervous condition, pacing the floor and threatening to jump out of the window." Another of the young men, according to the bellman, told him not to worry, as his friend was perfectly well, and they promised to look after him closely.

Sometime after the bellman left, the three men retired for the night, with Mayfield sleeping on a blanket on the floor. After he had been asleep for about half an hour, Robert Phillips was woken by the sound of Leigh Marlow getting out of bed and stumbling around the room. Phillips sat up and switched on the bedside lamp just in time to see Marlow, in his underwear, climbing onto the ledge of the open window, pausing for a moment, then plunging out.

When police searched the room, they found a pint of gin and nine empty wine bottles that had also contained gin. Phillips and Mayfield were detained on the charge of violating the Volstead Act, and a Prohibition agent was summoned to discuss the provenance of the contraband liquor with the two young men. Family connections no doubt played a part in the outcome of the case, since Phillips and Mayfield were released without charges, and the coroner decided that an inquest into Leigh Marlow's death would not be necessary. Since Marlow was under the influence of alcohol at the time, the coroner concluded, it was impossible to be sure that he intended to take his own life. Perhaps he was looking for the bathroom and, drunk and disoriented, stepped out of the window by mistake. The verdict in this case was not suicide, but accidental death.

Leigh Marlow, plunging from a lower height than Rey Rivera and launching himself from a standing position from the window ledge, still landed halfway across Charles Street, a distance of at least twenty feet from the side of the building. While such a distance certainly suggests a high velocity upon takeoff, it is not enough to require a running jump, nor to preclude a push.

According to Dr. Melissa Brassell, the assistant state medical examiner who conducted Rey Rivera's autopsy, he had been dead for at least a week when his body was found. There were no signs of a struggle and no evidence of foul play, though after eight days of decay, it was impossible to be sure. No drugs were found in his body, and the small amount of alcohol found could easily have been produced during the process of decomposition. "Injuries at the time of the autopsy were consistent with the fall from a height," concluded Dr. Brassell in her report. "Because the circumstances surrounding the incident are unclear, and it is not known how the deceased came to have precipitated from a height, the manner of the death is best classified as undetermined."

To a medical examiner, deaths fall into one of five categories: natural death, accident, suicide, homicide, and undetermined. A death is ruled undetermined when, after a careful investigation, even if the majority of the evidence seems to point one way or another, the cause cannot be conclusively ascertained.

The role of the medical examiner is to record the verifiable facts. The ME's report is based entirely on the condition of the body rather than on who or what caused the lethal injury. It is not the business of the medical examiner to speculate or to offer personal opinions of what might have happened to the victim. Whether she was aware of it or not, however, by classifying Rivera's death as "undetermined," Dr. Brassell made things much easier for the police. The vast majority of Baltimore's homicides are gang and drug related. In comparison to these deaths, the circumstances of Rivera's demise are remarkably obscure. If Dr. Brassell had classed his death as a homicide, the resulting investigation would have required a huge investment of time and resources, with possibly little chance of the crime being solved, or of any arrests being made.

Of the 4,323 bodies autopsied at the office of Baltimore's chief medical examiner in 2006, 36 percent were concluded to have died as a result of natural causes and 23 percent by accident; 20 percent were ruled "undetermined"—almost as many as were ruled to be homicides (13 percent) and suicides (8 percent) combined.

Stephen Janis, the only investigative journalist in Baltimore who refused to let go of the Rivera case, believes it is possible Rey was killed by someone who chose to disguise the murder as a suicide. "The fact that the medical examiner has classed it as undetermined means nobody's going to ask any questions," Janis told me, when we met in the Owl Bar to discuss the case. "This is what they do rather than admitting that they're out of their depth. They just have too much work to handle. I think there's enough evidence with Rey's death to call it a homicide. If they'd just done a little more work and ruled it a homicide, it could have been a whole different case."

What convinced most people that Rey Rivera took his own life, however, was the announcement by police that a note had been found at Rivera's home. It is true that Rey left behind a piece of writing, but this was a document rather than a personal note. It was, according to an FBI report on the case, "a piece of paper covered in printed type that had been reduced in size, most likely by a copy machine, placed in a transparent document protector, folded into a square, and taped to the side of Rivera's desktop computer at home." Is this why he returned home for a moment—to tape this paper to his computer? If so, why? Was it a message to someone, or a warning? Did he know he might not be coming back?

Interestingly, Rey had left his computer running. On his screen was a site that showed the time at which the sun rose and set in Baltimore. This apparently unconnected piece of information led to the circulation of a rumor that Rey had been keeping a log on his computer of the best places to see the sunset in Baltimore. From this, a connection was made to the chair that was seen on the Belvedere's roof. Some people speculated that Rey had been sitting on the roof watching the sunset when, for some reason, he made the decision to jump. This seems unlikely to me. I think the mysterious chair on the roof is, so to speak, neither here nor there. I imagine it was brought there by one of the bartenders at the 13th Floor who wanted to sit and smoke, and that it was later blown off the edge by a heavy wind.

The cryptic document left behind by Rivera is addressed to "Brothers and Sisters," refers to "a well-played game," and begins and ends with the maxim "Whom virtue unites, Death cannot separate," which is used by the Freemasons. Mel Blizzard, a former Baltimore police commander and a specialist in behavioral assessment, reviewed the document at the request of the reporter Jayne Miller, and described it as "a weird stream of conscious [sic] writing." Blizzard also said that the document's author "could be writing some kind of code to someone about something. That's possible."

The note mentions "the current participants," and refers to the actor Christopher Reeve (who had died the previous year) and the director Stanley Kubrick, as well as a long list of Rivera's friends, colleagues, and relations, with a request to make them (and himself) "five years younger." This is followed by a list of recent inventions and technologies: Portable Data Assistants, Flash Drives, the Human Genome, Genetic Engineering, Viagra-type drugs, the Fuel Cell, Bluetooth, Overnight Express Shipping, Airbags, Computer Operating Systems, Thermal depolymerization, Horizontal Drilling, Wi-Fi, the da Vinci Surgical System, Hybrid Engines, Muscle Milk, and Heads-Up Displays. It also includes a series of media-related abbreviations (VCD, DVD, HDVD, HDTV, jpeg, mpeg). Accompanying the document is a blank check, drawn on the account of Rivera's video company, Ceiba Productions, which he had named after the official tree of Puerto Rico, whose firm trunk and spreading roots were once believed to connect the underworld, the terrestrial realm, and the spirits of heaven.

Local detectives, confounded, turned the document over to the FBI Behavioral Analysis Unit. The FBI report, which I obtained by means of a Freedom of Information Act request, has little to offer. Rivera's personal risk of being a victim of violent crime is assessed to be "low." There were "no guns available in Rivera's residence," Rivera "did not owe a large amount of money and appeared to be financially stable," although he "had recently borrowed $15,000 to support his production company." The document does not appear to be a suicide note, the FBI report concludes, since "legitimate suicide notes" (which are left in only 25 percent of cases) are generally left in a more conspicuous place or addressed to a particular individual, and they are written by the victim to explain the reason for their suicide.

The statement that Rey "recently borrowed $15,000 to support his production company" is baffling to Allison Rivera. She knows Rey never borrowed any money because she bought the video production equipment on her own credit card, and she has the receipts to prove it. Nor was the equipment bought "recently." Rey produced his first video in November 2005; Allison remembers him working on it when they went to Puerto Rico to get married. He finished the tape two days before the wedding, and the payment he received covered the cost of the production equipment.

As for the mysterious note, Allison says that Rey was always working on creative projects and writing down whatever came to mind. Whenever they went out to dinner, he would jot down random thoughts and ideas on his napkin. Allison still has boxes full of Rey's notebooks, small and large, as well as other scraps of paper on which he noted things he wanted to remember. His handwriting was so bad that there are many she has never been able to decipher. However, the note in question—typed, and laid out in an unusual way—is bothersome to Allison in that it seems different from Rey's usual spontaneous scribbles. She thinks it may be a communication of some kind, and that there may be a code in the allusions, the numbers used, or the layout.

"It seemed really bizarre," said Fred Bealefield, a former commissioner of the Baltimore Police Department, of the Masonic references contained in Rey's note. "Based on what we've seen, his interest in the Masonic order was not necessarily to do charitable work. Somehow, it was linked to the movie industry, and this theory that somehow there was some control being exerted by the Masonic order."

Allison Rivera admits that, in the time leading up to his death, the Freemasons had become a subject of fascination for Rey. She recalls that he spent the weekend before his disappearance reading Joseph Fort Newton's 1914 book *The Builders,* which connects the origins of Freemasonry to ancient Egypt and the early mystery religions. Earlier on the afternoon he went missing, Rivera purchased a book called *Freemasons for Dummies,* and kept an appointment with a member of a Maryland Masonic lodge, to discuss the possibility of joining the Masons. This gentleman said there was nothing unusual about the conversation at all, describing it as typical of someone who wanted to learn about the organization's membership. Rey thanked him for the meeting and said he would be in touch.

On Wednesday, November 8, 2006, six months after Rey Rivera's death, a partial solar occultation took place. In broad daylight, over a period of five hours, the planet Mercury began a leisurely westward creep across the face of the sun. If you had looked through a telescope, you would have seen the planet in silhouette, stealing by like a sly black moon.

For as long as I can remember, certain kinds of mysteries have enthralled me, especially those that contain an element of the uncanny—an odd coincidence; a mysterious stranger whose presence can't be explained; an element of missing time; a prophetic dream the night before. To me, these wonders are dropped stitches in the fabric of the universe, windows left uncovered for a moment, permitting us a quick glimpse into the unknowable.

All my life, I've wanted to experience something like this, something inexplicable. It does not have to be anything huge or dramatic. As Sherlock Holmes astutely observes to Dr. Watson, "The strangest and most unique things are very often connected not with the larger but with the smaller crimes, and occasionally, indeed, where there is room for doubt whether any positive crime has been committed." Going in search of strange experiences is probably not the best way to find them, but I am tired of waiting. I have sat for hours with my fingers on a motionless planchette; slept alone in graveyards; crawled through the windows of abandoned asylums; followed a hand-drawn map to an unholy megalith, where I observed a lunar eclipse. I have virtually handed myself over to be possessed, bewitched, abducted, or transformed, taken out of my everyday life, even if just for a moment. On my office wall, I have the poster made famous by the conspiracy-obsessed FBI agent Fox Mulder of the TV show *The X-Files*: beneath a grainy image of a UFO is the slogan "I Want to Believe." My temperament, however, is more skeptical than Mulder's. Before I can believe, something inexplicable must happen.

And now it has. The circumstances surrounding the death of Rey Rivera—his disappearance, his presence on the roof, the bizarre note, the distance between his landing point and the hotel, the Freemason connection—are strange enough for an episode of *The X-Files,* and it feels as though the mystery I have been seeking all my life has fallen, so to speak, into my lap. Yet while I am intrigued by the secret that seems to be hidden somewhere in this series of bizarre events, I know I have to watch my step. I have a tendency—perhaps a need—to suspect that hidden forces are at work in any as-yet-unexplained circumstances. I'm too keen to think in cosmic terms, too eager to find connections between unrelated episodes, desperate to provoke an epiphany.

But an epiphany can't be provoked. An epiphany produces itself. A forced epiphany is not an epiphany; it is epiphany's opposite. It is an apophany.

The word "apophenia" (from the Greek *apo,* away from, and *phaenein,* to show) was coined in 1958 by the German psychiatrist Klaus Conrad to describe those revelations that appear to provide insight into the interconnectedness of reality but that turn out to be the second phase of delusional thinking in schizophrenia. The first stage of delusional thinking, according to Conrad's system, is *Trema* (stage fright); at this point, the patient has the feeling that something very important is about to happen.

A sudden glimpse into the ultimate interconnectedness of everything sounds like spiritual revelation, not psychopathology. When does a metaphysical vision become a medical problem? If you are so convinced by a private revelation that you no longer care whether anyone else shares your beliefs—when, in other words, you are no longer a part of conventional social structures— have you achieved a heightened state of wisdom, or are you experiencing the first stage of a grave mental illness? If revelation and delusion turn out not to be opposites, but the same thing, then what might come next?

It might be a vision of the True God.

Or it may be Conrad's third and final stage of delusional thinking:

Apocalypse.

VI

JAYNE MILLER OF WBAL-TV is a local reporter who, I am told, is known for her tough approach to cover-ups and corruption. For some reason—perhaps the "y" in her name—I picture her as a glamorous blonde in her thirties, and I am slightly surprised to hear the voice of a hard-boiled professional when we talk on the phone.

Miller tells me Rivera's death is one of the most mysterious cases she has ever encountered in all her years as an investigative journalist. She gives me the number of a woman named Jennifer who was one of Rey's closest friends. I call Jennifer, who is fielding inquiries from the media, and she talks to me on the phone for a long time. She speaks quickly, in a slightly manic way, as if she were speaking in headlines, leaving me no chance to interrupt her or to ask questions.

Jennifer tells me she is unable to give out contact information for Rey's wife or his parents, as they are severely traumatized and are not ready to speak to anyone about the death of their husband and son. She warns me that if I continue to investigate, I could find myself in very serious trouble. She says the situation is very dangerous. The people who killed Rey will stop at nothing, she tells me. She mentions a local reporter who has been investigating the case. He came home one day and found his house had burned down. When he went to the police, they said it was probably an accident. After that, says Jennifer, he wanted nothing more to do with the case.

Jennifer strikes me as one of those people who enjoy inserting themselves into the center of a disaster. Her monologues are like a long strip of land bearing a sign that says "No Trespassing." When I ask for the name of the reporter whose house burned down and the name of his news organization, Jennifer says she can't remember any of the details. She has spoken to so many people over the last couple of weeks, she says.

Inwardly, I dismiss this anecdote as an exaggerated rumor. While Jennifer's paranoid digressions never reach the level of a fully formed rant, she tends to talk in circles, rambling and repeating herself in the style of those who post on Internet conspiracy forums, where the death of Rey Rivera is attributed to the Freemasons, the New World Order, the CIA, or the FBI.

Yet in some ways, Jennifer tells me just what I want to hear. Her story feeds my compulsion to question the consensus version of events. It is impossible for me to believe that someone who has just booked an editing suite for the upcoming weekend would suddenly throw himself off the roof of a fourteen-story building, especially if he has a well-known fear of heights. Like almost everyone else caught up in the case, I feel there has to be something more sinister going on. Rivera's death would make far more sense if he had made himself the enemy of a powerful underground cabal. When an event has far-reaching consequences, we assume its causes must be equally momentous, just as when we want to roll a higher number, we shake the dice harder, and for a longer time.

I do not believe that I will solve the mystery of Rey Rivera's death; nonetheless, I cannot help wanting to go deeper. I feel that my invisibility, humbling as it is to my vanity, may be useful to my inquiry. It will, I hope, give me the ghostly advantage of observing unobserved. But of course, there is more to it than this. Invisible or not, I am unable to look away.

Since we first met, seventeen years ago, D. has given me three framed cartoons from the *New Yorker*. Two are George Booth bulldog prints; the third shows a group of people standing around an accident victim in the street. A bald, bespectacled, official-looking man with a large briefcase is pushing his way through the crowd. The caption reads: "Let me through—I'm morbidly curious!"

The gift was intended as an affectionate joke at my expense. Those who know me well are aware of my dark side, although these days I try to keep it under wraps. Over time, I have learned not to talk about violent death at social gatherings. Just as the child who enjoys cutting the tails off cats and dogs may grow up to be a great surgeon, I have managed to sublimate my interests into such socially acceptable pursuits as reading and writing about true crime.

Still, those who get close to me eventually learn that I'm fascinated by suicides, accidents, death scene photographs, forensic accounts of bizarre fatalities. I am not alone. I have encountered many others who find these things alluring. My dermatology nurse, my hairdresser, two of my graduate teaching interns, and a cosmetologist friend—all women—share my secret passion. We recommend podcasts and documentaries, exchange books and movies. We are like a secret sisterhood.

A colleague of mine, F., a philosopher, cannot understand my interest in the macabre. He constantly presses me to explain myself, as if he is looking for some moral reckoning. Whenever I remind F. that I am hardly alone in my pursuits, he insists, "Yes, but with you it is different. With you, it is an obsession." He finds it difficult to leave the subject alone. Every time he brings it up, his voice gets louder and his face grows slightly flushed. He seems to think I am refusing to confront something about my personality; perhaps he believes me to be a misanthrope, a brute, or a sadist. He may be thinking of Nietzsche's comment that "in all desire to know there is already a drop of cruelty."

One might argue that my fascination with accounts of violent death signals a desire to contemplate the pain of others—my revenge, perhaps, on those who find me invisible. On the other hand, such interests are not unusual for one born, like me, with Neptune in Scorpio. Such types tend to be deep thinkers who are often fascinated by secrets, mysteries, and dark subjects—death, murder, violence. They may be fixated on the occult.

In an 1811 lecture titled "On the Pleasures of the Mind," the famous Philadelphia surgeon Dr. Benjamin Rush described "persons who take delight in seeing public executions" as affected by a kind of "moral perversion." According to Dr. Rush, these instances of moral depravity "do not belong to the ordinary character of man. They are as much the effects of morbid idiosyncrasy, as a relish for fetid odors, or putrid meats is, of the same state of the senses of smell and taste." Dr. Rush is wrong to dismiss morbid curiosity as a vulgar, uncivilized impulse. There is more to this urge than is suggested by his disdainful sketch of the gleeful crowd at an execution, but we rarely consider its more refined variations: the subtle shades and nuances of that which makes the flesh crawl. And why should we? The English language has no aesthetic vocabulary for these refinements beyond the medical lexicon of the coroner, the euphemisms of the police, and the black humor of the cleanup crew.

Let me share an example I recently came upon. The retired police detective Vernon Geberth, in the fourth edition of his handbook *Practical Homicide Investigation,* refers to the scene of a suicide he once investigated in which the victim had shot himself in the head with a long-barreled shotgun. The ceiling, we are told, is a bloody mess. To make his point, Geberth includes a picture taken at the scene, drawing attention to a feature the reader might otherwise easily overlook. "In this photo," he notes, "the victim's dental plate has been driven into the ceiling along with the blood and brain matter."

This sentence stopped me in my tracks; the detail was so unexpected that it gave me an almost physical jolt. The scene engaged my imagination so much that when I went to bed that evening, I could not stop thinking about it, and had to get up in the night to write down my thoughts. What touched me so much was not only the shock of the uncanny (the familiar dental plate appearing in a place where it should not be), but the way this unpredictable image suddenly materialized in the formal prose of the police report. It was like discovering a ghost orchid growing in a gravel driveway.

My interest in these things is not an obsession, as F. believes. Obsessions are an impediment to life, not an enrichment of it. I believe that if I were feeling suicidal, thinking about that dental plate driven into the ceiling could re-engage me with the world, giving me a reason to go on. If my pursuits appear unhealthy to the modern eye, that is simply because they are no longer fashionable. Mine is the unhealthiness of the modern-day ascetic, the anchorite, the mortifier of the flesh. These moments I seek are my *mementi mori*, ritual injunctions reminding me that my own death is a little closer every day.

I am not a gawker; I am a connoisseur.

I take my investigation to the next level by learning everything I can about Rey Rivera. Mostly, I gather this information from public records, newspaper archives, and Internet forums, where I find the email addresses and Facebook profiles of some of his friends in Maryland, Florida, and California. I make contact online but speak only to one or two people. Two things get in my way. The first is that the idea of telephoning a stranger out of the blue to ask personal questions about their recently deceased friend makes me sick with anxiety. So, I conduct most of my interviews by email.

The second difficulty I have is that nobody will go on the record. Everybody is afraid. Most of Rey's friends appear to believe that he was murdered by a group of people so wealthy and powerful that they can kill anyone with impunity, and will not hesitate to kill again. It is not just one or two people who believe this, but everybody I contact. Some are convinced of it; to others it is merely a suspicion; still, nobody seems to believe that Rey's death was a suicide.

Rey Omar Rivera was born on Sunday, June 10, 1973, in the U.S. Air Force Base hospital in Madrid, Spain, where his father, Angel Rivera, an Air Force officer, was stationed at the time. His mother, Maria, was so certain she was having a girl that she had no name ready when the baby turned out to be a boy. The Riveras, who both came from Puerto Rico, already had one son, Angel Junior, so Rey's name was chosen virtually on the spot. The daughter Maria had been expecting, named Elena, arrived two years later, when the family was stationed in Arkansas. There they lived for a few years before Angel retired, at which time they moved to Winter Park, a northeast suburb of Orlando.

Rey, a typical Gemini, was creative, cheerful, outgoing, and extremely friendly, even as a young child. He grew into a tall, smart, good-looking kid who loved sports; he had an aptitude for basketball and a special talent for swimming. He also had an impressive memory and a love of learning. When Elena took piano lessons, Rey learned to play by ear just by listening to her. When visiting family in Puerto Rico, as a young man, he impulsively decided he wanted to learn to play the *cuatro,* a small guitar used at parties and other gatherings, and soon became a practiced player.

As his mother said, when Rey wanted to do something, he just went right ahead and did it.

In his junior year at Winter Park High School, Rey won a place at an Olympic swimming camp in California. That was the year he discovered water polo.

In the *Orlando Sentinel* of January 13, 1991, when Rey was eighteen, the sportswriter Bill Buchalter wrote, "I've had the opportunity to watch Winter Park get better and better at the sport and watch Rey Rivera become a budding national caliber junior performer. He's a complete player." The Winter Park High School water polo team, the Wildcats, was highly competitive right from the start, but within the team itself, according to their coach, there was no jealousy or competition.

In only their second year playing the game, the Wildcats went to Miami and won the state championship. Rey scored four goals, including a breathtaking clincher that changed the game and brought Winter Park to victory with just thirty-nine seconds to go. Coach Jack Horton kept in touch with Rey, who served as Horton's groomsman at his wedding; he remembers Rey as outgoing, funny, and quick-witted, exactly the opposite of the depressive, neurotic type who might be prone to suicidal thoughts. "Everybody liked him," recalls the coach. Rey was sensitive and thoughtful, he adds, not a "life and soul of the party" kind of guy. "The last time he came over to my place, you know what he did?" Horton asks me. "He alphabetized my record collection. He just sat down on the floor and that's what he did. He was just a super guy."

In his senior year, Rivera was offered a full water polo scholarship to the University of the Pacific, in Stockton, California. He left for Stockton in 1992. At college, he majored in English, since he also loved to write and had a talent for it, though his heart was in water polo. His name is still in the Pacific Tigers Water Polo Hall of Fame—he scored a hundred goals in Stockton during his college career. But his ambitions went beyond the college level. Rey wanted to play on the U.S. water polo team, and he came tantalizingly close. In 1994, in his junior year, he was chosen to compete in the Summer Olympic festival in St. Louis, an event dedicated to developing up-and-coming U.S. athletes, many of whom would go on to be selected as team members at the next Olympics. After Rey graduated from college in 1996, the Royal Spanish Swimming Federation hired him to play in Barcelona.

P., a teammate of Rey's there, told me about the atmosphere. Rey loved the tough training and the competitive games, said P. After matches, the guys would stay out late, drinking and exploring the city's nightlife. Rey's Spanish developed a Castilian accent, and since his family was rarely able to send him extra cash, he earned drinking money by giving English lessons. P. described Rey as a smart guy with a big smile and a great sense of humor who loved to tell jokes. He teased and kidded around a lot, according to P., but he was also tough and had a reputation for getting into fights when he drank.

Rey left Spain when he got the call he had been waiting for his whole life—he had been chosen as a contender for the U.S. water polo team at the 1996 Atlanta Olympics. At twenty-three, he returned immediately to LA to begin training. Unfortunately, he was still young enough that his temper often got the better of him. The way P. described it, Rey had a falling-out with the coach around two weeks before the men were due to leave for Atlanta, and was cut from the team. Those who knew him say it was the biggest regret of his life.

A few years after Rey's death, at a Yahoo group forum for the California water polo community, I find an archived email announcing his memorial mass, which was held on Friday, June 2, 2006, at two p.m., in Santa Monica ("The service will be approximately an hour. Dress attire is neat and casual—khakis and a nice shirt are good—ties and jackets are not necessary"). The email was sent to around twenty people, mostly men. I look a few of them

Rey Rivera

up online. Each seems to be more handsome, charismatic, and successful than the last. One is head coach of the U.S. women's water polo team. Another was featured in a *People* magazine "Olympic Beauties" issue. Yet another is head water polo coach at a major university in California. I email them and eventually, hear back from five. They all write affectionately about Rey. But they prefer me not to mention their names here.

Looking at the profiles of these striking, athletic men, I cannot help wondering whether Rey would have been one of them, had he lived. For the most part, his peers in the world of water polo have, it seems, worked hard and achieved their dreams. From what I've learned about Rey, he was also a hard worker, driven and ambitious; he must have been devastated at being dropped from the team.

It is hard to think of Rey Rivera as a has-been. But the world of professional athletics is cruel; the brute-force, raw-power strength that comes with youth is still the benchmark, and once you're past your peak, if you want to stay in most sports, the only decent jobs are as coaches and commentators, and they're almost as difficult to get as spots on a team. Rey had already moved over into teaching, screenwriting, and film production. Did he to a certain extent feel as though he had missed the main chance?

This sense of one great chance missed is not uncommon. It is perhaps the most comfortable way of explaining why a life hasn't lived up to its youthful potential. It is, no doubt, why Mary Louise Dean ended her life in a room in the Belvedere at the end of February 1945.

When Mary Louise was a child, the world was always on her side. Her family connections had meant she was almost royalty. Mary, who was known as May, was a direct descendant of Elijah Dean II, who served in the Revolutionary War under George Washington. Like many young ladies of her class, May was sent for a year to finishing school in Switzerland. Upon her return, she married John Marvin Gates, a law student at Yale. And this was when the charmed life came to an end.

The marriage ended in divorce, after which May never managed to regain her youthful spirit or artless joy. In time, however, she did begin to recover her need for activity. She trained as a nurse and accompanied a Christian mission to Labrador, where she tended to the suffering and distributed humanitarian aid to the poor. Eventually, she began to rally and regain her interest in life, and on October 17, 1941, at age thirty-seven, she married again, this time to Frederick Frick of Baltimore. As Mrs. Frick, May continued with her nursing, working as a recreational supervisor at the Phipps Clinic.

In the middle of February 1945, when she was forty-two, Mrs. Frick unexpectedly gave notice at the clinic and took a trip to visit her mother and sister in Putnam County, New York. She returned to Baltimore on Wednesday, February 28, but rather than returning home, she checked into the Belvedere. Two days later, her sister, Elizabeth, received a disturbing letter from May written on Belvedere notepaper, and, becoming alarmed, wired May's husband, who, until he received the telegram, had assumed his wife was still in Putnam County, not in a nearby hotel room with a .38 in her purse.

When Frederick Frick called the Belvedere, the desk clerk confirmed that May Louise had checked in two days earlier. The clerk called up to her room. When the call went unanswered, a chambermaid was sent to knock on the door. This failed to rouse Mrs. Frick, so two bellmen entered the room with a passkey. There, lying on the floor with a bullet hole in the left breast and a .38 caliber pistol by its side, was the body of Mrs. May Louise Dean Frick. She had left two notes, one addressed to her husband and the other to the hotel staff, apologizing "for the necessity of causing this trouble."

Those who knew Mrs. Frick assumed that she had never truly recovered from her divorce, but in fact, she had an even darker secret in her past. Frick told the police his wife had suffered from "a nervous disorder" ever since something that had occurred in 1931, many years before they had met. He had learned about it both from his wife and from her sister, Elizabeth. The incident happened just after May returned from Labrador while she was staying with Elizabeth, Elizabeth's attorney husband, N. Stephen A. Van Ness, and their two children in Putnam Country, New York.

The family had planned a family hunting trip to Maine. On the morning of their departure, May had appeared at the top of the stairs with her shotgun in her hand. She had cleaned it herself, she said, and as she came downstairs, she had called gaily on her brother-in-law to "admire its perfection of balance." To show it off, she had swung the shotgun around. It fired—either by the inadvertent touch of May's finger, or by being knocked against the banister as it was swung. Either way, the result was the same:

Stephen's right shoulder, chest, and lung were peppered with buckshot.

Just as Elizabeth appeared at the top of the stairs, Stephen, losing consciousness, managed to rasp that the shooting had been "an accident." He died from his wounds nine hours later.

In time, I begin to realize that if Rey Rivera was murdered, he must have been taken up to the roof of the Belvedere at gunpoint. However, it is difficult to imagine anyone being led up the fourteen long double flights of fire stairs against his will. Even if he was in great shape, the gunman could not have climbed all those stairs without stopping for breath, thus taking the risk that Rivera would shout for help, run through the fire doors into a residential hallway, or, given the likelihood that he was far larger than his assailant, turn around to push him back downstairs.

If Rey was taken up in the elevator, however—and assuming the elevator was locked, as it should have been—the perpetrator would have needed an access card. I begin to wonder: Does Rey's murderer live in the Belvedere? Is one of our neighbors responsible for his death? I begin to watch everyone more closely, paying careful attention to their comings and goings. And while sometimes I begin to wonder whether I have crossed the line into obsession, most of the time I know this is a game I am playing in order to convince myself that my life is more mysterious and exciting than it really is.

Other people fascinate me, but I enjoy them most from a distance—through binoculars or, metaphorically speaking, under a microscope. I suppose that, like many writers, I am something of a voyeur, eager to know all I can about others without putting myself at risk or exposing myself to judgment. I observe while remaining hidden, like a stranger who, on a dark night, looks through the lit window of a neighbor's house. While I can happily lecture to a large group, I am increasingly uncomfortable talking

about myself to a person I do not know well; as a result, it is difficult for me to open myself up to new relationships. If, then, I have
become invisible, perhaps I have only myself to blame. On the other
hand, being unseen has its advantages. As every detective story
reader knows, the alienated outsider makes the best investigator.
Edgar Allan Poe's Dupin also prefers to remain invisible. He is, he
says, "enamored of the night for her own sake," and never leaves
home until the "advent of the true Darkness," when he can go
"seeking, amid the wild lights and shadows of the populous city,
that infinity of mental excitement which quiet observation can
afford." He is also something of a voyeur, boasting, "with a low
chuckling laugh, that most men, in respect to himself, wore windows in their bosoms."

Like Dupin, I tend to look at things from an oblique perspective. In Rey's case, I am unwilling to accept the official narrative.
If anything, it makes me even more curious and confused. I keep
wondering how I would feel if someone I loved suddenly went
missing, out of the blue; if their body was found in mysterious
circumstances; if the cause of death was registered as undetermined; if the police seemed unwilling to investigate. How long
would I spend trying to understand what had happened? Could I
really put the loss behind me and go on with my life?

Then again, what choice would I have?

I notice that Mr. Holloway has also gone missing. To tell the
truth, I have not minded his absence. He is a person both D. and
I go out of our way to avoid—a short, loud, moody man who
lives down the hall. He has a low brow, puffy eyes, and a chin
cleft like a hoof. When either of us meets him in the hallway or
the laundry room, we cannot escape his loud, angry tirades
against the condominium board. He is also obsessively, madly in
love with my dog, whom he grabs at every opportunity, lifting
up the poor animal and trying to kiss him on the mouth, calling
him "sweetie" and "darling." Once, when I was going to the

laundry room, I left our apartment door open, and my dog followed me into the hall. Unfortunately, Mr. Holloway happened
to be on his way to the elevator at the same time. The moment he
saw the dog, he chased it straight through the door of our apartment and into our living room, where he grabbed it and began to
fondle it mercilessly.

He was clearly in need of someone—or something—to love.
Once, a young man with blond hair stayed over in his apartment.
Mr. Holloway introduced this boy to D. as his son, but we never
saw this young person again.

I ask after Mr. Holloway the next time I see the elderly sisters
in 505, Miss Helen and Miss Teresa. They are walking down the
hall slowly on their way to the elevator, Miss Teresa leaning against
her walking frame.

"He passed," says Miss Helen.

"God is good," says Miss Teresa.

The death of a near stranger can still leave a vague discomfort
in our daily life. It is odd how little we know about our neighbors. Yet in life, as in the crime scene, according to forensic scientist Dr. Edmond Locard's principle of exchange, every contact
leaves a trace.

Mr. Holloway's obituary states that "he was unmarried and
left no children. He had an interest in antiques."

"So much for his 'son,' " says D.

I ask Gary Shivers what happened to Mr. Holloway. Gary gives
me a hangdog look.

"He was real sick," he says. "At the end, I was carrying him in
and out, to the hospital and back. He had nobody else to take care
of him. He had all kinds of diseases. And when you're mean, it
don't help none."

Gary also tells me that Miss Helen and Miss Teresa, who share
the same last name, are not sisters, as D. and I have always

assumed, but mother and daughter, though which is the mother and which the daughter is anyone's guess.

At the age of twenty-seven, Rey Rivera decides to teach while he works on breaking into the movie business as a screenwriter. In 2000, he is hired by John Burroughs High School, in Burbank, to teach Spanish as a second language and to coach the school's water polo and swim teams. He is a huge hit with the kids, but even working two part-time jobs, he has trouble covering the bills. Eventually, he takes a third part-time job in admissions at the Los Angeles Film School. As a perk of his job, he starts taking screenwriting classes. Since his college days, Rey has always kept notes, journals, drafts, and outlines of potential novels and plays. He barely has time to write, but he is ambitious and a hard worker, and before long has managed to turn out his first screenplay, which he calls "Virtuoso." It is a surreal horror story about a Puerto Rican piano player. Rey commissions storyboards for the script. The production designer loves it, and thinks it will be a fantastic movie.

The film is something like a Puerto Rican version of *Tommy*, only rather than playing pinball, the protagonist plays the piano. Like Tommy, he is autistic; unlike Tommy, he turns violent whenever he sees blood. His manager, a man in a white suit who smokes a cigar, is also his antagonist, who deliberately instigates Tommy's acts of violence and directs them toward particular goals. The whole project has a bizarre undertone. "Sometime after I got done with the storyboards and illustrations, the Director was murdered or something in the Belvedere Hotel in Baltimore and the 'Virtuoso' movie never got done," wrote the production designer on his website. "Unfortunate and tragic, I say. Rest in Peace, Rey Rivera."

Rey meets Allison Jones through a mutual friend in Los Angeles in 2000. She is a tall, athletic brunette, a sales executive and volleyball player. In 2004, two years after they move in together, Rey proposes, and Allison says yes. But they both know it is too soon. Rey is virtually broke. He can barely even afford a ring, let alone support a family. If he really wants to settle down, Rey knows he is going to have to do something radical.

And this is where Porter Stansberry comes in.

VII

PORTER STANSBERRY WAS a goalkeeper on the Winter Park water polo team and a longtime friend of Rey Rivera's. They grew up together. Those who knew the pair describe Stansberry's childhood relationship with Rivera as one of "idol worship." Rey was big, striking, a model of athletic prowess. Stansberry, although he played sports and hung out at the beach, was, by his own admission, not especially distinguished as either sportsman or scholar.

After high school, Stansberry attended the University of Florida, graduating with a degree in political science ("It's completely worthless," he said in a later interview. "I learned all about how to drink beer and hit on girls"). At college, he demonstrated no special talents and was not especially ambitious; after college, he worked as a lifeguard for a while, then delivered pizza. None of his classmates would have voted him most likely to succeed. And yet somehow, by the age of thirty, Porter Stansberry had become rich. How this happened is difficult for those who knew him at college to explain, but it is important to understand the kind of business Stansberry was involved in when Rey Rivera went to work for him, how the company was established, and the people Stansberry was affiliated with.

In 2015, as a guest on a business podcast called *The Self Made Man,* Stansberry tells the host, Mike Dillard, his life story, in brief. First, though, he sums up where he is today.

> I'm not trying to be falsely modest, but if you'd told me fifteen years ago that the business that I'd started on a borrowed laptop computer, on my kitchen table, when I was living in a third-floor walk-up apartment in Baltimore's most notorious slum, would end up being a hundred-and-fifty-million-dollar-a-year-plus-revenue company with two hundred employees and customers in a hundred and fifty countries, I would have thought that you were completely insane.

Stansberry's biological father, he reveals, was killed in Vietnam, and his mother married a man named Frank Porter Stansberry, "a man of impeachable [*sic*] ethics and character." Frank Porter Stansberry adopted and rechristened Stansberry and his brother when they were small, naming the older boy after himself (Porter Stansberry's first name is also Frank, but he goes by Porter to distinguish himself from his father).

On the podcast, Stansberry explains that, after leaving college, he worked as a "very poorly paid junior analyst" at what he describes as "a very poorly run research company down in Florida"; then, in 1996, "one of our very few clients, William Bonner, bought the business, fired everybody except myself and [my friend] Steve Sjuggerud, brought us to his company in Baltimore, and gave us the chance to write large-circulation newsletters." Bonner's company was Agora, Inc., a quietly complicated affair. And this is where the story starts to get tangled.

Agora was founded in 1978 by William Bonner, who began his career working for the National Taxpayers Union; the company's early stable of products included three financial newsletters. One of these, *Strategic Investment,* was co-edited by Bonner, his friend James Dale Davidson, and their British colleague Lord William Rees-Mogg, a former editor of the London *Times* and a member of the BBC's board of governors and, of course, the House of Lords.

The marketing of *Strategic Investment* pushed the assumption, always tacit, that Rees-Mogg was in bed with MI5, which is just one of the many purported connections between Agora and government intelligence operations. (In fact, followers of the conspiracy theorist Lyndon LaRouche picketed the company's headquarters because of these alleged MI5 links.) Although Davidson and Rees-Mogg (until his death in 2012) remained loosely affiliated with Agora through various business concerns, Bill Bonner has for many years been the company's CEO. *Strategic Investment* briefly rose to national attention during the Clinton administration when its subscribers were sent copies of a small paperback "bookalog"—a marketing pitch in the form of a free book— titled *Who Killed Vince Foster?*

Another of Agora's original publications was a newsletter called *International Living.* An ardent Francophile, Bill Bonner owns two châteaux in France as well as a ranch in Argentina. In the late 1980s, during the craze for offshore investing and retirement abroad, *International Living* did so well that Agora launched a second, similar newsletter, *Passport Club,* which sold investment seminars on how to set up bank accounts in places like Switzerland and Hong Kong. A main aim of these two newsletters was tax avoidance via the international diversification of assets (Agora even had an early newsletter called *Tax Avoidance Digest,* which, for legal reasons, was later renamed *Tax-Wise Money*).

After two years at Agora, Stansberry, who admits he has always had problems with authority, was fired by his supervisor for general insubordination; through a Florida colleague named Mark Ford, he got a job as a junior editor at one of Agora's subsidiaries, the Oxford Club. Here, Stansberry did well enough that in 1999 he was given permission to launch his own Agora subsidiary, which he called Pirate Investor, LLC. This eventually became the company he still runs; it is now known as Stansberry Research LLC (formerly Stansberry & Associates Investment Research), and describes itself as "a subscription-based publisher of financial information and software, serving millions of investors around the world."

Most of us have a particular narrative that we tell ourselves (and others) about how we came to be who we are. Perhaps because he has told it so often, Porter Stansberry's story has been honed over the years, its outcrops and protuberances smoothed away until it has become almost a fairy tale, with an archetypal setting and characters: The true father killed in battle; the poor but honest stepfather; the borrowed laptop; "Baltimore's most notorious slum"; and, at the heart of it all, the orphan boy who, even after his rags-to-riches transformation, stays down-to-earth and never forgets his childhood friends. In fact, the more I listen to Stansberry's interview on *The Self Made Man,* the more I get the sense that he is the kind of person who lives by such stories—he not only believes them but also finds them stirring and romantic. Indeed, it is by crafting such tales that Stansberry has become rich.

"I was good at writing stories," he tells Mike Dillard. "I'd always been a writer, even since I was a little kid." The second secret to his success, reveals Stansberry, is that he only hires people with "great character," even if they have "very little or no experience." Yet when he describes his test of "character," it becomes clear that he is confusing it with something else—charisma, perhaps. His test is to ask himself, "If you were stuck in an airport for five hours with this person, would you be happy about that, or would you be miserable about that?"

In other words, rather than hiring uninteresting but experienced advisors or investment experts, Stansberry called on his old high school friends, as well as the guys he admired and modeled himself on. Most of us take it for granted that our old friends, simply by virtue of *being* our old friends, are people of value and integrity. Hercule Poirot offers a worldlier picture: "Every murderer," he points out, "is probably somebody's old friend."

Stansberry set out to teach himself how to sell financial products by writing persuasively, and he soon found he had a talent for convincing people to buy. In fact, he was a little too persuasive. On May 14, 2002, using the pseudonym Jay McDaniel, he sent out to PirateInvestor.com, his company's email newsletter, what he referred to as a "Super Insider Tip Email," letting subscribers know that a certain company's stock was about to rise on a particular date. In return for an extra $1,000, subscribers were offered a "Special Report" that, "McDaniel" promised, would give them the company's name and the precise date of the price spike.

"See how this works? It's a total insider deal," wrote "McDaniel" in the email. "Hey, I know it's dirty. But I don't make the rules. . . ." The email went out to around 800,000 people, and 1,217 copies of the "Special Report" were sold. In short, this one email netted $1,217,000, of which $200,000 went directly to Stansberry. As he noted in an internal memo to his copywriters, "If we're able to sell this to 250 people and it works, we'll be able to charge almost whatever we want next time." But "McDaniel"'s tip did not pan out. Many subscribers were angry. About two hundred of them demanded their money back. Some complained to the Securities and Exchange Commission.

On April 18, 2003, the SEC filed a civil complaint charging Agora, Pirate Investor LLC, and Porter Stansberry with securities fraud. A bench trial was set for March 2004. The complaint was based not only on the "Super Insider Tip Email" but also on a venture known as the "Oxford Club—Chairman's Circle," which, according to a direct-mail advertisement, offered "lifetime access" to annual "private teleconferences," at which "the world's most knowledgeable experts" would give advice about "important strategies." Members could also consult a "Chairman's Circle private researcher" and would be given the "private [telephone] numbers" of "The Oxford Club's Executive Director, Research Director, and members of its Investment Advisory Panel." The price to join the "Chairman's Circle" was $5,000, and additional sums were due annually.

Although this description of the Oxford Club may bring to mind an elite society where gentlemen sit around drinking claret and chatting about cricket scores and private financial opportunities, the "Club" is, for the most part, a newsletter that gives advice on investments, living abroad, and how to avoid paying income tax. In the 1980s, under the name Royal Society of Liechtenstein, it was one of more than a dozen direct-mail financial newsletters recommending assets whose investors, according to a *New York Times* article published in 1992, "frequently found themselves holding worthless shares."

The Royal Society of Liechtenstein was founded by Joel S. Nadel of Boca Raton and his sidekick Mark Ford; one of their earlier direct-mail ventures included an audiocassette tape on which a man with an English accent who called himself "Charles Lloyd" described the exclusive assembly as "one of the least-known organizations in the world," whose sole purpose was to "amass substantial wealth for its members." Those interested in joining were told to send a check for $100, along with a membership application form, to "our U.S. dispatch address." The recording concludes:

> If I do not receive your application within thirty days, I will eliminate your name from our invitation list, and you will never hear from me again. This is Charles Lloyd from the Royal Society of Liechtenstein. Please destroy this tape now.

In April 1991, after a U.S. Postal Service investigation into an illegal sweepstakes program run by Nadel and Ford, the government froze $6.6 million of Nadel's assets. In June, he paid $100,000 to settle a two-year-old SEC complaint that he had violated securities laws by failing to tell his newsletter subscribers that several stock promoters, since convicted of fraud, had paid him to tout their companies. One of the businesses that Nadel was paid to promote was Goldcor, a "gold-extraction company" whose founders claimed they had invented a way of turning a twenty-mile strip of black volcanic sand in Costa Rica into gold. "The sands that are removed from the beach are replenished by tidal action only after a few days," ran the pitch.

It was, of course, all a huge scam, costing an estimated three thousand investors a total of at least $50 million, of which $13 million was never recovered. In August 1991, two days before he was due to stand trial, Goldcor's president, Richard Brown, fifty-one, was found at his home in Daytona Beach, Florida, shot in the left side of the back of his head. No gun was found at the scene. His death was "probably a murder," concluded investigators, though it could theoretically have been a suicide. Brown's death, like Rey Rivera's, was ruled "undetermined."

Sand cannot be turned into gold. High profits come only from long and substantial investments. In this case, the old farmer's adage proves correct:

> Fruit out of season
> Death without reason

In response to subscriber complaints that the Royal Society of Liechtenstein was not a society and had nothing to do with Liechtenstein (which, being a principality rather than a country, actually has a "sovereign" rather than a "royal" family), Nadel and Ford rechristened their project the Oxford Club and, shortly thereafter, sold it to Agora. Ford was hired by Agora as an "executive consultant," and his talent for embellishment launched the company's meteoric rise as a marketer of investment newsletters. From Boca Raton, under the pseudonym "Michael Masterson," Ford began publishing a series of financial and business self-help books, and established various Agora-affiliated and Agora-owned businesses, including several publishing companies, a stock promotion business, a program training people how to write promotional newsletters, and a travel agency devoted to arranging subscribers' trips to conferences and to the foreign destinations where they might eventually retire.

Mark Ford, now known as Michael Masterson, is Porter Stansberry's personal mentor.

Over the years, Stansberry invited a number of people he knew and admired from high school to join Pirate Investor. In spring 2003, Brad Hoppmann, another member of the Winter Park high school water polo team, moved from Florida to Baltimore to work for Stansberry; Hoppmann bought a house on Lanvale Street, in the genteel neighborhood of Bolton Hill. Other friends of Stansberry's who moved to Baltimore to work for one of Agora's subsidiaries include Steve Sjuggerud, Aaron Brabham, and, in early 2004, Rey Rivera.

For Rey, it was never intended to be a long-term job. Porter sold him on the idea of moving out to Baltimore for thirty days to work on a special writing project. At first, Rey wasn't enthusiastic. He had settled in California, and Baltimore did not sound like his kind of place. He needed sunshine and access to the ocean. On the other hand, he was not getting any younger. It was too late for him to make it in the world of competitive water polo, and he had been unable to generate any studio interest in "Virtuoso," his screenplay about the piano player. In Baltimore, he could make money. He also knew that a nine-to-five job would give him the discipline to work on his screenwriting every day. He hoped eventually to support Allison and their future family from his creative work.

When he first moved to Baltimore, Rey lived in the Peabody Court Hotel in Mount Vernon, the historic district a mile or so north of the harbor where Agora is located. Initially, Rey planned to fly back every week to see Allison, who was working as a financial controller for a company in LA that distributes professional hair care products to salons all over the country. She was not happy about Rey moving to Baltimore, but for thirty days, she felt she could deal with it.

Yet to those who knew him well, Rey's move seemed to come completely out of the blue. Rey's friend B. tells me that Rey said he was going to work for a man who told him he could make a lot of money out there. B. thought Baltimore seemed a very strange place to move, since Rey was such a California guy. B. was not in favor of the move, though he didn't say so. But according to B., all his friends thought it was weird.

Another friend of Rey's I talk to on the phone—an old buddy from Florida—asks me whether I have a theory about his death.

I tell him that I do not have a fully formed theory, but I have been considering some possible scenarios. As I am speaking, he interrupts me.

"Are you nervous right now?" he asks.

I tell him no, I am not nervous.

"This is going to sound weird," he tells me, "but I'm going to say it anyway."

There is a long pause.

Then he says: "Be careful."

At first, things go pretty much as Rey and Allison planned, apart from the fact that they miss each other more than either of them had anticipated, and the project Porter had hired Rey to work on turns out to be a lot more demanding than he had originally expected. Stansberry thinks it will probably take more like ninety days. Rey continues living at the Peabody Court Hotel and flying back to visit Allison every month, when she's not in Baltimore.

One weekend, on a return flight to Baltimore, Rey and the woman next to him start to chat. The woman, Cynthia, is a generation older than Rey; still, they have an almost instant connection. They talk about the cities they have both lived in: Madrid, Los Angeles, Baltimore. After their conversation on the plane, Cynthia feels as though she has known Rey all her life. When they get back to Baltimore, Rey visits her, and he brings Allison when she's around. Allison has an aunt who lives in Ellicott City, a small town about ten miles outside Baltimore; Cynthia also lives there, so they always drop by when they're in the neighborhood. Cynthia calls around to see Rey whenever she's in the city. They have things in common and enjoy each other's company. Cynthia starts to feel as though she loves him like a sister.

"Rey was this really big, handsome man with a huge big bright smile," Cynthia tells me. "He was very predictable and very reliable. He had enormous confidence." I ask her for some of her favorite memories of him. She doesn't have to think for long. "Once," she tells me, "I was sitting outside by the harbor drinking coffee, and I saw this person smiling, walking toward me wearing lime green. And I thought, you have to have a lot of confidence to wear a color that bright. And this person got closer and closer, and then I saw him, and I realized, oh, of course, it's Rey."

Meeting Cynthia is a relief for Rey because apart from the people from Florida who now work at Agora, he knows nobody in the city. This is tough, because Rey is the kind of guy who makes friends easily and is used to being part of a crowd. For some reason, he seems unable to make any really close connections in Baltimore. He thinks it might be because he is flying to LA so much. Things are tough for Allison as well.

After ninety days, Porter Stansberry is so pleased with Rey's

work that he offers his friend the chance to write his own financial newsletter, something Rey has never done before. Actually, he
knows little or nothing about the money market. Still, he gives
it a shot, and the sample he produces turns out to be so successful
that Porter offers him a full-time job. Rey accepts, for the moment;
while their long-term plans remain unclear, he and Allison decide
that flying coast-to-coast is getting too expensive. It makes more
sense, they realize, for Allison to join Rey in Baltimore. After some
renegotiation of her own job, Allison is offered the new role of
regional sales and brand manager, a position that involves traveling to meetings and sales conferences all over the United States
with potential vendors. In her new role, it makes very little difference where she's based.

And so Allison moves to Baltimore, Rey moves out of the
Peabody Court, and they both move in with Porter Stansberry.
No longer inhabiting a "third-floor walk-up in the slums," Stans-

Rey and Allison Rivera

berry has moved into a nicely renovated row house in Baltimore's up-and-coming Canton neighborhood, a stretch of redeveloped industrial waterfront. Still, the house is a little cramped for the three of them, and craving more privacy, Rey and Allison move in with Allison's aunt in Ellicott City and start looking for a place of their own.

VIII

IF YOU WERE not looking carefully, you would notice nothing unusual about the elegant old residences in Mount Vernon that make up Agora's headquarters, mansions that include some of the most architecturally significant buildings in Baltimore. All that connects them is the fact that most of them bear discreet iron plaques by the front door bearing the single word Agora. Also, if you look closely, you might notice that the woodwork on the doors and window frames gleams with fresh polish, and the leaded glass in the windows has been cleaned and restored. These properties include the former Marburg mansion at 14 W. Mount Vernon Place, the former Christian Science Building at 702 Cathedral Street, the former headquarters of the Episcopal Diocese of Maryland at 105 W. Monument Street, and the former Grand Lodge of the Order of the Sons of Italy at 808 St. Paul Street, currently the headquarters of Agora Financial.

The mansions give the company an era of permanence and respectability, yet Agora is, relatively speaking, a young organization. It is basically a holding company for various publishers of financial, health, travel, and special-interest books and newsletters, some of which are free, though most charge a subscription fee. Many contain investment advice for our "chaotic financial times," and suggest ways in which readers and subscribers can increase their personal wealth by buying certain types of stocks and shares. Under the Agora umbrella are more than sixty subsidiary companies, which publish newsletters (all with a strongly independent-libertarian slant) on travel, financial management, taxes, real estate, and health. As of 2017, Agora has thirteen affiliates in the United States, one in Ireland, one in South Africa, and four in England. Bill Bonner is still president of the company.

Stansberry Research is one of many subsidiaries of Agora that send subscribers emails giving investment advice. The newsletters published by Stansberry Reasearch are headed by different high-profile employees: accountants, investors, traders, venture capitalists, and bankers. These are the "Stansberry Analysts," thirteen white men in dark suits; their grinning but humorless headshots are lined up on the Stansberry Research website like the Apostles at the Last Supper. Their master, Stansberry himself, is conspicuously absent.

The Disciples include Stansberry's old Florida friend Steve Sjuggerud, founder of *True Wealth Systems*; Dan Ferris, editor of *Extreme Value*; David Eifrig, editor of *Retirement Millionaire*; and Brett Aitken, lead analyst for *Stansberry Alpha*. Every newsletter follows a particular formula, building apparent credibility through a numbing overload of technical details, always pushing an us-against-them mind-set. "They" are the "mainstream financial media," the "White House," or the "Wall Street fat cats," and "we" are, by implication, white American males, getting on in years, distrustful of government, politicians, banks, mass media, the Internet, and computers in general.

One of Agora's most profitable branches is the health division. Its franchises include Dr. Marc S. Micozzi's *Insiders' Cures* (a monthly subscription newsletter) and daily e-dispatches (recent examples include "Cancer risks are statistically zero for smoking one or two cigars per day" and "Watch out for dangerous half-truths on the Internet") and Dr. Fred Pescatore's *Logical Health Alternatives* ("The infinite energy secret hiding in the world's most exclusive vineyards"). The rhetoric is all about independent thinking, but the promises are familiar: "explosive sexual power," "lightning fast pain relief," "antidotes to aging." On offer is nothing more than the usual generic nutritional supplements endorsed by charismatic-looking physicians. Many of the products seem to be aimed at older people in pain, or those suffering from a terminal illness. Significantly, each franchise has a legal department that employs a compliance editor, who ensures that the newsletters are litigation-proof. As a result, their "terms and conditions," in very small print, always contain the words: "The contents of this site should not be construed as personal medical advice or instruction. If you choose to utilize any information provided, you do so solely at your own risk."

On his podcast *Stansberry Radio*, in a 2014 interview with Bill Bonner, Porter Stansberry confesses that the biggest secret to his success, taught to him by Bonner ("the wisest man I know"), is that "you've got to give the other guy what he wants," with the important caveat that "often, what he wants is not what he says he wants at all." As an example, Stansberry refers to the "health group" at Agora.

> Part of what the health group sells from time to time is weight-loss strategies. And the science of weight loss is purely mathematics. . . . There's no mystery to it at all. You take in less calories, you burn more calories, you will lose weight every time. . . . And yet, Bill, as you know, the people buying weight-loss products don't necessarily actually want to lose weight. What they are really looking for, of course, is the excitement and the hope of losing weight. And what they want is, they want someone who can hit that emotional button for them again and

again and again and again. . . . What they want is to become the hero of their own story.

How does Porter Stansberry become the hero of his own story? How, for that matter, does Rey Rivera?

When a death is unexplained, we tend to sympathize with the deceased, even if we never knew them—partly because their absence dominates the story (they are everywhere), and partly because they no longer have agency. Omnipresence and vulnerability can be an intoxicating combination, and in the case of Rey Rivera, the deceased was also remarkably handsome.

Movies, media, lifestyle magazines, and real estate advertisements all encourage the primitive feeling that, since beautiful people seem especially blessed, their lives should also be happy and lucky. I sometimes think that, since I consider myself an average-looking person, I should not have a life that others find enviable and alluring. Rationally, I know this is not true; obviously, I have as much right to happiness as anyone else. But, like most ordinary-looking people, I have always overvalued physical beauty in others. When I realize that someone who looks the way I do can have lived such a fortunate life, while someone as handsome as Rey Rivera could die so horribly and at at such a young age, it feels as though the planets are out of line.

For all his imposing stature in life, Rey Rivera is now passive and defenseless, unable to speak for himself. His side of the story has to be told by those who knew him, and when someone dies young and in tragic circumstances, nobody has anything but good things to say about them. Nonetheless, I cannot help but believe that Rey Rivera really was a great guy. Like all of us, he had his flaws: his temper, his impetuous personality. But there was another flaw, too, which more than one person mentioned, using almost the same words every time: "Rey was terrible with money."

Which makes it even more surprising, perhaps, that Porter Stansberry should give Rey his own financial newsletter to edit. After some back and forth, they decide to call it *The Rebound Report,* since Rey was a huge basketball fan, and because the newsletter would focus on companies that were "on the rebound"— that is, after doing poorly and losing money, looked as though they were about to turn around.

At first, Rey is concerned that he knows absolutely nothing about finance. He is certain that anybody who so much as glances at *The Rebound Report* will know he's just guessing blindly, the way passengers in a car instinctively know when the driver is lost. But Stansberry reassures Rey. He is hiring Rey not for his skill as a financial analyst, but for his talent as a writer. After all, Stansberry himself has no business background and knew very little about investment when he started out. In fact, according to papers filed by the SEC, nobody who works at Pirate Investor seemed to know much about financial matters.

In its original judgment against Pirate Investor, an attorney representing the SEC cross-examined David Nelson, one of Stansberry's "experts," about how seriously the newsletters' investment advice was taken in general. He presented the following interview extracts in his notes:

> Essentially critics of the investment letters have argued that the advisors are ignorant, they may have no formal experience or education in investment . . . their investment record can be bad, dishonest, they can lie about their records. . . . Investors newsletters accurate as a coin flip. . . . Their advice was no better than throwing a dart at the stock quotes page of the Wall Street Journal and buying whatever it hits.

If Rivera feels uneasy at his new job, he also feels increasingly out of place in Baltimore, where he and Allison know almost nobody. They are used to being part of a large circle of friends, and suddenly the only people they know, besides Cynthia and Allison's aunt, are Stansberry, Stansberry's fiancée, Brad Hoppmann, and a couple of other guys from Florida. Porter tries to introduce them to people at Agora, but Rey and Allison have nothing in common with the Stansberry set, who are mostly capitalist libertarians. Rey and Allison both lean to the left.

Rey's friend B. remembers visiting him in Baltimore and being shocked that he would even be friends with someone like Stansberry. B. thought the two men had absolutely nothing in common. "Porter and his friends were like these businessmen in suits, with their Stepford Wives," B. recalls. "All they wanted to do was to eat at expensive restaurants, talk about politics, drink expensive wine, and throw their money around."

Rey never comes to feel better about his job. In fact, he only feels worse. While he makes decent money working for Stansberry, he also starts to dread writing *The Rebound Report* every week. He feels completely out of his depth. He signs his newsletters "Good Investing," but few of the stocks he recommends, which included Krispy Kreme and Independence Air, perform as he predicts. Every day, he is plagued by the guilt that his bad advice may be causing people to lose their life's savings. For a while, Allison is seriously worried about the complex mess Rey seems to have got himself into and the toll it is taking on him. He starts to suffer from insomnia. Every evening, when he gets back from a long, fretful day at the office, he stays up into the early hours of the morning playing video games to wind down. It is not like the normally laid-back Rey, thinks Allison, to be so uptight.

One of my greatest pleasures is taking my dog to Druid Hill Park, a couple of miles from the Belvedere.

We go every Friday, if weather permits. I prefer the older and more secluded areas at the northern end of the park behind the zoo; there, the roads are closed to traffic, my dog can run off leash, and some days we can hear the echoing bellows of the big cats. In

The Belvedere Hotel c. 1906, looking north from
Baltimore's Washington Monument

these parts of the zoo, ancient undergrowth covers a series of crumbling man-made ponds, including the former sea lion pool, its wrought-iron fences and stone steps barely discernible through tangles of vines. There's a small family burial ground here, dating back to the 1700s, with two broad flat tombs lying beside each other, one about twice as high as the other. The taller of the two contains the remains of Eleanor Rogers, who "died suddenly on January 1, 1812," the shorter one those of "her consort Nicholas," who died in 1822. If I sit on Nicholas and rest my laptop on Eleanor, I have a perfect outdoor desk, and can sit and write happily for as long as my battery lasts.

The tall spruces at the bottom of the park are home to what I always assumed were ravens but have since learned are crows. I learned they were crows when, one day, a gigantic black bird swept down and perched on a gravestone directly in front of me. He was almost the size of a vulture, as heavy-looking as my dog and almost as muscular, with a straggly mane of feathers around his neck and chest, and a huge black beak that looked as though it had been strapped on to the head as an afterthought, like the mask of a medieval plague doctor. He looked at me for a moment, then cocked his head. "I am a raven," he seemed to be telling me. "We are marvelous and unmistakable."

Iron railings circle the burial ground, so my dog can never stray too far, although most of the time while I write he digs happily in the shade nearby. He's unearthed the spinal column of a deer and the skull of a young fox, its teeth perfectly white and intact. I have always admired the teeth of animals. They are clean and proud, unlike our own teeth, those odd pieces of skull that show when we grin. The sight of a pulled human tooth gives me a queer sensation, its thick roots reaching down into the jawbone farther than the enamel protrudes above. In many cultures, extracted teeth are believed to be magical and dangerous. They should not fall into the hands of enemies. They should be buried in a secret place.

I used to enjoy visiting the old reptile house, which was separate from the zoo, and cost one dollar to enter. Then one summer, a large cardboard sign appeared announcing its closure. The zoo, I learned, could no longer afford to keep it open, and the reptiles had been sent to other zoos. The sign remained long after the building stood locked and empty, filled with the ghosts of geckos and iguanas. One day, I noticed it had fallen off and was lying on the ground. On impulse, I picked it up, put it in my car, took it home, and mounted it on the wall in our half-bathroom. In large green letters, it says, "Sorry, the Reptile House Is Closed."

Another place I like to go is the city courthouse. I will select a trial at random and sit in the spectator's gallery, where I am usually the only observer. One day I find myself watching a medical malpractice trial. It is endless, yet I cannot tear myself away. Surgeons, it seems, have removed the wrong part of Mr. S.'s anatomy, thus leaving him in need of round-the-clock care at a cost of $250,000 a month. Mr. S. is a skeleton in a suit. He sits slumped in a wheelchair, breathing into a tube, while his wife, stoical in high heels and a flowery blouse, holds up his head and from time to time wipes the drool off his chin.

"Now, I know it's uncomfortable," the plaintiff's attorney tells the jury, "but I have to discuss Mr. S.'s anticipated life expectancy."

The lights are dimmed. At the front of the room, a projected slide shows a diagram of Mr. S.'s bowels, colon, and intestines. The next slide contains a chart full of tables and mathematical calculations. I wonder whether the injury that has been thoughtlessly inflicted upon Mr. S. by the surgeons has affected his mind as well as his body, or whether he is able to understand every word as well as anyone else in the room. I wonder whether we should hope his anticipated life span will be short or long.

We soon learn. He is expected to live another twenty-five years, at least.

The pause that follows this sobering news is broken only by the gurgling noises from Mr. S.'s breathing tube and the snoring of an overweight woman on the jury bench.

IX

ON THURSDAY, DECEMBER 30, 2004, Rey Rivera and Allison Jones take possession of a handsome old Tudor-style townhouse in Original Northwood, a tree-lined family neighborhood of quiet residential streets about a twenty-minute drive from the city center.

Their combined salaries allow the couple to take out a mortgage on the $280,000 property; their monthly payments are less than the rent they were paying in LA for a nine-hundred-square-foot house with one bedroom. Buying a home sounds like a commitment, but to Allison and Rey, it is an investment. Of course, at over two thousand square feet, the Northwood house is far too big for them—it has four bedrooms and a landscaped yard, which they rarely get the time to use—but there is plenty of space for friends from out of town to come and stay.

Buying the house is one of the ways Rey and Allison make life in Baltimore more tenable. True, Rey still feels uneasy writing *The Rebound Report* every week. True, Allison's job involves a lot of travel, and at first, when she is gone, she worries about leaving Rey alone in Baltimore, where there is nothing for him to do except go out drinking with Stansberry. But Porter is deeply involved in

Rey and Allison's Baltimore townhouse

Agora, and Rey has no interest in the crowd he mixes with. Plus, Porter and his wife, recently married, are busy house-hunting themselves.

Rey settles down in another way, too. He joins the informal water polo games held every week at the U.S. Naval Academy in Annapolis. On one occasion, the Naval Academy team plays against the Johns Hopkins team, the Blue Jays, and Rey gets talking to Ted Bresnahan, the Blue Jays' coach. Bresnahan, a tough, fatherly figure with a gray mustache, realizes at once that Rey, with his experience, insight, and charisma, may well be the secret to turning things around for the Blue Jays, who, while full of promise, have never been a standout team. When Rey asks Ted whether he needs any coaching help, Ted invites him to be the assistant men's coach, and Rey accepts on the spot. The players are thrilled to have an ex-pro on board, and so is Bresnahan. It soon becomes clear that hiring Rey is one of the best decisions he has ever made. Of the thirty tournament games played by the Division III Blue Jays in 2005, they lose only six, and those are all to top-20, Division I schools. The team ends up with a first-place national ranking in the season's final poll, and Bresnahan is voted coach of the year. The team's magical turnaround is attributed to the ideal combination of Ted's knowledge and experience and Rey's approach and tactics. Rey "made a big difference in our strategies and our conditioning," says the team captain, Jim Singleton.

Coaching at Hopkins also gives Rey a place to swim; in the pool, he can escape from his anxieties about work. Says Allison, "He was like an otter in the water. It was his natural element. Rey was much more settled when he was coaching. And the boys loved him." Around the same time, Rey begins working seriously on a new screenplay: the story of a young Latina water polo player who makes it to the Olympics. He calls it "Midnight Polo."

The couple also join a church, which helps tie their life in Baltimore more closely to the community. Both Rey and Allison were raised as Catholics and remain affiliated to the faith, albeit loosely. Rey's mother is deeply religious, and Allison's parents are closely involved with a church at their home in Windsor, Colorado. While Rey and Allison would both describe themselves as "spiritual rather than religious," both are interested in the humanitarian causes that the Catholic church traditionally supports, and both feel that finding a welcoming, preferably youthful Catholic community might be a good way of forming a social network outside the insular and money-oriented world of Agora. It does not take them long to find the Church of St. Mary of the Assumption, on nearby York Road. It is only two miles from their new home, and they both warm to the Cuban deacon and his wife.

Lisa O'Reilly came to St. Mary's from Dublin to work as a youth minister and religious educator. She has been living in Baltimore for about a year when she meets Rey and Allison, in February 2005, when they arrive at St. Mary's for the annual Mardi Gras pancake breakfast. They are a striking couple, thinks Lisa, both tall and good-looking, and she can't help noticing how out of place they look at the suburban gathering. "As soon as I saw them, I thought, 'Oh great, new people, young people.' And they looked really different. Interesting, too. I couldn't wait to meet them," Lisa O'Reilly recalls. "Rey towered over you. He had this huge magnetism."

As transplants to the city, the couple have a kinship with O'Reilly, and although Rey and Allison do not attend church every week, they do so often enough for a bond to form. "My relationship with them was a ministerial thing," says Lisa, "but it was also a friendship thing."

Over the weekend of June 11–12, 2005, Rey attends Agora's annual conference in Vancouver. Here, perhaps because he has already decided to quit, everybody remembers him being especially fun to be around. The following month, he leaves his job at Pirate Investor. According to Allison, Stansberry is not surprised; he knows Rey dislikes writing *The Rebound Report* and is uncomfortable in a corporate environment. Rey loves to write, but he wants to write screenplays, not investment advice he knows nothing about. He has been making solid progress on "Midnight Polo," and that summer, after leaving Agora, he takes out a fifteen-thousand-dollar cash advance on Allison's credit card to buy video equipment and set up his own company, Ceiba Productions. While he hopes eventually to attract freelance work, in the short term he works on promotional videos for Stansberry, whose Agora subsidiary, in October of that year, acquires the rather more dignified name of Stansberry & Associates Investment Research.

This may have been an attempt to distance the company from the SEC fraud charges, which Stansberry is still battling. In May 2005, five months before Rivera leaves the company, a bench trial in Maryland Federal District Court concludes that Pirate Investor is guilty of securities fraud by "falsely claiming that a company insider provided the information in the 'Super Insider Tip Email.'" Stansberry is held liable for disgorgement of the profits of the scheme, and is fined prejudgment interest. Civil penalties are also imposed, and the court enters a permanent injunction banning Stansberry from similar activities. Still, Stansberry won't concede.

The case continues in litigation.

On November 5, 2005, Rey and Allison are married on the beach in Puerto Rico. It is the wedding they have been dreaming of. Rey's mother, Maria, somehow manages to convince Pedro Guzmán, Puerto Rico's most famous *cuatro* musician, to play for the newly-weds. Rey and Allison have the first dance, but pretty soon every-one joins in. "It was a perfect afternoon," recalls Maria. The only false note, people say, is struck by Porter Stansberry's absurd, tycoonlike entrance—stepping out of a private helicopter, chomp-ing on a huge cigar.

On the following day, November 6, there is a church ceremony to make things official, but Allison considers November 5 to be her true wedding date.

Four months after they get back from Puerto Rico, Rey and Allison start making plans to leave Baltimore. They are ready to start a family and eager to get back to their friends in LA. More immediately, Rey has finished "Midnight Polo." He is proud of the script, and can't wait to start pitching it to agents. With a sense of relief obvious to everybody who knows them, Rey and Allison announce their decision to put their house, which they have owned for just over a year, on the market and leave Baltimore as soon as they find a buyer. They assume it will not take long. It is 2006, and the real estate market is booming. They hope to make a decent profit.

That spring, Rey, who has always been politically active, is fired up by the immigration reform protests happening all over the country in response to proposed legislation to classify undoc-umented immigrants (and anyone who helps them remain in the United States) as felons. Rey finds the proposal outrageous and offensive. He sets up a blog to share his thoughts and ideas on this and other subjects. These are the early days of blogging, and

Rey's site attracts few readers, but in the comments, he enjoys sparring with his friend from St. Mary's, Lisa O'Reilly. They disagree about what kind of problem the immigration issue is. Rey maintains it is an economic problem, but Lisa believes the essential question is one of racism. "We used to have these great conversations about what we need to do for the country and what needs to happen," Lisa recalls. She wants me to know that their conversations were not critical of the United States, not doomladen and cynical, but just the opposite: full of hope for the future.

On March 14, 2006, Rey travels to Delray Beach for the weekend to film the Oxford Club's "8th Annual Investment University Conference" at the Delray Beach Marriott Hotel. By this time, the Oxford Club has more than 100,000 members, and the video will be sent to all those who can't attend the conference in person.

The conference organizer for the Oxford Club is Steven King, who still does not know Rey very well. At the Vancouver convention in June, he gets to know Rey a little better, and, while he likes him a lot, he still regards him as an old friend of Porter's rather than someone he knows on his own terms. But Porter is not involved in the conference in Delray Beach. Rey works closely with Steven King all weekend.

King has the job of introducing Rey to the guest speakers so that he can wire them up with microphones. After each day's events are over, the two men go out drinking, often with a crowd, and always have a great time. "A lot of socializing went on there, and Rey was the type of guy who never let you feel as though you were by yourself. He was very engaging. He had the best smile, and he knew how to make people feel special," says King.

I ask Steven for his favorite memories of Rey. "He was the sort of person that would immediately come up to you and give you a hug," he says. "I wish I'd got to know him better."

One thing, at least, King can say with no hesitation or regret: Rey loved his new job.

Widely described as reliable and predictable, Rivera clearly has an impulsive moment on the morning of Monday, April 10, 2006, when he leaves home on extremely short notice. Lisa O'Reilly calls him early in the morning. She tells him about a big immigration rally taking place that day in Washington, D.C. Lisa is going with some friends. Does Rey want to join them?

"He must have jumped up and left the house spontaneously," Lisa recalls, "because he met me within half an hour of my call." Then, about halfway through the march, Lisa found herself in trouble. "I'd brought an Irish flag to the rally, and it didn't go down very well," she told me. "At one point, this old Hispanic lady started shouting at me, and Rey defended me. They were arguing in Spanish. I don't know what he said, but he charmed the old lady. That's what Rey was like. He could charm anybody."

In the days leading up to Rey's death, a number of strange events occur. Allison notices that her husband is unusually anxious. Normally, he is completely self-assured, but for some reason he does not explain, Rey insists on being with her wherever she goes. He even brings a book and sits in the bleachers when she goes for her usual daily jog around an athletic track a few blocks east of their house on Westview Road.

One morning, Allison is doing her usual sprints when she notices a man beginning to come toward her. Since it is pouring rain, Ray is waiting for her in the car. As the stranger gets closer, Rey suddenly comes flying out of the car and runs toward Allison, only stopping when he gets to the track to watch the situation more closely. The man changes direction and leaves without incident. When she gets back to the car, Allison asks Rey whether he is okay and he says he's fine; but, for some reason, the stranger has terrified him. Allison cannot understand why her husband has suddenly become so edgy. When she asks him about it, he insists there's nothing wrong.

On the morning of Sunday, May 14, two days before Rey goes

missing, Allison and Rey go to church, a special service for Mother's Day. When they get back home and are walking up the front steps of their house in Northwood, Rey makes a phone call to someone who does not pick up, and leaves them an excited message. "Hey man, call me back," he says. "I finally got it all figured out!"

Allison does not remember whether anyone called him back. Later, when Rey is missing, Stansberry admits he was the person Rey called that morning. He plays the message for Rey's brother, Angel. Stansberry says he had no idea what Rey was talking about. Neither Porter, Angel, nor Allison can make sense of it. What has Rey finally got "all figured out"? And why would he call Stansberry to tell him so?

Suddenly, the security alarm in Rey and Allison's house starts going off in the middle of the night for no apparent reason. It happens on Monday, May 15, at one a.m., then again, according to the houseguest, Claudia, at three a.m. the evening Rey goes missing. By then, Allison and Rey have lived in the house for almost two years, setting the alarm every night (the neighborhood is a safe one, but after all, this is still Baltimore). They have never heard it go off before. The Northeast District police precinct is a short walk away, so the first time the alarm goes off, they ask officers to come and investigate. The cops suggest that maybe squirrels are triggering it. This sounds absurd to Allison. Even if she or Rey had left a window open, a squirrel would still have had to push out the entire screen to trip the alarm, and the screens are all intact.

But what makes even less sense to her is Rey's reaction. When the alarm goes off, Rey leaps out of bed, terrified. For the first time, Allison sees fear in his eyes. "He was a big Latin guy. He was macho. It wasn't him," she says. "Rey was scared."

To get a better picture of the events of the week after Rey went missing, I ask those involved in the search to recount for me what they can remember about those eight terrible days, and, in particular, at what point they first heard the word "suicide" being used.

Lisa O'Reilly remembers that on the afternoon of Thursday, May 18, she received a phone call from Allison asking whether she had seen or heard anything of Rey, as he'd been missing for two days. Lisa, shocked, goes over to Allison's house with her husband to help make "Missing" posters. Allison's parents are there, recalls Lisa, along with a couple of other families. When the posters are finished, Lisa and her husband drive around Baltimore taping them to utility poles and looking for the black Mitsubishi Montero Rey was driving. Lisa recalls the discovery of the car as a mystery in itself. "About a week later," she remembers, "somebody—either Allison's mom or dad—was going to the airport to pick somebody up or drop them off, and on the way back they decided to have one more look around the area near Mount Vernon, and that's when they found the car."

Lisa O'Reilly remembers everyone gathering at Allison and Rey's house on the evening of Wednesday, May 24, the day Rivera's body is found. All their friends and neighbors have brought food, recalls Lisa, and they have a sort of improvised wake for Rey. Lisa is in the kitchen when she first hears someone mention suicide. She remembers Rey's friend Marco, who has just flown in from Florida, responding angrily, saying, "There's no way." There was an awkward moment after that. "Most people in the kitchen just let it go," Lisa tells me. "But I thought, 'He's right, there's no way.' My God. Honestly, I can defend suicide. If it were even a possibility, I'd admit it." She knew of people committing suicide in a moment of irrationality. Then she remembered how calculated Rey's final movements must have been in order for him to get access to the roof of the Belvedere without being seen.

I ask Lisa whether, as someone brought up in a Catholic home, Rey would have considered suicide to be a mortal sin, but she says no. "He wasn't of that generation," she tells me. "He wouldn't have paid attention to those kinds of sanctions. Like I said, he wasn't really much of a believer." Lisa does not think Rey took his own life for the simple reason that he was always upbeat and happy, and had so much to live for.

That afternoon, the deacon of St. Mary's arranges a gathering for Allison and Rey's families and friends at St. Mary's. Then, at six o'clock, the church holds a memorial mass.

Cynthia also finds it suspicious that Allison's parents discovered the car, especially given that it was Rey's colleagues who found the body. "At that time," she says, "Baltimore was number one in the country for homicide. There was no investigation at all. The police just did not want to investigate anything." She, too, first heard the word "suicide" used in connection with Rey's death at the family gathering. At the time, Cynthia was in so much shock she managed to repress all her emotions. "I was just caught up in feeding everybody, making sure everybody was okay. I just kept busy. I was too busy to cry. But later, it all came out. I cried so much I got adrenal fatigue." When she overheard someone referring to Rey's death as a suicide, Cynthia was shocked. "That just seemed completely wrong to me. He was just too vital for suicide. He never even seemed depressed or anything. For them to say that—it's just so out of character."

Rey's mother, Maria Rivera, tells me, "When Allison called and said, 'Mama, Rey is missing,' we went over there, but we were not concerned really because we did not believe anything bad had happened. Nothing unusual had been going on in his life, really. Of course, we were worried, but we thought that he had an accident, got lost somewhere, or got sick, something like that."

What she tells me next sends chills down my spine. "The moment I went into his house, I could not feel his presence. And I just knew it at once. Oh my God, my son is dead." Naturally,

Maria says, she still went through with the search. But at the bottom of her heart, she tells me, "I knew. I knew."

Maria cannot remember when she first heard suicide mentioned in connection with the death of her son, only that she never countenanced the idea for a moment. "I know Rey would not commit suicide," she tells me. "I know because of my own observations of his behavior and because of things that came out of his mouth. When anyone we knew was depressed, it was always Rey that would help them, talk to them, give them reasons to live. And not only was Rey afraid of heights, but he'd never got over his fear of death. We had many conversations about it."

On Tuesday, May 16, 2006, Porter Stansberry is out of town. As soon as he gets the news that Rey is missing, he returns to Baltimore and joins the search, offering a (rather chintzy) $1,000 reward for information leading to his friend's whereabouts. When, by Friday, there are still no leads or clues, he raises the reward to $5,000, noting the increase at the bottom of the "Missing" posters. Stansberry, it appears, is as desperate as anyone else to find Rey.

"He's a happy guy," Porter tells Nicole Fuller, a reporter for the *Baltimore Sun*. "He and his wife had just booked a trip to go to New Mexico in a few weeks. This is not a man that wanted to leave. I've got to find my friend. I can't imagine my life without him. He's my best friend." But at some point on Wednesday, May 24, when Rivera's body was discovered, Stansberry's demeanor changed. He was at work when he got the news, and according to the FBI report on the case, he sent his employees home, hired a number of attorneys and, because of security concerns, a private detective, and refused to speak to the police.

In a podcast interview with Bill Bonner, Stansberry describes Bonner as "an incredible friend." He continues, "You know you really have a great friend when you're at the low point in your life, and you get a phone call—I think Bill's called me once in my entire life out of the blue—and it was during a very tough period in my life when I'd just recently lost a very good friend." A few years later, in an entry from *Bill Bonner's Diary* about the proliferation of "fake news" in the Trump era, Bonner mentions the newspaper accounts of Rey Rivera's death as an example of the trend. "In one sad instance," he writes, "an ex-employee committed suicide, distraught over a personal problem." The article continues:

> It happened at a time when one of our groups was being investigated by the SEC. (The case ended up as a legal fascination . . . complicated, but inconsequential . . . and later largely repudiated by the courts. . . .) The ex-employee was in no way associated with the alleged wrongdoing. And the infraction had nothing to do with the SEC's usual beat—front-running or market manipulation. But the reporter couldn't resist: "Suicide at Troubled Baltimore Publisher," read the headline. The reader was left to conclude that the poor fellow offed himself because he was implicated in a trading scam that had never happened or even been alleged.

My curiosity is excited when I read that Bill Bonner knows for a fact that Rey "committed suicide, distraught over a personal problem." Since the Rivera case is, officially, still open as a homicide, I wonder whether Bonner has reported his information to the police. What could the "personal problem" have been? Why did Bonner, Porter Stansberry's boss, know about it, when Rey's wife and friends did not?

On Wednesday, August 2, 2006, Porter Stansberry and his wife purchase a house in the country suburb of Cockeysville, about fifteen miles north of Baltimore. According to property records, they pay $1.5 million for the 4,587-square-foot house, which sits on a lot of 2.77 acres. Like Stansberry's other visible assets—his clothes, his car, his cigars—this property is a sign of the man's success.

Porter Stansberry

It is a snowy night. I am talking to one of my graduate students over drinks in the Owl Bar downstairs in the Belvedere when the electricity starts to go out gradually as the generators fail, one after the other. First the kitchen goes dark. Then the small lobby area where we are sitting; then the main bar; finally the whole place goes dead.

We finish our drinks by candlelight; then my student leaves and the evening concierge, Freddie, leads me to the stairs with a hurricane lamp. He shows me up to the second floor and guides me to a door that I've never seen before or since. The door leads to a broad landing at the bottom of the fire stairs. I stumble blindly up to the fifth floor, where I emerge into the dark hallway.

The entire Belvedere is pitch-black and almost completely silent. I light candles in the apartment. It is beginning to get very cold. When I go to brush my teeth by candlelight, I hear strange noises inside the bathroom walls: irregular dripping sounds, fragments of whispered conversations coming through the water pipes, the echoing footfalls of people climbing the fire stairs and back passageways: the building's inner organs and alimentary canal. After brushing my teeth, I take the dog downstairs for his evening walk, meeting residents I do not recognize in the dark hallways, nervously clutching their flashlights or cell phones.

The power usually goes out twice a year, whenever the circuits get overloaded: once in the winter and once in the summer. When it happens in the summer, there is a different feeling. Things are friendlier. People congregate outside, where it is still light and there is a chance of catching a breeze. The Owl Bar, which has its own mini-generator, will sometimes stay open when everywhere else is in complete darkness, though only to those who can find their way through the darkness of the lobby and around the back hallway. These special nights remind me of the tales told of the days of Prohibition, when the Owl Bar was a notorious speakeasy—there are apparently still bullet holes in the walls—and the eyes of the bar's two owl figurines would flash on and off when a liquor delivery had safely arrived.

That February night, when I get outside, I discover it is not only the Belvedere that has lost power, but the whole block. Something electrical has "blown" underground, according to the concierge, and "a part has to come from Philadelphia." As I climb through the thick, silent snow, I see that the traffic lights on Charles Street have been wired up to a makeshift generator. A soft white veil covers everything, blurring boundaries between sidewalk and street. Icicles hang from the canopy over the front steps of the Belvedere. I hear a sound normally smothered by the noise of traffic: the moan of foghorns out in the bay.

Rey's body is so decomposed that if Allison wants to bury him, she can do so only in Baltimore. Understandably, she does not want to lay her husband to rest in a city of so many bad memories, so after consultation with Rey's family, she has his body cremated and takes his ashes back to LA with her when she returns. For a long time, she is unsure where to bury the urn. She visits Madrid, planning to bury Rey's ashes in the city of his birth, but somehow it does not feel right.

After a great deal of thought and searching, she finds the perfect place. Rey's ashes are in a vaulted cave by the edge of the sea in Puerto Rico, so close that when the tide comes in, the waves wash over his urn.

One day, out of the blue, I receive an anonymous email.

"Mikita: with respect, I have a family and prefer to stay out of this. Rey did not kill himself. Be careful."

X

ON TUESDAY, DECEMBER 15, 2009, three years and seven months after Rey Rivera's death, the U.S. Court of Appeals for the Fourth Circuit concludes that Porter Stansberry did not obtain his "Super Insider Tip" from a private source, as he maintains. Deciding that, although Stansberry may have spoken to such a source, his claim to have received a tip from that person is a fabrication, the court finds Pirate Investor guilty of securities fraud.

To protest the decision, Stansberry and his attorneys draw up an appeal from a final judgment, requesting a reversal of the court's decision, arguing that Stansberry obtained what he believed in good faith to be a real financial tip, which he subsequently sold to the subscribers of his email newsletter. Stansberry himself was not a company insider, they argue; nor did he buy any of the stock he endorsed. Like other journalists dealing in speculation, his attorneys argue, Porter Stansberry has a right to get things wrong. In fact, they claim, this is a right protected by the First Amendment.

The Court of Appeals disagrees. It upholds its decision, reasoning that Stansberry clearly knew that what he was doing was wrong at the time: "Stansberry's conduct undoubtedly involved deliberate fraud, making statements that he knew to be false." At last, Stansberry is out of options. Pirate Investor is ordered to pay $1.5 million in restitution and civil penalties.

The Court of Appeals is seriously mistaken in its judgment, believes Stansberry. He will not accept defeat. In one final and powerful push, he persuades a number of publishers to sign various amicus briefs in his defense in an attempt to persuade the U.S. Supreme Court to reverse the decision. These petitions, signed by representatives of some of the nation's most reputable publishers (including the New York Times Company, the Hearst Corporation, and Forbes LLC) argue that a guilty verdict in the case will be "a significant threat to the free dissemination of news about the financial markets and specific investment opportunities," and could lead to a situation that "would be contrary to the spirit of our system of a free and independent press." A *New York Times* editorial published on July 3, 2010 ("The Right to Be Wrong") observes that "the implications of the SEC's action are potentially profound: newspapers or Web sites promising their paying readers stock information that later turns out to be untrue suddenly leave themselves open to fraud charges. Any financial commentator who passes on bad information in good faith could be sued."

But the Fourth Circuit Court does not believe that Stansberry passed on "bad information in good faith"; rather, the court holds, he made statements that he knew at the time to be false. And "punishing fraud does not violate the First Amendment."

The case of Rey Rivera, like most unsolved mysteries, is in the news for a day, two days, a week at the most, before fading out of sight. For the first couple of years, on the anniversary of the day Rey's body was found, Jayne Miller presents a brief news feature for WBAL-TV, reminding us that the case is still unsolved. After this, there is no follow-up investigation. When Rivera's death is brought up in online conspiracy-theory forums related to

Agora (and to these there is no limit), it is either dismissed as "obviously" a suicide, or regarded as equally "clearly" a murder—committed by whom remains unclear, but the question generates an intricate web of speculation and paranoia, which, since it cannot be penetrated or even approached, is essentially another kind of dismissal.

By the time five years have passed since Rivera's death, I decide it is no longer inappropriate for me to try and reach out to his family. After searching online, I find what I believe to be the email address for Allison and the phone number of Rey's brother, Angel. My email to Allison does not bounce, but I get no response. I call Angel and tell him I am interested in writing a book about the death of his brother. He tells me he is in a meeting and will return my call in an hour or so. He never does. Clearly, he does not want to talk.

I am persistent but, despite days spent writing letters, sending out emails, and making phone calls, I get nowhere. In one direction is a roadblock; in the other is a brick wall. I call the Baltimore police archives to see how I can get a copy of George Rayburn's 911 call reporting the hole in the roof, but I am told that it is too late—the police destroy all 911 tapes after six hundred days. I arrange for a disgruntled Agora ex-employee to talk to me off the record; though I wait up by the phone, he never calls. The form I fill out requesting a copy of the police report asks for an "incident number," which I do not have and cannot find. The phone number for the Baltimore City Police Central Records Office is either out of date or out of service: I call and call, but nobody picks up. One day I call to find the line is dead, although the number listed on the website remains unchanged.

I realize I will have to go down to the office in person. It is an overcast December day, and I am reluctant to leave the Belvedere, where D. is grading a pile of student papers with the dog snoring contentedly by his side, providing a noisy counterpoint to Rachmaninoff's Second Symphony which is playing on the radio. Loath to quit this peaceful scene for the bleak chill outside, I put on a pair of heels and wrap myself in my pink fur coat to have something bright and warm around me, something to make me visible in the fog.

The police records office website lists a downtown address. I park some distance away and continue on foot. I pass through the Block (Baltimore's red-light district), past Circus and Club Pussycat, then down Water Street and Custom House Avenue, past old dockside buildings, former banks, insurance offices, and counting houses—once-genteel Federal structures, now in crumbling disrepair. I emerge in a slightly more respectable precinct, pass the Two O'Clock Club, and finally arrive at a large concrete edifice that I assume is the building I am searching for. In fact, it is not the police records office, but the police headquarters, which is not open to the public—at least, not according to the belligerent policewoman who sends me back out into the cold when I walk through the front door. She then buzzes the intercom.

"What do you want?" she asks me.

I tell her I am looking for the Central Records office, and she comes to the door, opens it slightly, and hands me a form—the same document I downloaded from the website.

"Fill this out," she demands. "Then take it to the Central Records office." She gives me an address that is different from the one online. "Then they call you when they get your record. It could take a few months."

"I can't," I tell her. "That's why I came down here. I don't have an incident number."

"Hold on," she says, retreating inside. For a moment, I actually believe she is going to help me. Then she returns with another copy of the same form.

"I'll give you two of them," she says. "You'll probably mess up on the first." Then she closes the door and turns the lock.

I walk back through the mist to my car and make my way to the address given to me by the policewoman. It's about five miles away, in another part of town. At first, I think I must have got the wrong place. The building looks like an industrial warehouse. There is nothing to identify it as the police records office, and what appear to be the doors—at the side of the building, opening onto the parking lot—are locked.

As I stand there wondering what to do, an older cop with a gray mustache and a winter coat over his uniform comes out for a cigarette. He tells me they are closing soon, but he will help me if he can.

I tell him about the Rivera case. I have written down the name, the date of the incident, and the precinct involved. "I've been trying to get hold of the police report," I tell him.

"What's the case number?"

"That's what I am trying to get hold of," I tell him. "I have the autopsy report number, if that helps."

"That's the medical examiner's report number," he says. "They use a different system. Let me take a look."

He takes the piece of paper out of my hand, finishes his cigarette, and invites me to take a seat on a plain metal bench in the bare reception area of the records office. I sit there waiting for fifteen minutes or so. There are no magazines, no plants, no decorations, nothing but an overflowing ashtray, a soda vending machine, and a pot of burned coffee hissing on a hot plate in the corner. From the warehouse-like office space to my rear, I can hear raised voices, shouting, and loud male laughter. It sounds like a sports bar full of men watching a football game.

Finally, the cop with the mustache returns, empty-handed.

"You sure there even was a police report on this?" he asks.

"There must have been," I say. "It was an unexplained death."

"Let me take another look," says the cop, before disappearing back into the records office.

I wait for ten more minutes. Every officer who comes out of the room to go for a smoke or to get coffee gives me a friendly smile and asks me whether I am being helped. For a moment, I can't help but feel warm toward these kind and friendly men—but only until I remember that, to them, I am a quiet white woman in a pink fur coat who has asked for their help. I am just the kind of person they like to assist. In fact, helping me is what they are trained to do.

As it turns out, they are no use at all. The cop with the mustache comes back empty-handed again. "I can't help you with this," he says.

"Where else can I go?" I ask him.

"You could check the police archives in Annapolis," he suggests cheerfully. "Though a lot of records from back then were lost in the flood."

As a member of the general public, I am not allowed to set foot inside the Baltimore Homicide Section of the Crimes Against Persons Division, so all my dealings with the officers in this unit are by email or phone, although "all my dealings" is not a very accurate summary of the matter. In fact, I am trapped in an infinite loop of dismissal. Every one of my letters and emails, even those in which I ask questions as innocent and innocuous as "How would I go about finding a police report number for an incident?" elicit the same cold, impersonal, responsibility-dodging phrase: "We are unable to provide assistance with your request." In retrospect, after dealing with the Homicide Division, my experience at Central Records seems not friendly but dead sinister—the bare, unmarked warehouse; the male laughter; the loud camaraderie; the smoking men coming in and out of the door smiling at me, the records "lost in the flood."

And then, after I have lost all hope of ever obtaining a copy of the police report, when all my requests have been ignored and my checks returned uncashed, the report suddenly appears in my mailbox, like a magic trick.

The detectives named in the police report are no longer working for Baltimore Homicide. Michael Baier, Marvin Sydnor, and James Mingle have all retired. This should have been good news.

Retired detectives are generally more helpful than those still on the force, whose jobs can be put at risk if they discuss a case with an outsider. From public information searches, I find the home addresses of the three retired detectives and write them each a personal letter about my interest in Rivera's death, giving them my email address and phone number. I tell them I would be very grateful to hear from them. When this approach yields no results, I try the more direct method of making "friend" requests on Facebook. My requests are ignored.

I email Justin George, a police reporter for the *Baltimore Sun,* asking him where I might obtain contact information for retired detectives. He suggests I call the Fraternal Order of Police Lodge 3. When I do so, the lady who answers the phone tells me condescendingly that she is not permitted to release information about individual members of the order. She suggests I call the Baltimore Police Department media liaison officer. I do so. His assistant tells me he is unable to help me because I am not "media."

I file Freedom of Information Act requests with the FBI for everything related to the Rey Rivera case. Six months after filing the request I receive a letter informing me that the FBI possesses eighteen pages of documents about the case, but that because of "sensitivity of information," the file is confidential. However, according to the accompanying letter—which implies this is a great privilege—two pages of the file (thick with redactions) are being "released" to me. These turn out to be the first two pages of the 2003 SEC civil action against Agora, Pirate Investor, and Frank Porter Stansberry. I have long been in possession of the entire document. It is, in fact, available at the SEC's own website.

The Rey Rivera case is utterly perplexing. I cannot even find out if it is open or closed. No one will talk about it. But there are problems on my end, too. I am awkward and self-conscious, aware of my inexperience and lack of credentials. I am a literature professor and a writer, not an investigative reporter, definitely not a journalist. I have no connections, no clout, no names to drop.

Exploring a distant area of the city I have never been to before, I discover grand old streets lined with what must once have been splendid brownstones, their doors and windows now boarded up with plywood. I slip down an alleyway behind backyards filled with old mattresses, cable spools, abandoned strollers. Nearby, somebody is playing a saxophone. It is not the poverty that fascinates me so much as the grandeur. These nineteenth-century houses, built to last forever, stand proudly despite the neighborhood's collapse into decrepitude. The finely detailed brickwork, cast-iron balconies, and sturdy porticos seem a denial of the truth around them, a refusal to acknowledge that the kind of people they were built for left the neighborhood long ago.

The back streets here are, as always, full of surprises. I discover a mural of constellations surrounding the head of a man in a leopard mask riding a tiger; chickens and a rooster in a pagoda-shaped hutch; a sign outside a church declaring "Jesus Has Your Back"; a gang of stray cats gathering on the front steps of a house that looks inhabited. Are they waiting to be fed? Perhaps they're seeking shelter. They know a storm is coming. The air is thickening, the sky growing hot and black. The wind rises suddenly; sheets of plastic and cardboard are blown from the roofs of patched-up buildings. Thunder roars. The sky flashes violet through the vacant windows of ruined buildings, then turns black, as though night has suddenly fallen in the middle of the afternoon. The scene reminds me of an old painting I once saw of the fall of Rome.

When the rain hits, my dog and I escape down the forsaken main street until we come to a lone store whose front window is lit up, as if offering refuge. In the front window is a crowded pageant of African masks, dolls, and fetishes. Everything is jammed together in a big pile—voodoo masks, pendulous-breasted Yoruba deities, Egyptian idols, paintings of Haile Selassie and Malcolm X, a bust of Obama, an Aunt Jemima figurine. Many items are on their sides or upside down. A second window display by the front door contains old press and newspaper photographs of black musicians, all neatly labeled: Count Basie, Ella Fitzgerald, James Brown, Smokey Robinson, Jackie Wilson, Aretha Franklin, Jr. Walker and the All-Stars. Next to the window, a large blue hand-painted sign reads, "No Loitering. King Syrup Sandwich 20c. Inqurer Within." The K and S in "King Syrup" are topped with ornate crowns.

When we burst through the door, we bring a gust of rain inside with us. The door slams behind us in the wind. The owner, a middle-aged man with waist-length dreadlocks, introduces himself as E. He says I am welcome to stay in his store until the rain stops.

As I am thanking E. for his hospitality, my dog, who loathes rain, indulges in a strenuous, indignant shake, almost lifting himself off the ground in his frenzy, but E. shows none of the aversion some people display at the smell of wet dog. In fact, he appears to regard the dog as one of my personal effects, like a backpack I happen to be carrying.

He asks whether I would like some tea. I thank him. While the storm rages outside, we drink tea, and E. smokes a thin cigar.

"Do you play chess?" he asks me.

"I know how, but I haven't played for years," I confess. "I'd be terrible competition."

We sit in silence for a while. The shop smells of patchouli and sandalwood. Streams of rain run down the outside of the store-front windows. My dog sniffs around for a while, then settles down at my feet.

"Is there much of a market here for African artifacts?" I ask E.

"Hell, no," he says. "Never was. This place is just where I store my merchandise." He blows out a thin line of smoke. "Nobody lives 'round here anymore," he adds. "Most of these houses are empty."

"Some of them look well kept up."

"One or two," he agrees. "But those people don't come in here. Those people think I'm some kind of witch doctor. The only people who come by here are the rich white people from Jewtown, and the mailman. Eighty percent of my goods I sell on eBay."

"That's very smart of you."

E. asks whether I want to know how he got so smart.

I guess: "From some magic herb or root?"

"No." He smiles. "From playing chess. Chess teaches me always to be thinking three moves ahead. My magic is not so good for making people smart. I have magic for blessings and curses, but the curses work better than the blessings."

I ask, "How do you know?"

"More bad things happen than good," says E.

I can't help thinking that perhaps that's just how life is.

E. does not try to force any of his potions or fetishes on me, or persuade me I need to be healed, but this does not mean I trust him. Nor, on the other hand, does it make him a fraud. There is no clear line between charlatan and magician.

E. has nothing that works to solve mysteries, or to summon up the dead. But he says I need no special tools or concoctions to contact the Other Side. I just need to sit with a pencil in my hand and wait for the message to come through.

Back at home that evening, I make my first attempt at automatic writing, sitting in the dark, waiting to feel the gentle touch of spirit fingers. I sit for hours waiting for a hint, a sign, a clue, but nothing happens. Not a breath.

Perhaps I am caught up in my own expectations, trapped by my own idea of what ought to be happening, what the writing should look and feel like, what it should say. It may be the same problem I had with my old psychoanalyst, Dr. B.—the inability to let go of my expectations and allow my mind to wander. Have I been resisting what I cannot control, shying away from my fears, unbeknownst to myself? Or perhaps my faith is just not strong enough. I am not sure I believe in life after death, or even that I am capable of such faith. My temperament may be too gloomy and cynical. Yet as I sit there silently, pencil in hand, I can feel something growing in me. I hope it is faith, but it could be despair.

Curious to learn more about automatic writing, I begin spending time in the George Peabody Library, a few blocks from the Belvedere; it's a beautiful and cavernous space once described as a "cathedral of books." The southeast corner on the top floor houses the books classified as 130 in the Dewey Decimal System: parapsychology and the occult, dreams and mysteries.

Here are some things I learn:

Things are fifty times more interesting on the Other Side than they are here.

Those who have passed over would not come back, not for anything you could give them.

Many people who pass over will not believe it for weeks. They think they are just dreaming.

It is natural to find yourself a little confused, even a little depressed, when you first wake up. It is like finding yourself in a strange city, with strange people all around you.

You can have pets on the Other Side.

It is so surprising how many people come up to you, shake you by the hand, and speak to you.

Everyone seems to be interested in you, and wants to say "How do you do?"

The following week, D. and I visit an exhibition of artifacts recently unearthed from Faiyum, a city in Middle Egypt, whose people worshiped Sobek, the crocodile-god.

That night, I dream I have managed to convince a judge to order the exhumation of Rey Rivera's body. Uncharacteristically, I am terrified of seeing the corpse. The idea fills me with horror, but I know I have to follow through with my investigations. I wake with a sense of deep dread, and it takes me a few moments to recall, with some relief, that Rivera was, of course, cremated.

Only in retrospect do I connect my dream with the unearthing of the artifacts from Faiyum. The terror may have been compensation, or perhaps wish fulfillment, since the Egyptian exhibit was crowded and disappointing. The statue of Sobek, the crocodile-god, was especially unimposing. Only fragments remained. Even so, as the informational plaque pointed out with no shame, "the snout is a modern reconstruction."

On a conspiracy-theory discussion forum, I find a post by a man named Carlos, who claims to have been affiliated with Agora, discussing the Rey Rivera case. I send him an email letting him know about my project and asking whether he can help me.

Two days later, Carlos replies, telling me that he is no longer involved with Agora. "Unfortunately," he writes, "I really would have nothing of any value to offer to your project: I never once met, knew, or talked to Rivera, nor do I know any more about his death than was published in the papers. I would not even have enough knowledge to engage in speculation." Tantalizingly, he concludes: "It is true that certain 'sources' have been keeping up a steady drum beat of conspiracy over the years, but I have no reason to believe this was anything but a tragic suicide, [or] that those continuing that line of thought are any more than nutjobs themselves."

"OK. Well, thanks anyway for getting back to me," I reply, jauntily concealing my disappointment. I cannot help but wonder whether Carlos might be including me among the "nutjobs," a diverse squad whose key player is a blogger who goes by various aliases, including, most frequently, Beau Brant (which may in fact be his real name). Brant, who admits he incurred heavy financial losses after taking investment advice from one of Agora's newsletters, has been bombarding the Internet for years with increasingly opaque conspiracy theories detailing Agora's connections to Israel, the CIA, the Rothschild family, and the US government. Whatever pseudonym he chooses, Brant's long, semi-dyslexic sentences always give him away. There is no concealing his idiosyncratic style. Here is a typical example:

> It may have been no coincidence between that [sic] death of Rey Rivera and the fact that his name had been placed on Porter Stansberry's latest penny stock fraud promoton [sic] rag called "The Rebound Report" at that time, and that none of the sleazy pump and dump "public companies" it promoted "rebounded" from their worthless share prices any more than Rey Rivera "rebounded" when he crashed through the roof of the building below the Belvedere Hotel, but instead plunged even lower thus defrauding anyone who took their advise [sic] to buy!

I am disappointed that Carlos has nothing to share with me and that such a promising lead has taken me nowhere at all. Two days later, however, he contacts me again.

"Strangely enough," he writes, "I was reminded of your project today when reading a Chinese text from about 1247 (translated title *The Washing Away of Wrongs*):

> The similarities between those who jump into wells, those who are thrown in, and those who lose their footing and fall are very great. The differences are slight. . . . If the victim was thrown in or fell in accidentally, the hands will be open and the eyes slightly open, and about the person he may have money or other valuables. But, if he was committing suicide, then his eyes will be shut and his hands clenched. There will be no valuables on the body. Generally, when someone deliberately jumps into a well, they will enter feet first. If the body is found to have gone in head first, it is probable that the victim was being chased or was thrown in by others.

I think again of Auguste Dupin, who proclaims in "The Murders in the Rue Morgue," in his clumsy English: "Truth is not always in a well. In fact, as regards the more important knowledge, I do believe that she is invariably superficial."

I wonder: Am I making the error Dupin warns of, looking too deeply into the mystery and ignoring the surface truth? Rivera's autopsy says nothing about whether his hands or eyes were open at his death, but he did land feet first, which, according to this ancient Chinese text, would indicate suicide. But such metaphysical forensics would not stand up in today's courtroom. One might as well, like the fortunetellers of ancient Egypt, attempt to descry the future by gazing into a pool of ink.

I arrange to meet Carlos in the Owl Bar. He is a short, heavyset gentleman dressed in a dark suit without a tie. His shirt is open at the neck. He has a strong Hispanic accent. There is a streak of gray in his hair. He reminds me of a well-fed badger.

Carlos is extremely helpful in explaining to me the history and origins of Agora—what the company does, how it works, how it makes so much money, and details of the SEC ruling against Stansberry. When I tell him that I have encountered many people who are paranoid about the influence of Agora, Carlos says he is not unfamiliar with such sentiments. He knows people who believe Agora has hired secret agents to follow them, bugged their phones, hacked into their computers, and worse.

When I asked him whether there is any truth in these rumors, he says there is none at all. Agora, says Carlos, is just the kind of company that attracts nutty speculation and conspiracy theories because it has expanded so quickly and makes so much money without creating any tangible product. Agora also keeps a low profile.

"Most people don't understand what goes on there," Carlos tells me. "They call themselves a publishing house, but what they publish, for the most part, are hyper-aggressively marketed newsletters selling secret systems for predicting stock prices. It's not

The Owl Bar, 1934

surprising that people become suspicious of a company that boasts that it deals in clandestine information."

"So Agora doesn't employ any secret agents?" I ask him, slightly disappointed.

"No. In fact, Agora themselves circulate such rumors in order to give readers of their otherwise very mundane investment letters the impression that the company is connected to all these underground sources of knowledge."

"So it's just a sales tactic," I say.

"Correct," says Carlos. "Everything else is nonsense." He gives me a sly smile. I am not sure what it is, but something about him wins my trust.

I email Jayne Miller and ask whether I can speak to her again about Rey Rivera's death. She agrees, and gives me a time to call. A week later, we talk on the phone.

She has no memory of speaking to me before. This is hardly a surprise, considering the number of people she must speak to every day. But I am taken aback to learn that she barely seems to remember the case itself. After we hang up, I realize that, as an investigative journalist, Miller must cover many different stories every month, whereas for me, it is always the same story over and over again. But then I recall the words she used when we last spoke: "This is one of the most mysterious incidents I've ever encountered in thirty-five years as an investigative reporter." Was she exaggerating? If not, how can she have forgotten everything so completely?

When we speak on the phone, Miller tells me that most of her notes on the case come from her conversations with Michael Baier, one of the two homicide detectives initially assigned to investigate Ray Rivera's death.

Miller recalls that Baier was reassigned because his superiors thought he was spending too much time on the case, investigating it as a homicide when everybody else thought it was a suicide. She noted that Baier thought the story was a lot more complicated than Rey just going off the roof. There is no evidence that he slipped. Rey's wife knows Baier and has kept in touch with him. She also made a note of the fact that Baier thought it was important that Rey was a movie writer, and that he traveled a lot. Baier, she recalled, thought the case was too overwhelming for the Baltimore police to sort out. She also noted that Rey was a swimmer.

Might he have thought the Belvedere's swimming pool was still in use?

I sense Miller is short on time. I ask her if she recalls anything else that might be important.

She continues to read aloud from her notes: "Baier thinks Rey's death may be connected to the Nicaragua situation. Agora was doing some development deal in Nicaragua at the time."

Then she pauses again.

"I have to be careful here," she says. "I assume you know about the SEC injunction against Stansberry?"

"Yes," I say.

"Well, in a news piece I did on the case for WBAL, I made a putative connection between Rivera's death and the SEC conviction, and right after it aired I got an angry email from Agora's lawyers."

I ask her if she can tell me what the email said. I realize I am pushing my luck. But she finds the email and reads it aloud to me over the phone.

"'Rey was a childhood friend of many people who worked at Agora, and the connection you are trying to make is deplorable.'"

I ask her if it would be possible for me to get a copy of the email.

"No," she says bluntly. "That's a private email sent from them to me."

Even though I'm on the phone, I blush. To cover my awkwardness, I say, lightly, "Well, I'm sure I'll be getting my own soon."

"I'm sure you will," says Jayne Miller.

The next morning, I am drinking coffee on the sofa before work, scrolling idly through my email, when my attention is suddenly caught by a message from Carlos: there is something he forgot to mention when we met; can I give him a call?

Short of time, I call him on the way to teach my morning class.

"I just remembered," says Carlos. "Agora did, in fact, have one intelligence connection—and I should tell you, I use the word 'intelligence' advisedly. Sometime in the mid-1990s, they hired William Colby, the former CIA director, to edit his own newsletter, *The Colby Report,* which was a complete flop, As I recall, it attracted less than a hundred subscribers."

"Can you remember why it failed?" I ask him.

"Probably because it was so badly written," Carlos says. "I can recall a particularly deplorable article on the 'banana wars' in Europe. It began, 'The banana, that delicious and nutritious fruit . . .' "

We both snicker.

"He was not there for long," says Carlos. "If I recall, he was supposed to join Bill Bonner's newsletter, *Strategic Investor*, as a contributing writer, but something went wrong. I can't recall exactly what happened, but it ended up in litigation. And then Colby died in mysterious circumstances. Rather interesting. You should look it up."

I do so. On April 27, 1996, Colby set out from his weekend home in Rock Point, Maryland, on a canoe trip, even though it was already dark. He went alone. Nine days later, his body was found lying facedown in a marshy area. Although his death was ruled accidental, others suspect suicide or foul play.

By this time, I know so much about Rey Rivera's death that I can tell you in what direction the wind was blowing on the roof of the Belvedere that night, the exact phase of the moon, what stars were visible, what planets were in transit. But none of what I have learned has shown me anything but further contradictions and complexities. All I really know is that Rey Rivera met his death when his body, precipitating violently from a height, crashed through the roof of the Belvedere's former swimming pool.

Suicides are sometimes misclassified due to investigative error; however, it is true that people have plenty of reasons for wanting suicides hushed up, including no-suicide clauses in insurance contracts, religious taboos, and the reputation of the family. The latter is more and more rarely a factor today, unless you are in line for a title or a throne, but it may very well have led to the conspiracy of discretion around what happened to Mrs. Ann Rieman Duval, who died in her suite at the Belvedere on Tuesday, February 17, 1914.

Mrs. Duval was the oldest daughter of Dr. John Hanson Thomas, a former slave owner, a Confederate sympathizer, a bank president, and the owner of an elegant mansion four blocks from the Belvedere, on the northeast corner of Charles and Monument. This splendid house was once the talk of the town. It had a hydraulic elevator, speaking tubes for the family to summon their servants, a Tiffany skylight, terrapin tanks in the basement, and—according to rumor—a mysterious chamber reached through a secret door, purpose unknown.

Mrs. Duval's husband, Colonel Henry Rieman Duval, was a Confederate veteran just like her father. He was president of the American Sugar Beet Company and a major investor in the railroads. Although the couple had houses in New York City, on Long Island, and in Florida, Mrs. Duval preferred to live quietly in the Belvedere, where she kept a suite and lived a dignified life with her secretary, two maids, a housekeeper, and a chauffeur. She also had a personal cook, even though the Belvedere's chef, Francis Vallagéant, was reputed to be the best cook south of the Mason-Dixon line. It would simply not have been appropriate for a lady of Mrs. Duval's standing to eat alone in a public restaurant, and women were not permitted in the hotel bar.

In the early afternoon of February 17, Mrs. Duval's physician arrived at the Belvedere in response to a call from her daughter Nannie, who was paying her mother a visit. Mrs. Duval, sixty-four, suffered from diabetes and had been in bad health for many months. Nannie told the doctor that her mother had apparently consumed an unknown amount of Holloway's Ointment, a greasy, strong-smelling cream containing turpentine and meant for rubbing on gouty or rheumatic limbs. The version of Mrs. Duval's obituary that was published in the *Brooklyn Eagle* included the information that her maid had left the Holloway's Ointment in a glass, into which her mistress had mixed an envelope of Seidlitz powders, a laxative and digestive aid containing bicarbonate of soda that, when stirred into a glass of water, made a carbonated drink. Why the maid had put Holloway's Ointment in a drinking glass remains a mystery.

The doctor administered an antidote. Before long, the patient had made a full recovery and was sitting up in bed working busily on a crossword puzzle. She seemed so much better, in fact, that Nannie decided to take the train to New Orleans to attend the Mardi Gras, as she had planned to do before her mother had taken to bed.

After her daughter left, however, Mrs. Duval became seriously ill again. According to her maid, she was sick all night. The maid kept asking whether she should call the doctor back, but Mrs. Duval repeatedly said that it was not necessary. According to the maid, Mrs. Duval started to "shake horribly." Then she stopped shaking and would not respond. The maid believed that Mrs. Duval had fainted, and "went to touch her lightly on the arm, only to discover her skin to be quite cold."

Everyone admitted that Mrs. Rieman Duval's passing was

A suite in the Belvedere, circa 1914

sudden and unexpected; her death, however, was attributed to "natural causes." Nobody said that she swallowed the ointment on purpose, and perhaps she did not. It was described in her obituary as a "mistake," and perhaps it was. Mistakes, like suicides, come in many forms.

XI

ANOTHER OF MY favorite places to explore in Baltimore is the neighborhood surrounding the high stone walls of Green Mount Cemetery, which, perhaps twenty feet high, are topped with another ten feet of barbed wire. Once the most fashionable resting place for Baltimore's prominent families, Green Mount Cemetery is now also a mausoleum for this lost world of gentility. The cemetery is surrounded by poverty, and city authorities are obviously concerned to protect its marble stones and sculptures, and to keep the destitute from sleeping there at night.

Wandering through Green Mount's sixty-three acres of monuments to military grandees, senators, judges, businessmen, and philanthropists, you may come across the resting place of the assassin John Wilkes Booth, the legless sideshow performer Johnny Eck, or the inventor Elijah Bond, whose tombstone is carved to resemble his most famous device: the Ouija board. Follow the outside of the cemetery walls and you will pass abandoned homes overgrown with bushes and tangled vines, vacant lots thick with wild grass, violet cornflowers, pale clover, white and yellow daisies, blue forget-me-nots, and, almost everywhere, the pale, creeping blooms known as devil's trumpet. What once were the pathways behind houses now look more like caves composed of a thick dark mass, half foliage, half detritus, in which finches and cardinals have built their nests. How rapidly the territory is ceded. Perhaps, in ten years, there will be coyotes roaming these alleyways; I might see a mountain lion sleeping lazily on a half-collapsed wrought-iron veranda. Yet even here, one or two of the houses still display the standard signs of legitimate inhabitation: the jerry-rigged satellite dish, the pit bull chained up in the feces-splattered yard.

There are no sounds here to trouble the dead in their graves but the twittering of nest-building birds and an occasional police siren. These are supposed to be the most dangerous parts of the city, but there is nothing disturbing here, unless you are afraid of rats. Still, staying away is one of those habits that are meant to keep you safe. You are also supposed to avoid people loitering in places they don't seem to belong, look through the keyhole before opening the door, ask for credentials, always take your phone and purse with you, and tell someone where you're going and when you'll be back.

Rules like these do not apply when you are invisible. The older I get, the more invisible I become. To be invisible is to be inconsequential. That is the downside. On the upside, since nobody cares about a person of no importance, to be invisible is to be invulnerable.

To be invisible is to be free.

It's early 2014. Almost eight years have passed since the death of Rey Rivera. I email Allison again, and this time, I get a reply. Surprisingly, her tone is cheerful and friendly. She identifies herself as "the widow of Rey Rivera." She has heard I've been "sending out inquiries regarding Rey" for a project I'm working on. She's interested in knowing what angle I'm taking, "since we did not know you."

I take great care over the wording of my reply. I want it to sound thoughtful and discreet. I explain to Allison that I live in the Belvedere and have done so since April 2005, that I was shocked and bewildered by her husband's mysterious death, and that ever since it happened, I've been unable to put it out of my mind. I tell her that I'm a writer and a literature professor; I give her information about some of my previous books, and let her know that I'm writing about Rey's death in the context of the history of the Belvedere. I give her my home address and my cell-phone number.

Allison does not reply. A month later, I email her again. Perhaps, I suggest, she does not want to be involved in a project that might involve opening up the deep wounds caused by her husband's death. If this is the case, I tell her, I can understand how she feels. If she ever changes her mind, I ask her to please let me know.

That afternoon, Allison leaves a message on my cellphone asking whether I have a landline we can speak on. I call and give her my landline number, and she calls me back. She explains that ever since Rey's death, she has been extremely security conscious. She says I need to grasp the enormous power and wealth of Agora. They will stop at nothing, she says. She is certain that someone at Agora is responsible for Rey's death, but the company has so much money and so many connections, even among the police, that she knows she could never prove it.

Allison tells me that, for the first couple of years after Rey's death, she was obsessed with solving the mystery of what happened to him. She spent all her time gathering evidence. She still has boxes and boxes of the notes she made. But every time she would start to think she was getting somewhere, she would come up against another brick wall. It almost drove her crazy.

I am taken aback by Allison's open and friendly manner. She sounds smart, interesting, even funny, which I definitely was not expecting.

Obviously, I cannot promise I will solve the case, I tell her. But

I have become obsessed with it, and when I am obsessed with something, I don't let it go. I'm curious, I tell her, and determined, and I live right here in the Belvedere. If nothing else, perhaps I can at least draw more attention to the case and maybe even get people to come forward.

Allison tells me that if I want her help, I will have to come out to LA and talk to her in person. She does not trust the phone, she says, and she trusts email even less.

I tell her I'll be happy to meet her in LA.

The first thing I need to do, she tells me, is get hold of Michael Baier. He was the first detective on the case, and he was helpful and sympathetic. She tells me that Baier knew immediately that Rey's death was a homicide, and a very complicated one. He was going to start looking into Agora and Pirate Investor immediately. But within three weeks of Rey's death, Baier had been taken off the case and replaced with another homicide detective, Marvin Sydnor, who was much more "hard core." When Allison asked Sydnor what had happened to Baier, Sydnor told her they'd taken him off the case because he was "getting too attached" to her. She said she spoke to Baier one last time, when he came to say good-bye. He told her the case was far too complex for Baltimore homicide to deal with and that she should get back in touch with him in seven or eight years, by which time he'd be retired; Rey's death would be a cold case, and they would finally be able to get some answers.

Before we hang up, Allison wants to be sure I know exactly what I am getting into. She reminds me that very bad things have happened to other people who tried to find out what happened to Rey. She mentions a journalist who lost her job after starting to investigate the case. I have to be very, very careful, she tells me.

I know, I tell her. I'm not afraid.

It's true. I'm not afraid, and I often wonder why not. Maybe part of me actually hopes I will get into danger, if only to give the finger to everybody who dismisses my obsession as misplaced, who writes off Rey's death as "just a suicide." On the other hand, despite the dark warnings and anonymous emails, I've now been investigating the case for almost eight years, and I have not been followed by anyone, or threatened, or even warned away (except by well-wishers).

Of course, my lack of fear is also connected to my sense of invisibility, my "paranoia with a minus sign," as Dr. B. astutely described it. When it comes to conspiracy theories, I oscillate between skepticism and belief, envying the conviction of the paranoid. Those who believe in conspiracies have confidence in a higher power. In my more pragmatic moments, I see this confidence as the result of repressed and projected anxiety. After all, the one thing worse than being constantly observed is having nobody care about you at all. The paranoid's real terror is not the fear of surveillance, but that they are all alone in the world.

What is the repressed anxiety, then, of someone who thinks she is invisible? I am not alone in believing myself to be under the radar. Inconspicuous people may not be noticed by the wider world, but we recognize one another. I see myself in the small, delicate lady in my yoga class who arrives early and always sits by herself in the back corner; in the elderly man with the curved spine I glimpse in the window of the bar down the street, drinking by himself; in the red-haired girl with the aloof expression who walks her wire-haired fox terrier through Mount Vernon; in the gentleman in the fez who sits on a park bench by the fountain; in the woman who reads the newspaper every morning in the coffee shop, dressed in medical scrubs. To me, these fellow creatures are the opposite of invisible: they may be discreet, they may be unremarkable, but I always notice them, and wonder whether their lonely habits are a choice they have made, or a trap they have fallen into (at what point does the first become the second?). To me, it is the rest of humanity that passes by in a blur—groups, friends, and couples, chatting together, well balanced, insulated and self-involved.

My feeling of invisibility is, I suspect, a way of repressing the precipitous awareness that I am, in fact, as noticeable as the occultist Aleister Crowley in the Hotel Café Royale:

> Laboring under the conviction that he was possessed of a magical cloak that rendered him invisible, Crowley delighted in walking past smart sets in the café, a cone-shaped, star-spangled hat perched on his head. Polite groups of the British public would look straight ahead, frozen, as the grave, portly figure drifted past them, like an enormous elephant.

At first, what baffles me about the "Stansberry Analysts" is their relentless and persistent references, in their podcasts, on their websites, and in their investment newsletters, to their tremendous wealth. If you are not used to people talking constantly about how much money they have, it can be as embarrassing as someone who incessantly drops the name of a celebrity friend.

"My annual investment goal never changes," brags Stansberry in his newsletter *The Crux,* on January 2, 2015. "There are two parts. First, I strive to save at least half of my after-tax income. I define 'saving' broadly. Buying cars doesn't count. Buying gold does. Buying land does, even if it's merely land for recreational purposes like hunting and fishing." Michael Masterson (formerly Mark Ford), another person Stansberry calls "the smartest man I know," admits he was once $100,000 in debt, but brags that he's now "a successful businessman with a *multimillion-dollar* net worth." In a 2016 newsletter, the Stansberry Analyst Brian Hunt crows that he "put a large chunk" of his net worth "in gold bullion" after taking the advice of his colleague Steve Sjuggerud, and it was "one of the best investment decisions of my life." Hunt asserts that, "normally, someone like Steve would work at a billion-dollar hedge fund or a mega investment bank. He would live in a

$10 million mansion near New York City or London." Instead, Sjuggerud plays the guitar and lives by the beach; like his old school friend Porter Stansberry, he declares himself an "avid surfer."

I wonder why these men, with their "*multimillion-dollar* net worth," continue to work so hard sending out their bromides, touting their self-published books about how they got to be so rich. The lives of these men (and 90 percent of them are men) are, it appears, devoted to sharing their investment secrets with the rest of us so that we, too, can become multimillionaires—"*virtually overnight!*"

For me, possibly for most people, the main advantage of great wealth would be to take away all concerns about money. Yet the Stansberry Analysts seem to think about nothing else. Finally, I realize that while individual Stansberry Analysts may indeed be wealthy, their income does not come from investing in the companies they tout (that would be against the law). Possibly, it does not come from investing at all. Stansberry Research, despite its name, is not a research organization but a marketing company that aggressively sells subscriptions to email newsletters containing tips about how to make money. The analysts' income has nothing to do with the advice they give or the success of the investments they recommend, but with how many newsletter subscriptions they sell. To keep on selling, they need to impress, convince, confuse, frighten, persuade, and convert gullible members of the public. And to do so, they use one of the oldest tricks in the book: they hide recurring credit-card costs in the small print. As long as the small print is there, the Compliance Editor has nothing to worry about. In such cases, deliberate fraud is notoriously difficult to prove.

Stansberry and Associates claims to have an A+ rating from the Better Business Bureau, and this is true, but only because someone from the company has responded to every complaint—and there are a lot of complaints. The BBB lists 105 total customer complaints against Stansberry & Associates Investment Research LLC since March 2014. Those who have grievances refer to "rude service," and "low quality research," but by far the most common complaints refer to misleading information about unauthorized recurring credit-card charges, the company's refusal to accept cancellation requests by email, and phone lines that are always busy or that drop their calls.

For most Agora publications, the "customer service staff" are the only personal point of contact between subscriber and publisher, and it is these stressed-out telephone operators who have to handle cancellation requests, demands for refunds, and the task of repeating long URLs, often at the top of their lungs, to elderly, hard-of-hearing customers who rarely go online. Most members of the customer service staff have never met the editors or publishers, who can hide away behind SEC regulations, leaving it up

Rey and Allison on their wedding day

to the telephone operators to handle the furious calls. "Good old bait and switch at its best," one customer concludes.

Driving through the city, I swerve to avoid hitting a stray dog wandering in the road, a foxy little creature with big ears. I park my car and follow her on foot, hoping I can slip my fingers around her collar long enough to see whether there's a phone number on her tag. An elderly gentleman helps me for a while, but his presence makes the dog nervous, and we lose her. Then, walking back to my car alone, I catch another glimpse of the animal running perilously in and out of the traffic. I follow her on foot again, sticking close this time, until she gets tired and sits down on someone's front stoop, at which point I sit down quietly beside her, let her sniff my hand, then gradually begin stroking the fur on her ears and the top of her head. I continue to do so until she becomes calm. When she seems completely relaxed, I gently take hold of her collar and twist it toward me so I can read her tag. But the moment she feels the pressure around her neck, she grows afraid and starts to struggle, baring her teeth and snarling. I keep a tight hold of her collar. She twists her neck around, looks at me with wild eyes, and sinks her teeth into my wrist. I cry out, relax my grip, and the dog runs right back into the traffic.

I am only a few blocks from T.'s place, so I stop by to clean up my wrist. My friend T. lives in a dark basement with his two cats, one of whom was born without a tail.

I turn on the tap in the kitchen and hold my wrist under the running water. T. goes into his bathroom to look for a bandage. His bathroom is about five by five, including the shower stall. For six years, his toilet has been sinking down through the floor into the sub-basement, descending another millimeter or two every time he sits on it. Recently, it has also begun to move back and forth, like a porcelain rocking chair. T. is increasingly afraid it is about to sink through the floor entirely. He rarely has guests.

Once the bleeding has stopped and the dried blood has been washed away, we examine my wrist. The wound is not serious. My skin bears the red marks of a row of small teeth, but only the canines have punctured the skin.

T. has heard that dogs do not bite unless the moon is full. I have heard this is true only of rabid dogs. We wonder if the dog might have been rabid. Unable to find any bandages, T. gives me a dark brown sock to wrap around my wrist, one of a pair his mother bought him that he has never liked. He does not want it back, even clean. He does not want to catch rabies, he says.

I tell him that in this country there is a greater chance of being hit by lightning than of getting rabies from a dog, let alone from a clean sock. On average, in the United States, there are only three deaths a year from rabies, and those all are from bat bites.

For all these glib statistics, as I write this sentence it strikes me that if the dog was in fact rabid, and if I had picked up a small amount of the virus, it could even now be incubating in my body, and I would not know it. A small amount of rabies virus can linger in the body from two weeks to six years before the first symptoms appear. By then, of course, it is too late. What appears to be a mild case of the flu quickly develops into fever accompanied by agitation, paranoia, confusion, hydrophobia, delirium, and finally paralysis of the facial and throat muscles. At this point, death by respiratory arrest is unpreventable and occurs within a few days—if the victim is lucky.

Dr. Henry Wilde, who regularly treats rabies patients at the Chulalongkorn University Hospital in Bangkok, has made the case that in his final days, Edgar Allan Poe, who was known to have kept a number of semiferal cats, showed all the signs of rabies. When he was found on a Baltimore street, dressed in a stranger's ill-fitting clothes, he was in a state of delirium. According to medical records kept by Dr. John J. Moran, who cared for him while he was in the hospital, Poe's symptoms included wide fluctuations in pulse rate, respiration, and temperature. He refused alcohol and had difficulty drinking water. All these are typical symptoms of rabies. Also, the median length of survival after the onset of such symptoms of rabies is four days, which is exactly how long it took Poe to die.

Not long after being bitten by the dog, I see a poisoned rat on the edge of a busy sidewalk. The rat is lying on his back and taking short, gasping breaths. Thick black fluid seeps from his mouth. I think of Poe's young wife, Virginia, singing to her husband while playing the piano. Her throat catches as she strains for a note. The catch becomes a cough. She reaches for her handkerchief, bleached and starched by her mother, and sprays it with tiny flecks of blood, almost black. Her husband recognizes the sign; he has seen it before, too many times. His wife is in the late stage of tuberculosis.

The rat is in the late stages of brodifacoum poisoning. He may have hours of agony ahead of him, but I do not have the courage or strength of mind to end his pain. If I had known how much this failure would haunt me—how many times I would revisit this scene in my head, how many times I would imagine myself returning to the dying rat with a large brick, crushing his head, and leaving his carcass to the flies—I believe I would have found the strength to help him.

Brodifacoum is an anticoagulant marketed under many names, most of which conjure up the image of scientific yet violent and permanent warfare against "vermin": Ditrac, Ratshot Red, Vertox, Finale, Havoc, Klerat, Pestoff, Ratak+, Rodend, Rataquill. It is used in rat poison because it stays in the body for a long time. A rat will return to eat the poisoned bait for up to ten days before he begins to feel the effects, which means that neither he nor his fellow rats will necessarily associate the poison with the agony it produces. They will, perhaps, continue to eat while feeling confused, wondering what is happening, who has turned against them.

The manufacturers of these poisons often claim there is no pain involved when rats die. Yet here is a list of symptoms provided by veterinarians for owners who fear their dog or cat may have swallowed brodifacoum by accident: wounds that will not stop bleeding; large bruises appearing on the body or gums; acute swelling of one or more joints; swelling of regions of skin; the sudden swelling of the abdomen (due to hemorrhaging into the belly cavity); difficulty breathing (due to hemorrhaging into the chest cavity or lungs); diarrhea, abdominal pain, and the coughing up, vomiting, and defecation of blood.

At this stage, if an antidote is not administered, your beloved pet's lung cells will become damaged and lose their integrity, allowing fluid from the blood vessels within the lungs to leak into the airways, causing heart arrhythmia and respiratory distress. This will be followed by tremors, convulsions, collapse, loss of consciousness, coma, and finally, at long last, death.

I have courted a flock of birds with whirring wings by placing a feeder full of thistle seed on the outside ledge of one of our fifth-floor windows. At first, I assumed the birds were pigeons. Now I know they are mourning doves, and they have shown me the beauty of the color gray, which, on their small bodies, transforms itself delicately here into lavender, there into blue. I think I can hear them now, cooing at the feeder. When it is empty, they will grow impatient, tapping on the window with their beaks like hungry children, demanding their breakfast. One of them once laid an egg in my planter, and immediately abandoned it, as if embarrassed by what she had done. The small white oval lay there for months, cold as a pebble.

Sometimes in the early summer, fledgling doves, sparrows, pigeons, or starlings will fall from their nests high in the Belvedere's quoins and embellishments. Occasionally, one of these baby birds will land in my window planters ("to the mouse and any smaller animal, [gravity] presents practically no dangers"). Whenever this happens, I keep the fledgling in a box and feed it with milk from a dropper until it is old enough to fly. One summer I take in an injured homing pigeon that I find in the street outside. A tag on its leg provides a phone number and a registration number.

I call the phone number. It is answered by a gentleman who asks me for the registration. When I read it to him, he asks me to slow down.

"And speak up," he adds. "I'm ninety-one."

When he looks up the pigeon's registration, he discovers the bird is on its way to Coney Island.

"What should I do with it?" I ask him.

"I'll get the man with the books to give you a call," he says.

I make the pigeon a home in my closet and give it a dish of bread and milk. "The man with the books" never calls, but the next morning, the pigeon is much stronger. I put it on the window ledge and it seems eager to be on its way. It totters out, tests its wings, flutters and flaps for a while, then launches itself into the air. Its first attempt at flight is a brief one; it lands on the annex roof, takes a short rest, then flies off again, heading in the wrong direction. I hope it made it home. I still think of that pigeon now and then.

Another time, the bird that landed on my window ledge turned out to be a furious baby hawk. It lived for two days in my closet until two gentlemen from the Maryland Raptor Rescue, wearing big black gloves with wrist protectors, arrived to retrieve it. On two March days six years apart, I have found a woodcock in the gutter outside the hotel. Both times, I learned, the birds' spring migration had been disastrously interrupted by a heavy winter storm, leaving them starved, unable to find or forage for food in the snow-covered city. Or perhaps they had crashed into the building, mistaking the reflection in its windows for the sky ahead. One was freshly dead; the other, although beautifully plump and healthy-looking, was seriously injured, and died later that night in my blue scarf.

XII

WHEN I FLY out to LA to meet Allison Jones Rivera, I take a red purse, nothing more. The plane is almost empty. I fall asleep in a snowy Baltimore winter and wake up in the spring sunshine of California. We have planned to meet in the coffee shop of a hotel close to the airport.

I recognize Allison at once. She looks the same as she does in the two photographs I have seen of her, both taken almost ten years ago, at her wedding. She is tall, slim, and graceful with shoulder-length red-brown hair, angular, expressive features, and an easy laugh. She has brought a friend, a striking strawberry blonde with blue eyes and freckles whom Allison introduces as Megan. I am dressed for the cold, in a denim jacket and green knit cap, and feel distinctly grungy beside Allison and Megan's bright glamour.

We order coffee and talk for a long time—over four hours. Allison and Megan have both brought yellow legal pads, and we all make notes as we chat.

Again, Allison tells me that Rey's death left her frozen with grief. Then, she says, her sorrow turned into anger, and she grew obsessed with trying to find out how and why her husband was killed. But eventually she realized it was not helpful for her to be stuck in the past, and when she stopped thinking about the crime, she found herself starting to feel better. And the less she was consumed by the circumstances of her husband's death, the more interested she became in how she could honor his life.

Allison says there was a time at which she decided she wanted to write a book about Rey, so she joined a memoir-writing group. At their first meeting, the teacher, an older gentleman, went around the class asking everyone what they planned to write about. When it was Allison's turn to speak, she said that she was going to write about her husband, who had been murdered in mysterious circumstances while he was working for a financial organization in Baltimore. After she had finished speaking, says Allison, the teacher asked her whether she would mind staying behind at the end of the class. When they were alone, he wrote something on a piece of paper, folded it in half, and handed it to her. Then he told her to open the piece of paper, look at what he had written, and tell him whether those were the people who killed her husband.

Allison opened the piece of paper and saw the words "Stansberry/Agora." For a moment, she was struck completely dumb. When she could speak, she asked the teacher how he knew. He told her he used to be a lawyer, and his work involved prosecuting white-collar criminals. He knew the kinds of things those people could do. He said others had spent years trying to prosecute those people but could not even get close. His advice to Allison was to stay away. If she wrote her story, he said, she would be putting her life on the line.

Allison grows animated as she talks; her eyes light up and she brushes her hair away from her forehead. I start to wonder how often she has told this story before. It feels like a well-polished anecdote. I am also unsure why the man had to write down the name on a piece of paper, as if it were a magic spell that could not be said aloud. Nonetheless, it is a compelling narrative, and she tells it convincingly.

The afternoon shadows grow longer. Allison continues to talk about sinister events connected with her husband's death. She tells me that Michael Baier was thrown off the case for, as his accusers put it, "falling in love with her." She also describes almost being hit by a car emerging at breakneck speed from a Baltimore street.

I am not sure what to make of it all.

Megan is a documentary filmmaker, born in Britain and raised in Canada. Along with her brother, she co-owns a documentary production company. Megan and Allison are thinking about writing a feature based on Rey and Allison's story, with a strong female lead who goes in search of the truth behind her husband's mysterious death. They feel it's just the right time for a movie like this.

"When I got your email," says Allison, "it felt as though everything was falling into place. I thought: 'This was meant to be.'"

"Imagine the story," says Megan. "The handsome young couple with everything going for them. The guy just wants to make enough money to buy a ring, have a dream wedding, and introduce his family to his beautiful bride. He takes up an offer from his former school friend to make a lot of money in a short time. The couple move to a city where they don't know anybody, and it's nothing like they think it is going to be. The husband thinks the job's going to be one thing, but it turns out to be another. It's like a deal with the devil. They find themselves completely isolated. The girlfriend is traveling all the time, and the guy starts to get lured into this dark world and witnesses some very sinister things."

We agree to keep in touch. When we stand up to say good-bye, Allison and Megan both give me a hug. Megan is tall and slim, but when she pulls the material of her dress tight against her stomach, I see a slight bulge, which she smiles and pats affectionately.

"Yes, I'm pregnant," she says. "It's my second. I already have a little boy."

It strikes me as very ambitious to have a baby, write a screenplay, and make a film all in the coming year, but Allison and Megan both seem full of energy and vigor.

In fact, the two of them radiate so much life that later, back in my room, I feel lonely and depleted. I return to the hotel coffee bar, which has a relaxed and welcoming mood, and position myself at the counter. Even though it is evening, I order oatmeal. The waiter who serves me, a Hispanic man, has an avuncular charm.

"You like oatmeal? I like oatmeal, too," he tells me. "People think oatmeal is just for breakfast, but no, not at all."

The television on the wall above the bar is showing a basketball game with the sound muted. The conversation around me is a gentle hum. On the other side of the lobby, someone plays a Cole Porter tune on the piano. The baristas are teasing one another in Spanish above the mechanical buzz of the dishwasher and the purr of the espresso machine. Every so often, the headwaiter will ring up someone's check at the cash register, and every time he does so, he says the same thing:

"Your signature right here, my friend, and we're in business."

When someone has committed a murder and wants to get rid of the corpse, they usually bury it, dump it in a body of water, burn it, cut it up and dispose of it piece by piece, or dissolve it in chemicals. Rarely do they hide it. When this happens, according to homicide investigators, particular attention should be paid, especially when the body is kept close by, as this suggests the perpetrator has the blind self-confidence of a Hitchcock villain, and may have killed before. The forensic literature includes, by way of example, a body discovered after ten years under the concrete patio of the killer's house; a corpse encased in a concrete block and hidden in the murderer's attic; two bodies buried in concrete on a local golf course; and a cadaver found after two years walled up in the basement of a house the killer had put on the market. The bodies of murder victims have been found within a mile of the perpetrator's home hidden in wells, sewer systems, water tanks, pits, compost bins, elevator shafts, trash cans, dumbwaiters, barrels, air-conditioning systems, chimneys, the trunks of cars, and the sewage tanks of portable toilets. They have been found shoved inside mattresses and rolled up in carpets. One corpse spent twenty years in a deep freeze. Another spent ten years inside a sofa. Bodies have been hidden in the box mattresses of motel beds, and even under the beds themselves, in one case for as long as seven weeks, with no recorded complaints from guests although the rooms had been cleaned and rented several times in the interim.

Given his landing place—almost forty feet from the wall of the Belvedere—and the fact that he landed feet first, it seems impossible that Rey Rivera was pushed directly from the roof. I learn this from Rod Cross, a retired forensic physicist affiliated with the University of Sydney, and one of the world's leading experts on falls from a height.

"A feet-first jump usually results in a feet-first landing, unless it's a low-speed somersault or a head-first dive," Cross told me. "A push from shoulder height would result in significant rotation through the air." For Rivera to land where he did, Cross concluded that he had to have taken a running jump.

Experiments conducted by the authors of an article published in the *Journal of Forensic Science* show that "the two-hand push of a normal individual to other individuals (154lb of body weight) can generate an initial velocity of up to only 9mph." These experiments were conducted in Taiwan, where 154 pounds is the average male body weight. Rey Rivera weighed 242 pounds; still, his initial velocity was around 11 miles per hour and, according to the authors, "an initial velocity exceeding 6mph or so becomes the criterion for the running jump that is distinguishable from being pushed or slipping before falling from a height." The authors conclude that "an initial velocity of over 6mph in a voluntary jump suggests that the attempt to commit suicide is considerable," which is true only if we assume that a running jump has to be voluntary. Is this something we should take for granted, or are there circumstances under which a person could be forced to take a running jump against their will? If so, what would those circumstances be? If threats were made against the lives of the victim's loved ones? If he was forced at gunpoint? If the alternative was something even worse?

But if someone made Rey Rivera jump, even if they insisted he take a running leap, the layout of the back of the Belvedere is such that no one could have predicted exactly where he would land. If he had landed a few feet to either side, or closer to the building (and both seem far more likely than his actual landing place), his body would have been visible to everyone on the east side of the Belvedere and the parking lot on the other side of the annex. The moon was full that night, but even if we suppose that Rey's body was not seen that evening, it would certainly have been noticed early the next morning, when those like us, with east-facing windows, went to open their curtains or blinds. If she had been able to examine the body within a day of death, the medical examiner could have given more precise estimates about things like Rivera's blood alcohol level, the presence of drugs in his bloodstream, the wounds on his head, and other important facts that are currently unknown due to the extent of decomposition.

Even if it had been possible to predict that Ray's body would land on the swimming pool roof, no one could have predicted that the roof would give way under his weight, or that his corpse would lie for a week on the floor of an empty office. Even in the Belvedere, few people knew that the former swimming pool had been made into office space; even fewer were aware that this space had been divided into two rooms, and that the east one was empty. And if Rivera ran and jumped at gunpoint, the person pointing the gun must have been sure—since there was a strong chance that the falling body would be seen—that they could get down from the roof immediately and make their way through the Belvedere without being observed, or suspected, or caught on camera.

More to the point, if someone was planning to force Rivera to jump at gunpoint, how could they be sure he would not simply refuse, opting to take a bullet (he was afraid of heights, after all) or—since he had nothing left to lose—try to tackle his assailant and take him down as well? With his huge height, strength, and athleticism, I imagine it would be well worth the odds. And who is to say that the two men would not be seen on the roof, or that Rey would not draw attention to them by crying out for help? He could not have been sedated; if he were, how would it have been possible for him to take such a determined and vigorous jump?

The only other possibility that makes any sense is that Rivera's body was dropped after dark from a helicopter; but again, it would have been impossible to predict how or where the body would land, and surely Belvedere residents would have seen or heard a low-flying helicopter on the night of Rivera's death. Plus, airspace security would definitely have picked up on an unidentified aircraft flying in such close proximity to the center of Baltimore after dark, as the airspace above downtown Baltimore is subject to air traffic control, and any airborne vehicle must be explicitly cleared before it can enter. Of course, this does not exclude the possibility that the body was dumped from a helicopter that had already been cleared by air traffic control, but why take the risk of dropping a dead body into the middle of a busy city rather than, say, into the Chesapeake Bay? If weighed down, it might never have resurfaced. And even if it did resurface, drowning would seem a far more likely method of suicide for a man who feared heights and loved the water.

The investigative journalist Stephen Janis told me he thought there was enough evidence surrounding Rey's death for the medical examiner to have come up with an alternate conclusion. "If they'd just done a little more work and ruled it a homicide, it could have been a whole different case," Janis told me. "All you have to do is to introduce a little ambiguity into a death, and it will be labeled 'undetermined' and remain uninvestigated, because the Baltimore police already have enough homicides on their hands."

In the world of Baltimore City homicide detectives, according to Janis, "unusual circumstances" is anything beyond a bullet wound to the head. He told me about an investigation he and a colleague did into five unsolved cases of women who were strangled in 2008. "Strangulation is just a little too esoteric for Baltimore City homicide," Janis told me. "And then one of them had drugs in their system; others had criminal records, primarily convictions for prostitution or drug possession. So they were considered in 'high risk professions,' and that's just kind of what happens. There are so many homicides that are just not even investigated."

Out of the 966 "undetermined" deaths reported by the Office of the Chief Medical Examiner in 2006, 718 were attributed to "narcotics" and 248 to "other."

High-profile murders are solved by eliminating the innocent suspects one by one, as in most detective fiction, until the murderer can be arrested and charged. In such cases, even apparent suicides are sometimes revealed to be disguised murders. But in reality, particularly in a city like Baltimore, victims and murderers are almost always part of the same culture and environment. Frequently, today's suspect is tomorrow's victim; often both have comparable criminal records.

If Rey's death was a murder, there is another mystery to solve: *cui bono*?

It is true that *The Rebound Report* had not been a great success, and those who chose to invest in the stocks Rey recommended no doubt lost more money than they gained. But he stopped writing the newsletter almost a year before his death. And all Agora's investment newsletters—perhaps all investment newsletters in general—have their dissatisfied subscribers. If giving bad stock tips put one at risk of murder, the entire financial industry would collapse.

More plausible is the theory that, after leaving Stansberry's company, Rey had, whether intentionally or not, learned something potentially incriminating about Pirate Investor, or about someone working at Agora. Perhaps he was planning to take this information to the police or to the SEC; perhaps not. But when news got around that he and Allison were planning to move back to LA, did someone decide that Rey had to be silenced? Did this person hire a contract killer? If so, the crime must have been calculated to take place while Stansberry was out of town. And when Stansberry got back to Baltimore and learned about Rey's death, was he rewarded for his silence? An anonymous comment on an article about the case by Stephen Janis posted at the *Baltimore Examiner* website puts this theory in a nutshell. "Rey was a very inquisitive man, a truth-seeker. He had information that threatened something larger than himself and was murdered for it."

Some have suggested to me that Rey's death was connected to the death of a gentleman named Thom Hickling who worked at Agora. Rey had become especially close to Hickling, who was killed in a car accident while visiting his daughter in Africa. His death is often mentioned as a turning point for Rey, who apparently found it suspicious. Rey's mother told me that Rey and Hickling were good friends. "Rey liked him very much," she said. "He talked to me about him. He said he was a real person. Honest. And this guy died somewhere overseas—I don't remember where. All I remember is that it was a very weird situation in which he died. And Rey got very concerned."

Others have suggested that Rey's death may have been connected to developments in Nicaragua, where Agora owns a large stretch of coastline. Those who have studied the case often refer to "Nicaragua" in cryptic terms. Jayne Miller wrote in her notes that "Michael Baier thinks Rey's death is somehow connected to the situation in Nicaragua." In an email to me, Stephen Janis wrote,

"I'll never forget what police spokesman Donny Moses said when I asked about the case: 'Don't mess with the Nicaraguans.'"

In fact, for those who enjoy conspiracy theories, "the Nicaraguans" are just the tip of the iceberg. I have now spent years of my life following Internet threads by angry speculators, investors, muckrakers, and "independent thinkers" of dubious sanity, a bizarre path of loosely connected breadcrumbs that has led me to the edge of nowhere and back again. There are those who have "irrefutable evidence," for example, that Agora is connected to everything from 9/11, to the "Jewish domination of Wall Street," to the CIA, to the Rothschilds, to George Soros, to the Taiwanese triads, to the murder of African political leader Patrice Lumumba in the Congo in 1960.

Yet officials obviously believe there is no smoke without fire, since they continued to harbor suspicions about Agora's activities. In September 2003, Melanie Senter Lubin, the securities commissioner for the state of Maryland, served two subpoenas on Agora asking the company to produce its subscriber lists. When Agora refused, Lubin filed a motion to compel enforcement. A trial court denied the motion, arguing that the commissioner had failed to demonstrate a compelling need. The case went to the Court of Appeals of Maryland in September 2005, and the appeal was upheld.

Rey Rivera was given two separate memorial services: one in Baltimore shortly after the discovery of his body, and one on June 6 in Santa Monica. When Allison returned to Baltimore after the service in Santa Monica, which Stansberry did not attend, she went immediately to his office on St. Paul Street to find out the latest in the police investigation. To her shock, Stansberry told her he would no longer be cooperating with the inquiry. He wanted nothing to do with the police, he said. Because of the SEC investigation, he felt they would be against him from the start. Allison could hardly believe what she was hearing. Porter had been Rey's closest friend in Baltimore; the two of them had spoken on the phone the day before Rey's death. Worse still, when she went to speak to the police about the situation, she was told by Marvin Sydnor that Stansberry had made himself inaccessible to them. "He's five lawyers thick," Sydnor said to her. "We can't touch him."

It is very unfortunate that Allison Rivera received nothing at all from Agora by way of compensation for Rey's death. While compensation may not have been required, since Rey was no longer working for Stansberry except on a freelance basis, it does seem heartless to deny her anything, especially given the fact that, a few weeks after Rey's death, according to Allison, Stansberry began to act coldly toward her.

The discreet, low-profile, high-profit nature of Agora undoubtedly gives the company a secretive, cultlike feel. It employs at least a thousand people in Baltimore alone, and seems to make a baffling amount of money for a company that produces little more than emails. It is constantly advertising for new employees, indicating a very high rate of turnover, and is always looking to hire young people ready to work for entry-level salaries. In November 2016, the company purchased two more buildings in Mount Vernon: a five-story office building at 1125 N. Charles Street whose acquisition and renovation have been estimated to have cost at least $11 million, and the offices at 1001 Cathedral Street, above the popular City Café.

From this perspective, the story of Rey Rivera at Agora is a tale of David and Goliath: the huge, mysterious corporation versus the good, honest man seeking the truth.

Is it possible, however, that we can expand our imaginations widely enough to embrace both sides of the story? I have spoken to Agora employees who tell me that working for the company is the best job they have ever had.

"It's a great place to work," one employee, G., told me. "Everybody's young and full of energy. There are no strict work hours, no dress code, and you're encouraged to think out of the box. It's totally unique." The old mansions are beautiful places to work, and though their offices are physically separated, all the employees come together for social events like summertime receptions in the Mount Vernon parks, wine tastings, music recitals, and the end-of-the-year holiday party at the Belvedere. The company, moreover, offers a great benefits package, and encourages radical and independent thinking. And this is not a minority opinion. Agora is regularly included in the *Baltimore Sun*'s annual poll of "Baltimore's Best Places to Work." One year, every employee was given an iPad as a token of the company's appreciation. Employees praise the work environment and say there are lots of opportunities for anyone who fits the company model. Agora has contributed generously to the upkeep of the parks, fountains, and statues in the Mount Vernon area, as well as to the renovation of Baltimore's Washington Monument. It has established a health clinic/hospital on the tract of coastal land it owns in Nicaragua, for both the residents of Rancho Santana, its resort and residential community, as well as the local workers.

If Stansberry was involved in anything illegal, why would he invite his honest and ethical friend Rey to come work for him? No one has denied that, as soon as Porter learned that Rey had gone missing, he was terribly anxious; he offered a reward for any information about his friend's whereabouts and was eager to help with the search. And once Rey's body was found, is it really so surprising that Stansberry felt uncomfortable around Allison? After all, it was Porter who had brought Rey to Baltimore, where he was reportedly unhappy. If he had stayed in California, he might still be alive today.

It is natural that Stansberry should have been traumatized by his friend's death, and it is well known that people grieve in different ways. Some reach out to friends for comfort; others grieve in private, avoiding social contact, often to the extent of appearing cold and distant. There are even those who behave irrationally by going on spending sprees, for example, or buying an expensive new home. It is also natural, perhaps, that Stansberry should fall under suspicion, partly because of the way he avoided the police after Rivera's death, but also because he is so wealthy and successful. He is clearly the object of a great deal of envy among those who know him, or have worked for him. Those who are too conventional or not brave enough to take the kind of financial risks that Stansberry has taken might well resent him for his accomplishments, and feel that he must certainly be guilty of something.

For in some regards, Porter Stansberry is an accomplished man. In a small way, he is a public figure. Often, in Baltimore, I see people carrying bags or folders bearing the name and logo of Stansberry Research; I see cars bearing Stansberry Radio stickers on their back bumpers. Porter Stansberry himself has weathered the SEC fraud charges and emerged with his company not only intact, but thriving. No longer the cigar-chomping show-off of Pirate Investor, he has become more thoughtful and self-aware. On his podcast, the *Stansberry Investor Hour,* he takes nuanced and surprising positions, chatting to his guests with a cheerful confidence, describing himself as "a family man." He occasionally refers to his wife, their stable marriage, his two young sons, his dog. Longtime listeners of the podcast have heard Stansberry talk about his charter boat, a sixty-five-foot-long Viking Sportfish called *Two Suns,* which he keeps docked in Miami. They have heard him talk about his world travels, his many friends, his sailing and surfing trips, and they have heard him grow passionate about his favorite hobby, deep-water marlin fishing. While Porter Stansberry may be seen by some people as a

Stansberry and his team, "Two Suns," at the 2017 White Marlin Open

braggart and a blowhard, to his thousands of followers, he is a hero
and a role model.

When I ask the Baltimore homicide office yet again for their files
on Rey Rivera, I am told nothing is available, because the case is
still open as a homicide.

This is baffling. I watched the police retrieve Rey's phone and
flip-flops from the swimming pool roof in May 2006. They tossed
the items down to one another very carelessly. There was no sense
that they were working a crime scene. According to police guidelines, personnel at a crime scene should be kept to a minimum:
only the investigating officers and those who have a necessary role
in collecting and preserving evidence should be present. At Rey's
death scene, a whole battalion of police cadets marched through
the Belvedere. Viewing the body was part of a training exercise.

How could the security and integrity of the scene be safely maintained when at least twenty people were present?

Around six hours after Rey's body was removed from the Belvedere, the disused office where the body had been lying for a week was empty, the door unlocked and propped open, the room accessible to anyone who happened to be walking by. There was no crime scene tape, no chalk outline of a body on the ground. The scene was not secured. The medical examiner did not attend; the body was not studied at the site of death. The police obviously assumed Rey's death was a straightforward suicide.

In an article on death scene investigation, the forensic medicine experts Serafettin Demirci and Kamil Hakan Dogan advise officers arriving at the scene of any death to always be assiduous:

> Remember that onlookers, including the decedent's family, and news media may be at the perimeter of the scene, so do not say or do anything that would reflect poorly on yourself and the organization you represent. Trash (discarded gloves, etc.) should be placed in bags designated for investigators' refuse, and not in the garbage cans that are part of the scene because in actuality, they are evidence. Never remove items from a scene for souvenirs.

"It has been my experience that when police officers or detectives hear the word 'Suicide,' they go into what I describe as the *Suicide Position*," writes Vernon K. Geberth in *Practical Homicide Investigation*. "Suicides are non-amenable offenses that are not recorded in the UCR [Uniform Crime Reports] and therefore are considered less important than other events. . . . I have reviewed many suicide cases where it was apparent that the investigators did not take each point to its ultimate conclusion."

"I talked to some people in Homicide who knew about the case," Dr. Charles Tumosa told me in his office in the University of Baltimore's forensic studies program, "and they were of the opinion that it was a suicide." At what point, then, did Rivera's death become an "open homicide investigation"? Has it been one all along? If so, why was the scene of death allowed to be contaminated? Was this just a sloppy investigation? Why have Baltimore homicide detectives not apologized to Rivera's family for their thoughtless attitude to the crime? Why has there never been any active investigation of the case? If calling Rey's death a homicide was intended as a way of pandering to the Rivera family, it has not worked.

Many of the Belvedere's residents are concerned that restaurant and banquet waste in the loading-bay dumpsters is attracting rats. I am a concerned resident, but I am not concerned about the rats. I am concerned about the rodenticide.

It is wrong to generalize about rats. Their personalities are as individual as those of human beings. Anyone who has come to know a rat will tell you that these small creatures are surprisingly intelligent, playful, and affectionate. In a group, rats are sociable, altruistic, and have excellent instincts; they will take care of weaker members of their pack; they will lead around the blind and sick; they will stick together to avoid danger. Rats will tickle each other, emitting unique ultrasonic chirps that, when amplified, resemble human giggles.

Contrary to popular belief, rats are extremely clean. Like cats, they have rough tongues with the texture of sandpaper, which they use to wash themselves and each other, removing dust and dirt from their fur at least twice a day, taking care to clean behind their ears with their front paws, and tending to one another's nether parts as a quid pro quo. Clean rats have a subtle, sweetish aroma. I have never smelled it myself, but rat lovers I know describe it as reminiscent of grape soda. Others say it reminds them of fresh strawberries.

Rats carry no health risk to human beings. If you do not believe me, or want to get rid of them regardless, the only way is to remove any traces of food. Nothing else will work in the long run. You will only end up causing these friendly creatures to die in agony. Rats caught in glue traps will often break or chew off their own limbs in their struggle to escape. Snap traps are supposed to kill quickly, but rarely do so, often leaving the prisoners screaming in pain for hours.

The Baltimore Department of Public Works has a "Rat Eradication" page on its website informing citizens that if they have a "rat problem," they may call 311 and request a visit from the "Rat Rubout Unit." The page features an illustration of a nasty-looking rodent in a circle with a red line through it. The city employs fifteen full-time "Rat Rubout Workers." When called to a rat sighting, the worker will coat the outside of the rats' homes with brodifacoum, so it will catch in the creatures' fur as they come and go. Since rats groom themselves frequently, the poison is ingested quickly.

Imagine how it would feel to die alone in terrible pain, the way these poisoned rats die, in public, far from those who loved you, who fed you, who licked your soft fur until you smelled of strawberries.

The private exterminator who comes to rid the Belvedere of rats does not use poison, but live traps. Whenever I see him, I ask him how many dead rats he has "found" (i.e., killed) that month, and he always replies the same way—by asking me, with a ghoulish grin, "Why, do you want me to bring you a couple?" He reminds me of the "fat boy" in *The Pickwick Papers,* who says, "I wants to make your flesh creep."

Poisoning is the most common suicide method worldwide, no doubt because it is easily available to the average person, especially in impoverished countries, where the toxin most commonly swallowed is paraquat, a weed killer that is readily obtainable at low cost. A mere two teaspoons of paraquat is enough to kill a person of average size. However, in sundry times and places, among different social classes, other poisons have come in and out of fashion as instruments of suicide, including hemlock, aconite, belladonna, digitalis, mandrake, strychnine, arsenic, mercury, cyanide, phenol (carbolic acid), mercuric chloride, battery acid, and Lysol. In general, self-poisoning has always been used predominantly by women, which is not to say that it is painless; despite widespread assumptions, deaths by poisoning can take hours, even days of violent agony.

For example, in a case reported from 1920, a doctor treating a case of self-poisoning by bichloride of mercury, an extremely toxic substance, wrote the following of his patient one week after she took the poison: "Up to this time she appeared almost normal, but from that time she seemed to undergo a molecular or cellular death. The mind was clear but it seemed as if she were decomposing while still living. The odour from the body was nauseating, greyish pallor increased, and at the end of about two and a half weeks from the onset, she died."

Bichloride of mercury was also the poison of choice for Mrs. Winifred van Schaick Reed Tredwell, the wife of the American ambassador and diplomat Roger Tredwell. In 1914, Tredwell was stationed in England; in 1915, it was Italy (Turin, and then Rome). In 1918, he was imprisoned in Russian Central Asia by Bolshevik forces, and for a few months, he was famous all over the world. He was released in May 1919.

Mrs. Tredwell's life was far less exciting, although before her marriage she, too, had traveled widely. After going to finishing school in Switzerland, she studied art at the University of Florence, the University of Geneva, and Wellesley College. She was a talented art critic and historian; in 1915, six years after her marriage, she published *Chinese Art Motives Interpreted,* a book that was considered the authoritative source on the subject for many years to come. Yet while her husband's name was going down in history, Winifred Tredwell's world was growing narrower. While Roger was involved in dramatic adventures, his wife, along with the couple's four-year-old adopted son, went to stay with her widowed sixty-three-year-old father in Cincinnati, and it was here that, at age thirty-seven, she fell into her most serious episode of melancholia, a condition from which she had been suffering for several years.

In April 1921, Mrs. Tredwell informed her husband that she had arranged a trip to Baltimore to visit the Phipps Clinic, where she would be treated for depression. On April 17, she took the train from Cincinnati to Baltimore, but upon arrival, instead of taking a taxi to the Phipps, she checked in to the Belvedere. In the guest book at the reception desk, she gave her name as "Mrs. Royal Travler," and her provenance as Frankfort, Kentucky, a frail disguise that suggests she had already lost hope. However, that evening, she seems to have rallied. She made a call to the Phipps Clinic to let the staff know that she had arrived in Baltimore, and would be checking in the next day.

In the bleak morning light, however, Mrs. Tredwell's courage must have failed her once again. When a housemaid arrived to change the linen, assuming the guest had left, she was surprised to discover "Mrs. Travler" lying on the bed, clearly very ill. The hotel doctor had her brought to the Maryland Women's Hospital. Here, during intense interrogation by the doctors, she confessed that she had no desire to live and had taken 126 tablets of bichloride of mercury, whose effects are almost invariably fatal.

Mrs. Tredwell suffered in great pain for a week, during which time she confessed her true identity. When she died, around four thirty on April 24, the superintendent of the hospital, Miss Stella Sampson, called the police; Patrolman Herman Rosenthal arrived and spoke to the hospital staff about their patient's cause of death. At Mrs. Tredwell's request, Miss Sampson also called her brother, General C. Lawson Reed, an influential Cincinnati businessman, who came to Baltimore immediately and insisted that no one in the hospital say anything about his sister's death.

Mrs. Tredwell died in the Northwestern police district. When the district coroner, Dr. J. Tyrrell Hennessy, arrived at the hospital to fill out the death certificate, he asked Miss Sampson how the patient had died. Miss Sampson replied, "This is a very peculiar case and I cannot discuss it. We promised her brother not to give out any information."

After an initial examination of the body, Dr. Hennessy at first issued a certificate giving the cause of death as "acute nephritis with broncho-pneumonia as a contributory factor." He later said there was no evidence of Mrs. Tredwell having taken poison, but also admitted that certain poisons might have the same symptoms as acute nephritis.

The police were still suspicious. Detective John Day was sent to investigate further. Dr. Hennessy must have realized there would be more inquiries, because when Detective Day retrieved the death certificate from the coroner's office, he noticed that Hennessy had jotted on the back that Mrs. Tredwell "was a victim of dementia praecox (melancholia) and while in a state of excitement took 126 grains of poison." Opposite this statement was the word "suicide."

Detective Day went to ask Dr. Hennessy about his unconventional method of filling out the patient's death certificate. The doctor replied,

When I saw the body of Mrs. Tredwell, there was no evidence of suicide. Later, however, when I made a further inquiry I was informed by hospital authorities that the woman had taken poison before she came to the hospital. Further investigation indicated that when she swallowed the poison she was not in her right mind, and so I stated my conclusions on the back of the death certificate. I wrote that she had been suffering from "dementia praecox," and a person suffering with such a disease is not responsible for his or her act. When the officials of the health department talked with me I told them frankly what my investigation had disclosed, and when they asked me if the death could be classed as suicide, I said yes.

"Would you term Mrs. Tredwell's act one of self-destruction?" asked the detective.

"Well, yes," said Hennessy.

"Then the case is one of suicide?"

"Well, yes," the coroner agreed.

From this report, it seems that Mrs. Tredwell's brother attempted to persuade the coroner to fudge the death certificate. It is important to remember that until the 1970s, when they were replaced by medical examiners, coroners in Baltimore needed no qualifications whatsoever, rarely had any training, and were usually elected to the position. This was true in many places across the United States until much later than the 1970s. In fact, there are places where, even today, coroners are elected officials with no qualifications to deal with the deceased. The state of South Carolina, for example, only recently required that its coroners be high school graduates.

In the Middle Ages, suicides had a stake driven through their heart, and their bodies were buried at a public crossroads rather than in hallowed ground. In many places, it is still a crime to commit suicide, or to help another to do so. At the time of Mrs. Tredwell's death, the act of suicide was still shrouded in shame; how much more shameful would it have been, then, for a woman like Mrs. Tredwell—the wife of a national hero and the mother of a four-year-old child—to take her own life. Since it was assumed that no healthy, rational person would choose to kill himself, the coroner would often include on the death certificate of a suicide some such phrase as "while suffering from a temporary mental aberration," a convenient escape mechanism that transformed the suicide into a form of accidental death. This was important, since many workmen's compensation laws denied death benefits for self-inflicted injuries; many life insurance contracts still exclude death by suicide. In Mrs. Tredwell's case, however, since nothing more was at stake than the reputation of the family, the coroner's attempts to prevaricate did not stick.

The corpses of animals are everywhere, strewn across my path every day. I cannot avoid them. In street and alley, I step over the bodies of poisoned rats, laid out in the scrambled posture of their fall, flattened by traffic, dotted with flies. Just yesterday perhaps, these stiff cadavers might have been "gay young friskers, . . . Cocking tails and pricking whiskers," as Browning described the rats of Hamelin in his famous poem. Driving down the highway, I see the neatly severed front half of a doe lying by the side of the road, her coiled innards spilling over the concrete. A quarter of a mile later I pass the other half, standing comically by the crash barrier like the back end of a pantomime horse. To the preoccupied driver, the severed body is an everyday sight, forgotten as soon as it is glimpsed.

But to the turkey vultures, those black shadows perched in a row on the high-mast lights of the highway, the carcass is a feast that can be smelled from over a mile away. On summer mornings when I am driving out of the city for an early hike, I often see pairs of them waiting for the traffic to calm so they can move in on some roadside carrion. Vultures are bald-faced in more ways than one. They are brazenly practical, keeping themselves cool by pissing and shitting on their feet. If any creature bothers them, they vomit in its face. Along I-83, I have seen turkey vultures standing on the lights with their wings outstretched, a cooling posture known as the horaltic pose, after Horus, the falcon-headed god of the sky. Ancient Egyptians knew that dealing with the dead is a sacred task.

One August, in a small town on the Gulf of Mexico, I stopped my car about five feet from a dumpster to watch the vultures. I found them so compelling that I forgot my plans and sat there for an hour or two. One pair would dive into the dumpster while a second pair stood guard on its brim; then, after twenty minutes or so, the dumpster divers would return to a straggly pine while the sentries take their turn at scavenging. A group of vultures gathered together is called a wake. Clustered on the branches of the pine tree around whatever was rotting in the dumpster, with their black plumage and lowered heads, they did resemble mourners. But there was a difference. Death, to the bobbing, bouncing vultures, brought not grief, but joy.

XIII

THREE MONTHS AFTER I meet them in LA, Allison and Megan arrive at the Belvedere. They are here to do research for their screenplay. We meet in the Owl Bar for lunch. Megan is visibly pregnant by now. The two women have already been up on the top floor of the parking garage to take photographs of the swimming pool roof, and they have a meeting with Jayne Miller at half past three. I feel a little unnecessary. I wonder if they are ambivalent about me, suspicious, unsure whether I can be trusted, uncertain whether I am on their side.

One of the things we talk about over lunch is the hole Rivera's body made in the annex roof. On my laptop, I show Allison a photograph of the patched-up roof, tracing the outline of the hole with the cursor. It was covered up not long after Rey's death, and the pool roof was recoated a few years after that, but you can still see the shape of the hole quite clearly beneath the surface.

Or so I have always thought. But Allison tells me the hole was closer to the side of the Belvedere. She points to a different area on the pool roof.

I trace the hole again with the cursor. I point out what I believe to be its outline under the new coat of white paint. I describe to Allison how I watched the police on the roof from my apartment window. I even watched the contractor patch up the hole.

Allison says she will show me exactly where her husband landed. She puts her finger on my trackpad and moves the cursor to a slightly different area, outlining what appears to be another faint circle underneath the layer of white. As I dig for my glasses in my purse, I begin to realize it is far more likely that I am the one in the wrong. Rey was Allison's husband, after all. She has obviously spent far more time studying the circumstances of his death than I have. Still, it is difficult for me to believe I could be so wide of the mark.

Allison is engaging and animated, as before, but as she talks, I am unexpectedly overcome by a feeling of great listlessness and disappointment. I manage to go on smiling, nodding, and making the appropriate noises, but it seems as though all the energy has been drained from the mystery, leaving nothing but a series of repeated anecdotes and memories that lead nowhere.

Allison is staying with her aunt in Ellicott City; Megan is staying in a hotel. They plan to call around the following day to look at the documents I have collected on the case.

The following afternoon, I meet them in the lobby of the Belvedere. It is mid-July, and outside, the temperature is rising, but the lobby is cool and quiet. Both women look tall and glamorous in the sleeveless maxi dresses that are fashionable that summer, Megan's in red and Allison's in navy blue with white stripes. We take the elevator up to D.'s and my apartment. Megan has brought her video camera; she is filming location material to help her with the screenplay. She wants to take some footage out of the window through which, I told her, I watched the police pick up Rey's flip-flops and cell phone from the annex roof. We walk through the apartment—D. makes friendly conversation—and I show Megan the window. She leans out, squints, and points her camera. Of course, the "real" hole, whose location Allison pointed out at lunch the previous day, is scarcely visible.

Over lemonade, we study the folder of documents I have accumulated. I offer to make copies for Allison of anything she would like to take back with her, and I am surprised to find I have many papers that she has never seen, including the police report of the crime scene—basic documents that were nonetheless uncannily difficult to obtain. Allison and Megan are especially interested in the Freedom of Information Act document I received from the FBI telling me that, of the eighteen pages they have on the Rey Rivera case, they are prepared to release only two. Allison and Megan both believe this has to be because Michael Baier is working on the case behind the scenes in his new capacity as an FBI agent; to release all the information right now, they say, would jeopardize his progress. Given the uselessness of the documents the FBI has agreed to release, I cannot help thinking this is overly optimistic of them, but not wanting to crush their hopes, I keep my skepticism to myself.

Next comes the most difficult part of the visit, at least for Allison—a visit to the roof. When I have been up there in the last few years to take photographs, I have always taken the elevator to the twelfth floor and walked through the kitchens, but today, for some reason, all the elevators, including the freight elevator, have their locks set and will take us no farther than the eleventh floor. It is very unusual for the elevators to be locked on a Sunday. We get out at the eleventh floor, which is nonresidential, only to find that the door to the fire stairs is also locked. We study the windows for a while. Megan has been harboring a theory that Rey could have been lured to one of the offices on the eleventh floor and chloroformed, and that his body was then tossed out of a window there, but the eleventh-floor windows turn out to be not only too small to accommodate a body the size of Rey's, but sealed shut.

Still hoping to get up to the roof, I suggest that we go down to the Belvedere office and ask for the elevator to be unlocked. If Allison identifies herself as Rey Rivera's widow, and explains that she has come to revisit the scene of his death, I am sure no one could possibly object. But when the elevator arrives back in the lobby, Allison's bright face has lost its color and softness. She looks pale and grim.

"Let's forget about the roof," she says. "I guess it's just not meant to be."

I feel as though I've let them both down.

"Curiosity killed the cat," adds Allison.

The two women leave a little abruptly. The experience has been hard on Allison, I think.

The fact that the elevator is locked probably means that housekeeping is preparing the twelfth-floor ballrooms for an event later in the day. While there are a few private parties, office get-togethers, and corporate gatherings at the old hotel, the Belvedere's soaring ceilings, elegant ballrooms, and glittering chandeliers make it one of the city's most popular venues for wedding ceremonies. For a few years, when D. and I first moved into the building, a room was kept free on the fifth floor for the bride and her attendants to dress in before the wedding. On more than one occasion, a drunken wedding guest, opening the wrong door, blundered into our apartment in bow tie and tux only to find us sitting watching a movie in our pajamas.

In the hotel's early days, the Belvedere's bridal suite was popular among newlyweds who would leave for their honeymoon from the station the following morning. On Tuesday, October 29, 1918, however, this set of rooms was the location for a celebrated scandal that seems to have little to do with romance. On the other hand, as George Bernard Shaw pointed out, "When we want to read of the deeds that are done for love, whither do we turn?" His answer: "To the murder column."

At around two thirty in the afternoon, one of the Belvedere's housekeepers reported that the bridal suite needed to be cleaned but the door was still locked. According to the front desk clerk, the guests had not yet checked out. A bellman was sent up a ladder to peer through the transom, and he descended with an alarming report. The newlyweds, he said, were lying in the bed "as still as the tomb," and although there was a bottle of whisky on the table, "they looked more dead than drunk." Since the fire escape did not pass by the windows of the honeymoon suite and the master key could not be found, the manager, John Letton, called a carpenter to come over with a saw and cut out the transom window. He also summoned the hotel physician, Dr. Thomas, and placed a call to the police.

According to the guest registry, the couple had signed in as Mr. and Mrs. C. P. Webster of Philadelphia (the names were their own, but they were both Maryland residents). They had arrived at three p.m. on Saturday, October 25. The hotel staff had seen very little of the honeymoon couple, but the bellmen who had worked on Saturday night had a different story. They both agreed something very peculiar had been going on in the bridal suite. Mr. Webster, it seemed, had been unusually thirsty. First, he wanted a glass of ice water. Then he wanted a glass of milk. Then he wanted another glass of ice water. Then he asked for another glass of milk. The two bellmen who responded to Webster's calls both said the same thing. When they got to the room, Webster had been nowhere to be seen. Mrs. Webster, on the other hand, had been very conspicuous. She had been wearing something, the bellmen recalled, but not very much. Each time they had been called, they had both left the room very quickly. They both said it "felt like a set-up."

The carpenter sawed out the transom window and lowered it down to Mr. Letton, who made sure the glass was perfectly intact. A bellman was then sent up the ladder to squeeze through the gap and open the door from the inside.

Bride Strangled By Husband

Mrs. Bernice Chaney Webster, Washington Times, *October 29, 1918*

The scene in the bridal suite that day was anything but romantic. The bride lay dressed in a thin nightgown. A sheet covered her lower half, and the part of her that was visible bore evidence of a long, hard fight. Her face was purple and swollen, her neck was badly scratched, and a trail of dried blood led from her nose to the bedclothes, which were stained almost black. Her tongue protruded gruesomely two or three inches out of her mouth

She was unequivocally dead. Her husband looked done for, too, until Dr. Thomas took out his stethoscope and discerned that he was still breathing, at which point the doctor leaned over and shook the groom firmly by the shoulder.

"Mr. Webster, are you all right?" he asked in a loud voice.

Webster opened his eyes. He had a boxer's face, thick and square. When he saw the crowd standing around his bed, he sat up abruptly, like a resurrected corpse.

"I'm dying," he declared. "I've taken poison."

"Did you kill your wife?" asked the doctor.

"Yes," he said. "I murdered her. And now I'm going to die."

The police made Webster get out of bed and try to walk. He got to his feet without much trouble. In fact, he did so well they marched him down to Mercy Hospital in his bathrobe, where he confessed he'd swallowed five tablets of mercury, and asked for his mother. "Judging by appearances," wrote a reporter for the *Baltimore Sun,* "he did not especially want to die."

Police found two letters on the desk of the honeymoon suite, both written on Belvedere stationery. The first was a suicide note written by Webster sometime between strangling his bride and taking the mercury tablets. In the note, he explained that he had quarreled violently with his bride when he discovered—so he claimed—that his suspicions were true and she was not a virgin. "I have believed it and now I know it," he wrote. "I have loved her so much. We are even with the world and will die together."

The other note was from Webster to his mother, giving the same story, though the wording was less starry-eyed. He had "found out" his wife, wrote Webster, so he was going to have to kill her, and then himself. In closing, he asked his mother to pay off his debts. The attempted setups with the bellmen, it appears, were a pathetic attempt to corroborate his story that the new Mrs. Webster was "a loose woman" (it also made it very clear that Webster had planned the murder in advance).

Carlyle Webster was thirty-two and his bride, Bernice, just twenty. According to the autopsy, Mrs. Webster's cause of death was "compression and obstruction of the carotid arteries." The papers wanted to know whether Mrs. Webster had been a virgin, but the coroner "did not testify as to the particular results of other anatomical examination." Her mother, Mrs. Chaney, told police that Bernice had met Mr. Webster just over a year ago. He had been a customer in the men's clothing department at Hutzler Brothers downtown, which had been her daughter's place of employment before her marriage. According to Mrs. Chaney, Carlyle was the perfect gentleman. He was good to the whole family, "and especially good to Bernice, who had been reared very carefully and there was not a blot on her character."

Webster's trial began on March 29, 1919. Though he remained under control, it was obvious he was suffering from terrible strain. When he took the stand, he claimed that he first realized his wife was dead when he awakened and found her "beside him in the bed." His defense attorney, W. Trickett Giles, put forward the argument that because of "insanity and drunkenness" Webster was not guilty, and he produced witnesses who testified that the accused often lost his memory when drunk.

Webster had been married before, it turned out, in 1912, and the marriage had ended about fourteen months before the murder. The former Mrs. Webster, née Callahan, was now Mrs. Virginia Trader of Salisbury, Maryland. At the trial, she offered the opinion that Carlyle was quite insane. She testified that his people came from Deal Island, in the Chesapeake Bay, and were "more or less inbred." His father and mother were first cousins, she said, adding that Carlyle was "subnormal as a child" and had confessed to her that "at least twelve of his relations were certifiably insane." She said he had an uncontrollable temper that came on at the slightest provocation.

Giles argued that Webster, weakened by inbreeding and "the cravings of his ancestors for alcohol," influences over which he had no control, was "in the grip of an irresistible force" when he strangled his bride. On behalf of the prosecution, the psychiatrist Dr. J. Percy Wade, superintendent of Spring Grove Hospital, gave his opinion that Webster was in sound mind when he committed the murder, and had known the nature of his act.

Most moving of all, according to witnesses, was the evidence given by the victim's eighteen-year-old sister, Miss Edna van Lear Chaney, who testified that she had known Carlyle Webster for some time, and that, while convincing the rest of her family he wanted to take care of her sister, he had systematically terrorized Bernice into submission. Edna went on to say that Bernice was very pretty and very popular, and that many men were interested in her. As a result, Webster had become fixated on the subject of her sister's reputation.

"Long before the wedding," testified Edna, "Bernice told me that there was something of a most depressing nature hanging over her and she believed she would be killed." When Edna asked her sister why she was planning to marry Webster, Bernice said "she thought things would be better after the marriage." However, the night before her wedding, according to Edna, Bernice had dreamed that Webster had tried to murder her, and told her sister "she feared that she had not much longer to live."

Calling the Baltimore homicide department has started to feel like knocking on the door of a semi-derelict building; there are occasions when someone responds, but when they do, they are as unhelpful as possible, and clearly want me to go away before I cause any trouble.

At a loss, I hire a private investigator, a former FBI surveillance specialist who says he has plenty of contacts among Baltimore homicide detectives, both active and retired. I will call him Stein. We meet in a coffee shop. It's in the middle of August 2016, ten years since Rey Rivera's death. The heat is overwhelming. I notice Stein as soon as I walk through the door. He is conspicuous not only because he is much older than all the students in their tank tops, shorts, and flip-flops, but also because he is wearing a jacket and tie. He is a stocky man in his midfifties, with slicked-back hair and a walrus mustache.

To his credit, Stein is completely open about what he can and cannot do for me. He says that the Baltimore homicide division is a very small world; it contains around forty detectives, and they all know one another, at least to some degree. He says he can put me in touch with the retired detectives who worked the Rivera case, though he cannot guarantee they will talk to me. He asks me for the name of the lead detective on the case. When I mention Marvin Sydnor, he gives me a broad smile.

"Do you know him?" I ask.

"Sure, I know him. Everyone knows Sydnor," says Stein. "He's a legend in Baltimore homicide. He's a real snappy dresser, known for his colorful bow ties. I'll go and see him right now, see if I can't fix up a lunch meeting next week between the three of us."

"But Sydnor retired ten years ago," I tell Stein.

"I know," says Stein. "But I know where to find him."

The following week, Stein gives me a call, and his tone has changed. He has spoken to Marvin Sydnor, he says, and was surprised to find he won't meet with me and won't take part in any interviews about the case.

"All he would say is that he felt Rey's family wanted the death to be ruled a homicide, although personally, he thought there was no evidence to support anything other than suicide," Stein tells me. "When I mentioned the case, he said that he just doesn't want to talk about it. I asked him why, but he wouldn't give me a reason. I'll try him again at another time, to see if he's had a change of heart."

The news about Sydnor reminds me of something the reporter Stephen Janis told me: when he was trying to get information on the Rivera case, he asked a police source to try to get hold of the homicide file. The source got back to Janis and said the file was not where it should have been, with the other homicide case files. Eventually, he learned there was only one copy, which was locked in Sydnor's desk. The source asked Sydnor in a casual way whether he could take a look at it, but Sydnor refused, and apparently seemed suspicious.

I wonder: Are the police covering something up, or do they just feel that they have made a mess of the case, and so do not want anyone reading about the botched investigation? I ask Charles Tumosa why a case that was initially treated as a suicide might still be listed as a homicide many years later.

"At times, it's a judgment call," Dr. Tumosa told me. "When I was in Philly, we investigated many deaths that we initially thought were homicides that turned out to be something else. Probably the original call came out as a homicide. When there's that much damage to the body, you make the assumption it's a homicide first. Somebody labels it a homicide, even if they later think it's a suicide, but if nobody's pushing for it to be reclassified, nobody's going to change it. We've got over three hundred homicides a year to deal with in Baltimore. Six months later, it's old news."

Stein learns from a Master Mason that Fred Bealefield, who was the chief of detectives during the Rivera case and later police commissioner, is also a Master Mason. This news does not surprise me. Many policemen are members of the Freemasons; it does not make either the police or the Freemasons especially sinister. I often invite Master Masons to speak to my classes about the history of their organization, which I have come to see as a benevolent fraternal charity with an archaic structure and hierarchy, not a malevolent force running the universe, or even the city. In other words, I think the Masonic angle is a red herring. I believe Rey's interest in the group was part of his research for something new he was writing.

Stein next talks to a retired Baltimore homicide detective who is familiar with the Rivera case, though he did not work on it himself. This detective, Stein tells me, has three theories about Rivera's death.

"First," said Stein, "it could be simply a suicide. Second, there could be some involvement by an outside element—a loan shark or some other criminal entity; third, it could have been a blackmail situation. Do you know if the victim was involved in any affairs outside the marriage?"

"Not as far as I know," I said. "He'd only been married seven months."

Stein is not so sure. "You know, the Belvedere has a long reputation as being a place where straight men can cruise for gay sex. The detective I spoke to immediately brought up that scenario," he tells me. "Even if Rivera's wife was sure he hadn't been involved with any men in Baltimore, that doesn't rule out the possibility of a gay relationship, or the possibility that he was about to be exposed. In light of that," he wonders, "did he feel the need to jump?"

No one I have spoken to has ever suggested there was any ambiguity about Rivera's sexuality. Everyone who knew Rey and Allison says the couple was deeply in love—"soul mates" is the phrase most often used—so a homosexual blackmail plot seems unlikely. If Rey had been interested in men, or if he had been involved with men in the past, even if it had been—for whatever reason—on the downlow, then once the news of his mysterious death got out, surely somebody would have mentioned the fact, even if just in the form of gossip.

More to the point, I have lived at the Belvedere for over ten years and have never heard of it being known as a place for gay-straight pickups.

I ask Freddie Howard, the Belvedere's longtime concierge, whether he has heard the rumor.

Freddie shakes his head. "I've never heard that before."

"Do you think it's plausible?" I ask him.

Freddie rocks backward and forward on his heels and thinks about it for a while.

"I never know everything that goes on upstairs, at the 13th Floor," he says, finally. "Also, the bottle club—I never knew what kind of things went on there, either."

Freddie is referring to Suite Ultralounge, a notorious gathering that used to take place in the basement of the Belvedere at weekends, and was closed down by police in 2010 after a fight in which two people were wounded by bullets and another stabbed.

After talking to Freddie, I email Stein and ask him where these hookups are supposed to occur: "Do they happen in a public place, like the 13th Floor or the Owl Bar, or do they take place somewhere secret, like the second stall in the men's basement bathrooms, or the corner table at Belvedere Bagels and Grill?"

He picks up on my skepticism, and replies flatly that "with regard to the Belvedere, it is commonly known through law enforcement community as a discreet place to hook up, and has been since the 80s."

I ask Rey's friend Steven King, who got to know Rey when he was working as a freelance video editor at the Oxford Club, whether he ever sensed that Rey might have been struggling with his sexuality, or hiding a secret gay past. King, who is gay himself, replies, "It never crossed my mind that he could be homosexual."

I am almost ready to dismiss the rumor when, at a dinner party, I mention it to the other guests. I'm curious whether any of them have ever heard it before. An attorney who used to be a reporter for the *Baltimore Sun* tells me, a little cryptically, that I should look up the case of Jonathan Oster.

On April 15, 1982, Oster, forty-nine, a former deputy Maryland attorney general and a partner in a prestigious Baltimore law firm, attended a dinner meeting at the Belvedere, which was followed by drinks in the Owl Bar. When Oster did not return home that night, his wife called the police; early the next morning, officers were sent to search the vicinity of the Belvedere, where the attorney had last been seen in the bar, talking to a man named Frank Tomasek Jr. Jonathan Oster's body was found in an alleyway off Maryland Avenue, just around the corner from the hotel. He had been stabbed to death and robbed. News broadcasts reported that Tomasek was wanted for questioning in connection with the death.

Later that day, a young man seeking financial assistance showed up in the office of Catholic Charities in Ravenna, Ohio. When asked, he gave his name: Frank Tomasek Jr. Someone who had heard the news broadcast recognized it and called the police. Tomasek told them that his car had run out of gas about thirty-five miles southeast of Cleveland. The car turned out to be Oster's. Tomasek, twenty-one, was charged with receiving stolen property and was held on bond, pending extradition to Maryland. He was subsequently convicted of second-degree murder.

Oster had picked Tomasek up in the Owl Bar. "The fact that the murder was not a simple robbery gone bad was hinted at but never explicitly laid out in public," my source told me later, by email. "There was an interesting newsroom debate about what to report. In the end, since the victim was married with two sons, the *Baltimore Sun* described Tomasek as a "hitchhiker." The *Washington Post* referred to him as "a drifter from the city's south side."

At a party, a woman I have met enough times for me to consider her a casual friend asks me where I live. When I tell her, she gets excited.

"Oh, I was talking to someone who lives in that building a few months ago," she said. "She told me she'd been researching all the suicides that had taken place there going back to the year it was built."

I smile and say nothing. Yes, I think. That was me. Who else would it have been? Am I really so instantly forgettable?

The man-sized crater in the swimming pool roof is the rabbit hole into which I have fallen. It is the doorway into the mystery of Rey Rivera's death. Like Auguste Dupin, I have always been "fond of enigmas, of conundrums, of hieroglyphics." Now I start to wonder: If I am wrong about the position of the hole, what else might I be wrong about? It is terrifying to learn that all my speculations until now have been so tentative that just the slightest change can send everything spinning into confusion.

I often think about how I went down to the disused swimming pool the day the body was found to see the place where it had landed. The scene feels fresh in my memory. I even took photographs of the collapsed roof and darkly stained carpet with the cheap digital camera I owned in 2006, before I had a camera in my phone. Digital pictures are so disposable. I take them all the time and delete them a few days later, wondering what ever compelled me to take photographs of an ordinary-looking tree, a disused water tower, an undistinctive chimney, a large stone lying on its side. I have no doubt that I deleted the photographs of the death scene from my camera a month or two after taking them. Why would I have wanted to save pictures of an empty office with a stained carpet and a hole in the roof?

I would do anything, now, to have those photographs back. This is a mistake I can learn from. Although my photos may feel like clutter, I remind myself how little space they consume, and try to resist deleting them. I have learned that, as each moment fades from my memory, its capital increases. Casually snapped images from nine or ten years ago are infinitely precious to me now, containing my only evidence of meals, trips, and parties I would otherwise have forgotten, of people who have died or moved away and are no longer vivid in my memory, which is proving itself increasingly unreliable as I get older. I remind myself that human memory is not a stable and unchanging source of information, like the memory on a phone or a laptop, but untrustworthy and incoherent, however much we find ourselves insisting otherwise.

My own memory must be unreliable, because since Rey Rivera's death, I have not been able to find the former swimming pool.

So many times, I have thought about my visit to the room after the body was removed—eleven years ago now—and sometimes I wonder whether it really happened. I can clearly remember going up a short flight of steps somewhere on the second floor and walking down a narrow hallway, but for some reason I have not been able to find those steps or that hallway again. I have wandered around the second floor many times—there is really not much to see—but I have never been able to find the short flight of steps to that mysterious door in the wall. I have found a door that fits this description, but it is on the first floor, down the hallway to the parking garage. It leads to an office used by the Belvedere's resident catering company. Sometimes I think I must have been wrong about the door being on the second floor. But Rey Rivera did not fall through the roof of this office, which is half a story lower than the swimming pool roof, and to the west.

The more I think about the hole in the roof, the more convinced I become of its importance. I realize I have been drawn irretrievably into the details of this case, spending months pondering and probing some moment or incident, but I cannot seem to make myself back away and consider the bigger picture. I am afraid this picture will look like a jigsaw that is missing certain crucial pieces. I do not want to think about whether everything fits together, because I am afraid it does not. I can feel the pull of the particulars, neglecting the fact that the particulars need to cohere into something larger. This is not a fragmented poem or an abstract painting, I remind myself, but an investigation into something that actually happened: the death of a man. I can start, I realize, by finding out where the hole in the roof used to be. But the more I think about this, the more it worries me, because the hole—this absence through which a man's body once fell—is at the heart of the mystery.

After Allison first sowed the seeds of doubt about the location of the hole, whenever I try to find it, I feel as though I'm in a frustrating dream, a mirror world where everything is the opposite of how it should be. I remember how things were, but I cannot remember how to get back to them. Worse, I cannot tell whether the changes are in the building or in me. I keep puzzling over it in my head; it is like an itch that needs to be scratched, and I worry it like an animal biting at a wound. If the hole was where I originally believed it to be, it would mean that Rey must have taken a running jump. If he did so, it is almost impossible that he was murdered.

At the worst point, my certainty about everything starts to erode, and the story I have been telling myself about Rey Rivera's death suddenly seems ill conceived, full of contradictions and mysterious blurs. In my head, the hotel's rooms and levels start to get confused. One morning very early, unable to sleep, I get up out of bed and go down to the second floor. I have a new theory about the location of the door in the wall; as usual, I am mistaken. Returning disappointed, I catch a glimpse of myself in a hallway mirror and am shocked. In my nightdress and bare feet, I look pale and mad, like the sleepwalking Lady Macbeth.

Perhaps the shock shifted something in my head, because when I wake up the following day I immediately realize: This is a puzzle that can be solved. Someone climbed a ladder and patched up that hole. In fact, I watched him do it. It was Richie, the Belvedere's on-site handyman, who fixes our leaks and unclogs our waste disposal units. I see him almost every day, working around the building. Not only did Richie patch up the hole, he recoated the surface of the swimming pool roof a few years ago. If anyone knows the exact location of the hole, it will be Richie.

I sketch a rough diagram of the annex roof—a rectangle with two arches for the barrel-shaped windows of the former swimming pool—and go in search of Richie. I find him having a smoke outside the front entrance, hand him my outline and a pen, and ask him to draw a cross at the location of the hole in the roof. Richie takes my sketch, squints, thinks about it for a couple of moments, then draws an X about four feet north of the first barrel-shaped skylight. The hole he draws is exactly where I remembered it to be. To reach this spot, Rey must have taken a running jump.

Later, I realize there is another way to confirm my memory of the hole. On my laptop, I have a downloaded copy of Jayne Miller's WBAL-TV 11 news clip that aired on the first anniversary of Rivera's death. This includes footage shot from the roof of the Belvedere that zooms in on the hole. When I watch it again, it becomes clear that Richie's X has marked the spot. I feel a tremendous sense of relief. My mind is back on track.

I feel even more excited when I learn from Stein that he has tracked down the elusive and shadowy Michael Baier. He plans to give him a call later in the week. I ask Stein to give Baier my contact information, and Allison's, and to ask him to contact me as soon as possible. I jump every time my phone rings, but Baier does not call.

To clear my head, I take a walk across the bridge into the dead part of the city. Exploring the world around me always frees my mind from its infernal loops. Along these empty roads, choked with the debris of the past, I can always find new ways to look at things. I find a cobblestoned street without a name (at least, without a sign) that seems completely deserted. It is so narrow that if it was accessible to traffic at one time, it must have been a one-way street with no parking, since it is barely wider than a car. On each side of the road are boarded-up two-story row houses with flat roofs; each house has five stone steps leading to its front door. A disused utility pole looms over the road; its shadow pierces the street like a spear.

As I explore, I listen carefully for sounds from the boarded-up houses, wondering whether anyone still lives here. I imagine people lurking in the shadows, but I hear nothing and see no one. This entire neighborhood is a ghost town, abandoned to the elements and to the trash, which is everywhere: broken bottles, plastic beads, buttons, candy wrappers, rusty hubcaps, the rims of tires, discarded food picked over by gulls and crows. Even in the summer, the weeds that grow in the sidewalks and in between the cobblestones are mottled and decayed, like plants that struggle at the bottom of a canyon. In the shade of the steps a strange fungus grows, smelling of rot and death.

I spend an afternoon in the federal courthouse, selecting a trial at random, as usual. I am lucky: it is completely absorbing. The plaintiff, a smart, neatly dressed, well-spoken African-American woman in her forties named Charlene Bishop, is suing her employers, an engineering company run by Karim El-Kader, for race and gender discrimination.

"Why," asks Ms. Bishop's attorney as I slip through the door and take a seat in the back row, "did Mr. El-Kader hire the young, unqualified Salma Ahmad rather than the older and more qualified Mildred Welles?"

"I think it's because she was pretty and Egyptian," replies Ms. Bishop. "Everyone said Salma was nice," she adds, kindly, "but we all knew she was completely incompetent."

Karim El-Kader's attorney, a slick, oily-looking fellow, asks Ms. Bishop whether she ever asked Mr. El-Kader why he did not hire the candidate she had recommended, Mildred Welles.

"I did," Ms. Bishop replied. "He sort of rolled his eyes and said, 'Can you imagine somebody who looks like that sitting outside my father's office?'"

"Were both Mildred Welles and Salma Ahmad on the short list of candidates you had chosen?" the attorney asks.

"Only Mildred Welles," Ms. Bishop replies. "But when I gave him the short list of candidates, Mr. El-Kader told me they were all too old. He asked me to give him the full list, and said he would screen them himself. And the final list he gave me—it was all Middle Eastern names, and they were all young girls with no qualifications."

Ms. Bishop went on to describe a culture of discrimination at the company—Middle Easterners were given preferential treatment; women were told to look at the floor and fold their hands together when they were being admonished. Mr. El-Kader's son asked Ms. Bishop whether she could call in some good-looking but unqualified interview candidates so he could "pick them up." When the company was hiring administrative assistants, male candidates were routinely thrown out of the interview pool, because Mr. El-Kader believed that "men do not belong behind a desk."

I'm transfixed. Charlene Bishop is a star. I could not imagine

The Belvedere's second-floor hallway

a stronger, more convincing case. But then I glance at the jury—a group of disheveled strangers, lost, tired, and defeated—and my hopes collapse at once.

It is a dark, rainy Saturday afternoon in January 2016, and I am down on the second floor searching, yet again, for the mysterious door. I walk quietly down the main hallway, with its red carpet, its walls painted in two soothing shades of beige, its crystal chandelier, its doors—to function rooms and doctors' offices—labeled with discreet gold plates.

Unexpectedly, I hear the bright ping of the VIP elevator, and out steps Mr. C., our neighbor from apartment 503, dressed for a workout.

Mr. C. and his wife are the founders and owners of the events and catering company that runs the Owl Bar, the first-floor and second-floor function rooms and offices, the twelfth-floor ballrooms, and the 13th Floor. One of the concierges recently informed me that Mr. C. and his wife have separated, which explained why D. and I were no longer running into him on the fifth floor or in the elevator, as we used to do.

"What are you doing down here?" asks Mr. C., curiously. The second floor contains only offices and ballrooms, and since most of the offices are closed, as it is a Saturday, I am unsure what to say. For a moment, I consider telling him the truth: that for the last ten years, I have been trying to find my way back to a room into which a body fell through the roof. But I do not. Mr. C. is a jolly type, always ready with a cheerful greeting, but I do not sense in him any touch of curiosity, morbid or otherwise.

"I thought I saw a massage studio somewhere around here," I tell him, which is the first thing that comes to mind—I have, in fact, just walked past a massage studio. "I've got a stiff neck from sitting at my desk all day."

"Let me call Bill and ask him," says Mr. C., ever helpful. He calls the Belvedere's manager, and it turns out there are three massage studios in the building, two in the basement and one on the second floor, but they're all closed on Saturdays.

"Never mind," I say. "I'll try on Monday."

We chat for a while. I ask about his daughter's puppy. Mr. C. scrolls through the photos on his phone to show me some new pictures. The puppy is now a large dog.

Mr. C. mentions that he is going to the gym.

"Do you use the gym opposite, Mount Vernon Fitness?" I ask him.

"Actually," he tells me, with a bashful chuckle, "we have our own private gym. When we first moved here, we thought that was the one thing the building lacks, a gym, and so we made our own, for me and my wife, our daughter, and our guests. Would you like to see it? It used to be the swimming pool."

"I'd love to," I tell him.

"Follow me," says Mr. C.

He leads me to the trash room, walks past the freight elevators, takes out a bunch of keys, and there it is: a door at the top of a small flight of three steps.

I had never once thought to look in the trash room. I had assumed it would be the same as all the other trash rooms in the building—a small area, around six feet by eight feet, with a window at the far end, and the two freight elevators on the left. But then I remember that the second floor is an annex, and different from the others. The raised door is where the window should be. Of course, it is the door I have been searching for. As Mr. C. unlocks it, everything falls into place. Here are the three stairs; here is the narrow hallway; here is the glass door that was left propped open to get rid of the smell.

Mr. C. is explaining the construction they had to do in order to cut off access to the pool: "We blocked off the whole passageway. Everything here used to be open. This hallway went all the way around here, you see?"

As I follow him through the door and down the hall, everything feels right. I am in control again. I can see the second floor from a new perspective. I follow Mr. C. like Orpheus returning to the underworld, already knowing what I will see: a line of electric lights set into the floor and forming a rectangle where the sides of the pool used to be, and a parallel rectangle of lights on a frame suspended from the ceiling.

Naturally, there are differences. The room is no longer divided, so it is twice the size of the room I remember. The carpet has been changed, no doubt more than once. The room is full of exercise equipment; at the front sit a huge flat-screen television, a sofa, and a shag rug. The ceiling, much higher than I remember, is open, the rafters and beams all visible. And although the space has been repaired and renovated, I can still see a couple of dented girders to the north of one of the skylights.

Human memory may be flawed, but the Belvedere has a memory of its own.

XIV

HERE'S THE THING about accidents. We make them happen, but we don't want them to. We say they happen "to us," which means we are not at fault. In legal terms, the closer our aggression is to consciousness, the more we are held responsible for it. There are degrees of intention, just as there are degrees of homicide; an act committed "with malice aforethought" will be punished more severely than one that results in an "accidental" death. Under the law, slips of speech, memory, or physical movement are never the consequences of motivation, however repressed.

Still, some accidents are incontrovertibly accidents. An article in *Forensic Science International* describes a case in which a group of middle-aged friends returned from a party to the hotel room they had rented for the night. The room contained a double bed and two Murphy beds. The following afternoon, while cleaning the room, the maid had trouble unfolding one of the Murphy beds. When she knelt down to find what was jamming the mechanism, she discovered a human arm hanging down between the bed and the wall. It turned out that, due to mechanical failure, one of the Murphy beds had abruptly folded up into itself during the night. The fifty-one-year-old man sleeping there, apparently still heavily intoxicated, was suddenly forced backward, head over heels, and crushed. The cause of death was given as "traumatic asphyxia." In the morning, upon seeing his bed neatly folded into the wall, the man's friends simply assumed he had checked out early. (And in a way, he had.)

Accidents can also be invisible. Death by the inhalation of hydrogen sulfide, better known as sewer gas, is particularly insidious because the gas's presence and concentration are unpredictable and it is neurotoxic at relatively low levels. Victims of sewer gas poisoning can be identified by the greenish discoloration of their skin and internal organs (liver, trachea, esophagus, stomach).

In one case I read about in a forensic journal, a sewer worker was overtaken by fumes and died shortly after clearing an obstruction in a wastewater cistern. When he did not return, another man was sent after him. He, too, was overcome with fumes and died. A third man was sent. Then a fourth. Then a fifth. Ultimately, six men died in the attempt to rescue their colleagues, falling one after another like a line of dominoes. One of the first effects of sudden exposure to sewer gas is the subtle paralysis of the olfactory nerves, so you are no longer able to discern the tell-tale stink of rotten eggs. At this point, as the authors of the case study put it, "death may come on like a stroke of lightning," sending you straight into oblivion.

I begin to wonder whether Rey Rivera's death could have been an accident. Of course, one does not "accidentally" take a running jump from the roof of a fourteen-story building. But what if Rivera did not fall from the roof of the Belvedere at all? What if his fall was only through the roof of the pool?

As he mentioned more than once, at the time of his death

Rivera was under a very tight deadline to finish editing his video of the Oxford Club's annual conference. The conference took place from March 15 to March 18, 2006, and Rey was planning to make DVDs to send out to those members who could not attend in person. On May 16, Rey reserved an edit suite for the weekend, sounding as though he was, according to Mark Gold, who booked the equipment for him, "under a crunch for work." On the evening he went missing, we know he was summoned at around four p.m. by a phone call from someone at Agora, which flustered him and made him leave home at once, presumably for either a last-minute meeting or a previously scheduled meeting he had forgotten about.

For a while, I wondered whether Rey might have somehow messed up the edits, accidentally deleted the tape, or found that he had made a serious recording error and his tapes of the conference were blank. Such a mistake would have cost him the money he had paid up front for equipment rental, crew, travel expenses, editing hours, and the duplication of DVDs, which Allison estimated came to around $70,000, not to mention reimbursement of the hundreds of subscribers who were waiting for their DVDs. Would Rey have committed suicide rather than face the consequences of screwing up on such an epic level? Was the phone call from Agora right before he left home a final request for the videotape he did not have?

This scenario doesn't ring true. No reasonable person would take their own life rather than confess to a mistake that would have been, essentially, an expensive inconvenience. Rey might no longer be asked to work for Stansberry, but the job was only temporary in the first place—he and Allison were planning to return to LA. Suicide would have made no sense for another reason, too: Rey would be leaving Allison with the burden of paying off the $70,000 (which, in fact, she had to do because it was on her credit card).

After the mysterious meeting with the person from Agora, Rey may have accompanied whomever he met for a drink afterward somewhere near the Belvedere, moving Allison's car to the lot on St. Paul once the attendant had left for the night, at six p.m. According to the medical examiner, the alcohol found in Rey's system could have been a by-product of decomposition, or it could have been consumed shortly before his death. Would it be possible that, after having a few drinks, Rey went up to the top floor of the Belvedere parking garage, perhaps to walk someone back to their car?

The parking garage is about forty feet from the street and twenty feet from the roof of the pool. Its top floor is on a level with our bedroom window. You might think that not much happens on the roof of a parking lot, and for the most part you would be right, but the space is sometimes used for unexpected purposes—as an impromptu viewing platform for the fireworks over the Inner Harbor on July 4, for the lighting of the Washington Monument in Mount Vernon Place at Christmas, and for the show put on by the US Air Force during Fleet Week. After dark, I have twice seen couples using the roof as a place to make out—and I have also seen suspicious-looking figures pacing, brooding, and waiting. One night, we were transfixed by a young woman in jeans and a leather jacket sitting on the wall at the edge of the roof overlooking the street. Was she about to jump? We thought about shouting to her, or calling the police, but she seemed calm and peaceful; much to our relief, after smoking a cigarette, she climbed down and walked off into the dark. When the roof is free of cars at the weekend, I have seen people use the flat expanse of the top story to practice yoga, to hula-hoop, to roller-skate, to film a video dance routine, to fly a kite and a remote-controlled airplane, and, once, to train a pet kestrel to come to the glove.

For someone with a serious phobia of heights, this surface would not be as terrifying as the Belvedere roof. It has walls at every side, so there are no exposed drops. If Rey went up there that night, he might have leaned over the waist-high wall of the top floor to check out the view to the west. If he jumped or fell from the top of the parking lot rather than the roof, could he still have landed where he did? I realize the question can be answered by means of a mathematical equation. I have no head for figures, but I know that in legal terms, they are the equivalent of facts— the only things that matter.

Once again, I contacted Rod Cross in Australia. He told me to go up to the top of the garage roof and drop down the end of a very long piece of string tied to something heavy (I used a shelf bracket), then measure the string. I also used a piece of string to measure the horizontal distance from the parking garage wall to the hole in the swimming pool roof. Cross compared these figures with the original calculations and concluded that "the jump speed is almost the same in both cases, and both are easy for any adult given a short run up. The speed is too high for a push." However, a running jump from the top of the parking lot would be impossible, as it is surrounded on all sides by a wall of at least four feet.

But there is another scenario. What if Rivera was leaning over this wall and his phone slipped out of his pocket and landed on the swimming pool roof, about twenty-five feet below? What if, instead of going to the front desk of the Belvedere, Rey decided it would be easier to climb down to the roof and retrieve the phone himself? Or maybe he went looking for the concierge and found nobody at the front desk to help him. This would not have been unusual in 2006. It happens now; it happened to me this morning when our newspaper was not delivered. All the concierges are overworked; they are regularly called on to fix leaks, carry packages, replace lightbulbs, clean spills, and deal with whatever else arises in the daily business of the building. Another possibility is that someone who had not visited the building in years could have

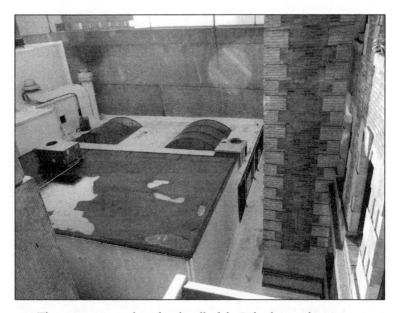

The swimming pool roof and wall of the Belvedere parking garage

told Rivera that the Belvedere had an indoor swimming pool, and Rey, in search of a place to swim, decided to check it out himself by climbing on the roof.

The parking garage is connected to the swimming pool roof by an enclosure that houses the garage stairs, the elevator shaft and machinery, and auxiliary structures for the building's mechanicals—pumps, boilers, furnaces, the HVAC system. There is also what appears to be a ventilation system containing two large, chimney-like exhaust ducts and a garbage or linen chute, along with pipes, shafts, coils, hoods, and compressors.

From the roof of the parking garage, it would not have been difficult for someone with Rivera's athleticism to climb down onto the swimming pool roof. At the time, this roof was old, its rubber membrane patched and worn. The steel girders that support the structure beneath were exposed. If one of these girders was weak and rusty from water damage—not impossible for the roof of a swimming pool—could the pressure of Rivera's substantial weight in the wrong place have caused the unsupported roof to collapse the moment he stepped on it?

Dr. Melissa Brassell, the medical examiner who conducted Rey Rivera's autopsy in May 2006, concluded that he "died of multiple injuries sustained as a result of precipitation from a 13-story building." I wonder if there is anything specific about the injuries to the body to suggest Rivera had fallen thirteen floors, as opposed to, say, eight. I try to speak to Dr. Brassell, but I am informed that, as a rule, medical examiners do not talk about anything outside the scope of the autopsy report, nor do they speculate or offer personal opinions.

I am certainly no expert in this area; I have never even witnessed an autopsy. However, I have read numerous articles by forensic scientists who, after studying the type and severity of injuries in hundreds of falling deaths, have created mathematical models by which medical examiners can determine the height of the fall. Unfortunately, these models do not apply to Rivera's case, since the roof would have slowed his fall and changed the pattern of his injuries significantly. Instead, I compared the injuries listed in Rivera's autopsy report with those commonly listed in studies of the injuries to construction workers who fall through a roof onto a concrete floor.

Such falls are often fatal, even if the height is less than twenty feet. One such study conducted in Denmark concludes that what distinguishes fatalities in such falls is the presence of serious head injuries (skull fractures and brain injuries). Rivera had multiple skull fractures and hemorrhages. In addition, the lacerations on either side of his chest, his broken leg and ribs, his internal injuries, and the absence of serious injury to his spine and arms, are all consistent with a scenario in which he fell through the swimming pool roof and landed on his feet. This is so whether he fell from the top of the Belvedere or just through the roof.

But there is a problem with my theory. Even if Rivera had

climbed down to the roof wearing nothing but a pair of flip-flops, why were they found on that roof, separated by at least sixty feet?

Stein continues to press his theory of homosexual blackmail. I am openly skeptical, but Stein invests all his faith in police knowledge. Still, even if Rey was having an affair with a man he first met at the Belvedere, why would they continue to meet there? Why not select a more discreet rendezvous, especially if the other party was planning to blackmail Rey? Why risk being seen and overheard? Surely Rey's death took place at the Belvedere because of its height and its proximity to where he was that evening, not because of its reputation in Baltimore's gay subculture—unless there was some kind of symbolic message in the choice of location, which, as far as I can tell, Stein does not seem to be suggesting. On the other hand, it is not out of the question that a married man might be driven to suicide by guilt over a previous or current homosexual liaison.

In 1929, shortly before noon on a cold February day, a concerned guest told the front desk clerk at the Belvedere that he could see what appeared to be the body of a gentleman on the roof of the second-floor sun parlor. When a bellman was sent to confirm the report, he returned with the news that the guest was correct; the gentleman on the roof was dressed in pajamas and appeared to be dead. He added that the window of a room on the tenth floor was standing open. A glance at the hotel guest book showed that this room was registered in the name of a Mr. William H. King Jr., who had arrived at the Belvedere the previous day in the company of his friend Mr. William Faison. Mr. Faison had already checked out of his room and was sitting in the lobby waiting for Mr. King. The police and coroner were called to the scene, and Mr. Faison identified the body as that of Mr. King.

To those who knew him, William Harvey King Jr., forty-six,

appeared to have a perfectly stable life, and he had recently made great advances in his career. Born in Portsmouth, Virginia, he had continued to live there until just prior to his death, when he and his family (wife Nancy and three children) had moved across the Chesapeake Bay, to Norfolk. In the early 1920s, the shipping lines and railways were booming. Mr. King had worked as private secretary to a series of businessmen of increasing importance. At the time of his death, he was secretary to L. R. Powell Jr., the president of the Seaboard–Air Bay Line Company, which owned both steamboat lines and railroads. It was a key position. King was well known in shipping and railway circles, and business frequently brought him to Baltimore. At the time of his death, he was moderately wealthy and at the height of his career.

King's companion at the Belvedere, William Faison, forty, also married with children, was the manager of the Atlantic Steel Castings Company. On February 1, 1929, the two friends were traveling together on business when they made a side trip to Baltimore to attend the annual Bal des Arts. This was a bohemian party held by the Charcoal Club, a group that had been formed in reaction to what many considered the prudishness of Baltimore's traditional art scene, where nude models were thought indecent. Under the leadership of such prominent citizens as the dentist and caricaturist Adalbert Volck and the architect Joseph Evans Sperry, the Charcoal Club was known for its progressive attitudes and ever-changing stable of nude models, both male and female. The Bal des Arts was a wild, all-night affair with dancing, jazz music, prizes for creative costumes, and a yearly theme—which, in 1929, was "Mount Olympus."

It is not known whether Mr. King and Mr. Faison attended the ball in costume, but according to the correspondent of the *Baltimore Sun,* "Apollo and Aphrodite led the lesser gods and goddesses in a jubilation that they will not soon forget." Inevitably, "all restraint was cast aside" and, disregarding Prohibition, the defiant

Mr. William King, the St. Louis Post-Dispatch, *February 2, 1929*

revelers drank and danced to the music of a "Negro jazz band" until three thirty a.m.

After the Bal des Arts ended, the two Williams must have found somewhere else to continue their revels: according to the desk clerk, they did not return to the Belvedere until around six thirty a.m. William Faison told police that when he got back to the hotel, he went up with William King to his room on the tenth floor, stayed for an hour or so, then returned to his own room. He managed to get a little sleep, then rose at nine, bathed, dressed, then went to the tenth floor and knocked loudly on his friend's door. There was no reply. Assuming that Mr. King was sleeping off his night of revelry, Faison went down to the restaurant, breakfasted alone, returned to his room to pack, and then tried knocking on King's door again. Finding himself unable to rouse his friend, he checked out of the hotel, bought a newspaper, and sat down to wait in the lobby.

The coroner, William T. Riley, estimated that William King had either fallen or jumped from the window of his room on the tenth

Mr. William Faison, Who's Who in Delaware County, *1925*

floor sometime between seven thirty, when Faison left the room, and eleven thirty, half an hour before his body was discovered. According to police, there were no signs of a struggle, but neither was there a suicide note, and those who knew Mr. King could think of no reason why he would want to take his own life. A wallet found in his clothing contained $83.

Mr. Faison did not believe that his friend was especially depressed. He thought that perhaps, opening the window of his room for a breath of fresh air, King may have attempted to sit on the sill, lost his balance, and toppled out. While the window was too high to step through accidentally, the sill was broad enough for a man to sit on, though it is hard to imagine why he would do so, since the temperature outside was close to freezing. Nothing was said in the coroner's report about alcohol, but Faison's story makes little sense unless King had been drinking heavily, since the Belvedere's window ledges are broad and it would be difficult to imagine sitting on the ledge then "toppling out of the window" unless perhaps, very drunk, you fell asleep for a moment and, waking up, lost your balance and plunged forward. Still, this is hard to picture.

The coroner agreed with Faison's speculation. He stated that to judge from marks in the dust on the radiator just in front of the window, "Mr. King lost his balance and fell to his death while opening the window to admit fresh air," adding that "the fact that his body was found close to the wall ten stories below indicated that he did not jump." The verdict was not suicide but accidental death, and it does seem possible that this was true. But there can be unconscious motivations for suicide. If the incident had occurred today, no doubt further questions would have been raised about the relationship between the two men, their night at the bohemian Bal des Arts, and the hour they spent together in Mr. King's room after returning to the Belvedere. In light of the men's social positions, families, and business connections, however, the relationship between them was left unexplored.

I get an email from Stein with the unfortunate news that Michael Baier is not comfortable participating in an interview. Baier is not working for the FBI, as he had told Allison he planned to do after he retired from Baltimore homicide. He is working as an investigator for the Maryland Department of Public Safety and Correctional Services. "He has concerns about jeopardizing his current position by making official statements, and is not willing to talk candidly," writes Stein, then summarizes his brief telephone conversation with Baier.

From this conversation, notes Stein, certain inferences can be made. First, Baier does not believe that Rey's death was a suicide. Second, Baier's statement that he would be willing to talk after he retired "indicates that there is more to the case than is reported." That Baier is unwilling to jeopardize his current career suggests that his suspicions are unpopular and could possibly land him in some kind of trouble. Third, he neither denies nor confirms any of the speculations surrounding the case.

I had asked Stein, if he ever found Michael Baier, to pass along

Allison's contact information, and let him know she has been trying to reach him for the last five years. But Baier told Stein that he did not want to be put in touch with Allison. In short, he did not want her bothering him and trying to convince him to solve the case.

All these years, Allison has believed that Michael Baier was working on the case of her husband's murder in secret, from an FBI office staffed with cold-case detectives. This has been her last and final hope: she continued to believe that someone, somewhere, was working to solve the mystery of Rey's death. When I let her know the truth, she is heartbroken. She cries for three days.

I, too, am taken aback by Baier's response. Why the casual dismissal? Was he surprised to hear from Stein? Did he simply lose all interest in the case long ago? Does Stein think Baier is hiding something? Since Stein has managed to track down the elusive Michael Baier, it should be easy for him to put me in touch with Porter Stansberry, who is, at least in a minor way, a public figure. Of course, I have tried writing to Stansberry many times—at Stansberry and Associates, then at his home address, then via his attorneys—but he has not replied, not even to let me know he wants nothing to do with my project. It seems counterproductive to keep pestering him, so for my portrait of Stansberry I have relied on his podcasts, blogs, and video interviews; on public documents; and on other people's accounts of him. I realize this has given me a certain impression of the man—one that is far from objective—so naturally, I am still eager to talk to him. And although he may not respond to me, I am certain that Stein, the professional, will be able to get a response from him at last, even if it is just a big fat no.

But I am unprepared for what happens next. Stein goes AWOL for weeks, leaving my phone messages and emails unanswered. When he finally gets back in touch, his emails include cryptic references to being "out of pocket," even though, according to the accounting statement I ask for, almost half of my two-thousand-dollar retainer remains unused. I ask him when we can meet. He puts me off with vague references to doctor's appointments. I tell him it does not have to be during the day. Finally, after some pressing, he agrees to meet me on October 20, 2016, at six in the Owl Bar.

I arrive early. The bar is not busy, but Stein is already there, sitting at a high table in the farthest corner, with his back to the wall. He nods at me from across the room. I realize he is probably carrying a gun.

"I took the liberty of ordering two drinks," Stein says: a beer for himself, and a margarita for me.

He must be showing me his detective skills by finding out from the bartender what I usually order. At least, so I assume until the bartender comes over and asks me what I'm having, at which point, I'm blindsided.

I ask for a margarita with lots of ice.

Stein, it seems, has ordered himself two drinks, a beer and a cocktail. I am no private investigator, but if I were, I would read that as a sign of nerves.

I ask Stein whether Baier was surprised to hear from him.

"Sure he was," says Stein.

"How did you find his number?"

"I'm a professional, Mikita."

I ask about some of his other cases. He tells me that much of his work involves staking out husbands and wives looking for evidence of infidelity.

"When you think somebody's cheating, they usually are," says Stein. He also does a lot of cybersecurity work and has recently been consulting for the police on a homicide case.

The conversation doesn't go as I had hoped. I ask Stein a lot of questions and press him for details, but either he is not a fluent raconteur, or he's unwilling to discuss his work, even off the rec-

ord. But he tells me enough to give me the impression that he sees
things through the lens of his own preconceptions. To Stein, people
are either innocent or sinful, and although he doesn't exactly put
it this way, he believes that even the innocent have their Achilles'
heels and that everyone, if tempted in the right way, can be led
astray.

In short, the impression I get is that he doesn't want to talk
about his job, but about his problems: his nagging sense of guilt,
his ex-wife, his mother, his current wife, his kids.

He keeps glancing at his watch as he talks. I find this so unnerv-
ing that I finally ask him whether he has to be somewhere.

He stops looking at his watch.

"I have all the time in the world for you, Mikita," he says.
Then he nods to the bartender and orders another round of
drinks.

Stein, I think then, is one of those men who have spent so long
learning how to flatter and manipulate women that they begin
flirting automatically, even when they have no interest in the
woman, and have nothing to gain. If I were more honest, I would
tell him that I find his smooth talk just as offensive as his discour-
tesy, but the fact is, I like being complimented. If I believed he
was being sincere, I might even have been able to play along for
a while, but everything about his conversation seems so calculated, from what he is prepared to reveal to his repeated use of my
name, that I squirm uncomfortably on my barstool and change
the subject.

I ask Stein about his surveillance work for the FBI. He tells
me that is confidential information, but says he joined the FBI
because working in the homicide division was starting to eat his
soul. He would watch the other cops dealing with dead bodies
every day, and noticed how they behaved after work.

"They all needed to wind down, let off steam," he told me.
"There's no way they could go straight home to their wife and

kids after dealing with that shit all day. They would do anything to take their mind off it. They had to get it out of their system before they went home. They'd drink, do drugs, fuck anything with a pulse."

Stein says he left the police because he did not want his soul to be eaten up like that. But by the time he got out, he said, not much of his soul was left.

I ask whether he can arrange for me to meet with Porter Stansberry. The phone call made to Rey from Agora that made him leave home in a rush, and the meeting that presumably followed, leave a huge hole in my investigation. What happened during this missing time is the seemingly unbridgeable gap in the chain of events—it is the key to the mystery, the smoking gun, the missing corpse, the vanishing clue, the unsolvable puzzle that, if this were a work of fiction, would be solved in the end after all. Someone at Agora made that call, someone met with Rey shortly before he died, and I believe Porter Stansberry knows who this person is.

"Easiest thing in the world," says Stein. "Are you free at lunchtime tomorrow? I'll set it up for you. I should be there as well, just in case."

I think: Just in case what?

Stein gets out his phone and fires off a few texts.

I ask for the check. Stein picks it up and pays it.

I don't see him again for almost two months.

The weather turns freakish overnight. It's eighty degrees in November, with the smell of decay in the air. Somebody moves out of the Belvedere, leaving a vintage wood-and-leather Chesterfield sofa by the dumpsters in the loading dock. I pay two men to bring it up to my apartment. When I sit on it, as I am doing now, it engulfs me like a leather tomb. I adore it. Still, I can't help wondering who owned it before me, and why they attached the four clawed feet to the frame with rebar, as though giving it a set of concrete shoes. And why, when I sit on it, do I start to itch? I bleach and scrub the couch incessantly, but the itching continues, and a rash appears on my arms and legs. I think of Walter Benjamin's aphorisms on late-nineteenth-century furniture. "The bourgeois interior . . . fittingly houses only the corpse. 'On this sofa, the aunt cannot help but be murdered.' The soulless luxuriance of the furnishings becomes true comfort only in the presence of a dead body."

It feels as though something dark has suddenly entered my life, has crept into the apartment inside the Chesterfield. All the inanimate things in my life seem to turn against me. The eucalyptus tree dies overnight. The piano goes off-key. I start to get terrible headaches. In that heightened state of consciousness that can be a side effect of intense pain, I lie on the Chesterfield for hours unable to move, listening to ice cracking and falling into the tray in the refrigerator, the dog's claws pattering on the wooden floor, the ceiling fan turning above me, the mourning doves scratching for seed on the sills. When the headaches come, I can do nothing but trace the progress of the pain; it starts behind my eyes and moves in terrible increments slowly backward, spreading the agony over the drum of my skull.

I become unaccountably edgy, checking the locks on the windows, noticing shadows under the door, jumping at sudden noises, sensing movement out of the corners of my eyes. I wake up in the early hours of the morning, drained from nightmares.

I go to the closet to take our rugs out of storage, and they fall to pieces in my arms. They are no longer fabric, but a huge nest of pupae: case moths, I discover. This, it turns out, is the cause of my itching.

A tarot card reader once told me that the Ace of Wands is the only card that has no bad in it. Life is not mostly good fortune, as people think, but mainly bad, with a bit of luck thrown in, more for some than others. But who among us is really prepared to take an honest look at the cards they have been dealt? "The creative mind is better off with hints than with extensive knowledge," wrote the society hostess Marion Hooper Adams, wife of the historian Henry Adams, who, on the morning of December 6, 1885, committed suicide at the age of forty-two, by swallowing a vial of potassium cyanide.

In December, feeling depressed, I decide to go up to the roof of the Belvedere. I think some dangerous exploring might bring me comfort. It usually does.

The door to the roof is unlocked, as usual. The ladder leading to the access door is steeper than I remember. When I reach the top, I step out into the bright winter sunshine, and there, maybe four feet in front of me, is the narrow edge of the building, "protected"

Rey and Allison Rivera

by a thin metal railing about two meters long. The rest of the perimeter is wide open.

I turn right, away from the edge, stretch, walk out into the sun, and look around me. A lot of work has been done since I was last here. A new white protective coating has been added to the surface, the chimney has been rebuilt, and the gutters have been unclogged.

The sun feels warm against my skin, and the city shines below me in the sunlight. If I were ready to die, I think, it would not be difficult to jump off the roof on a bright, clear day like this. I imagine how it would feel: like leaping into the sunshine. People rarely acknowledge how comforting the thought of suicide can be, especially the thought of suicide by jumping from a height. To

Rey and Allison Rivera

launch oneself into the abyss is to give the finger to the world; it is a way to cause trouble, to make an impact, to snub quiet discretion and an open casket. How tempting: to simply bring down the curtains on one's life. If I were to do it, I think, I would first get rid of my possessions, write a note to D., make sure my dog was well taken care of, then take a couple of Valium and a big shot of vodka. I think of opening my arms, closing my eyes, and running forward, straight off the edge of the building and out into the brilliant blue sky.

I have every reason to live, yet I can still feel the pull of the edge. When I lived in London, there was a time when I could not use the Tube. It was irrational. I was not unhappy. But as soon as I got to the platform I would become mesmerized by its edge, lose focus, miss my train, think about nothing but my body on the tracks.

I remember Poe's lines from "The Imp of the Perverse": "And because our reason violently deters us from the brink, therefore do we the most impetuously approach it. There is no passion in nature so demoniacally impatient, as that of him who, shuddering upon the edge of a precipice, thus meditates a Plunge."

It is time to go. Forcing myself to turn from the edge, I return to the door and turn the handle. It does not move. I turn it again. Still nothing. I push. I kick. Nothing. I shove my hip against it. I throw my whole body weight against it. It will not budge. The facts set in. The door has locked itself behind me. I am trapped.

My phone is downstairs. Nobody knows where I am. D. is out of town. How long before he gets back? Three hours? Four? Even then, will he assume I have gone for a hike or to visit a friend? If I wave my arms around, will anyone see me? If I scream, will anyone hear? In truth, I could be here for five or six hours before I am missed, and five minutes has been enough to make me feel the pull of the edge.

I turn around, and that's when I see it: another door, about three feet to the left of the one I've been trying to open. I turn the handle, and it gives immediately. I'd been trying to open the door to the elevator shaft. Weak with relief, I climb down the ladder and back through the loft.

I no longer go up to the roof.

XV

IT IS NOW eleven years since Rey Rivera was killed. In the Belvedere, life goes on. People move in. Others move out. A terrible smell has been pervading the fifth floor, like rotting meat or fish. It is especially bad at weekends. The couple on six are going through a nasty divorce. Someone's dog takes a dump in the freight elevator. A random drunk leaving the Owl Bar beats up James, the gentle concierge, and puts him in the hospital. After his Baltimore benefit concert following the riots in summer 2015, the singer Prince takes his entourage to the 13th Floor. Everyone says he is humble, extremely polite, and asks for vegan-friendly food.

On the steps of the New Deliverance Cathedral on the corner of Chase Street and St. Paul, I find the toe tag from a corpse. Cause of death: rosary pea poisoning. The jequirity bean, or rosary pea, is commonly used in West African witchcraft in order to ward off curses.

At a wedding, an ambulance pulls up and someone is carried out of the Belvedere on a stretcher. It's the chef, suffering from an allergic reaction to jalapeños. Inexplicably, no jalapeños are being served.

Stein's final report is a big nothing. I realize he had nothing to offer me to begin with, and I as should know by now, nothing will come of nothing. I get the sense he gave up on the case long ago. What is left of my retainer is spent on a straggling trail of useless questions, failed connections, and unanswered phone calls. The report, like much police writing, is a masterwork of pointless detail and redundant precision. I would have tossed it aside and happily forgotten about Stein were it not for one detail. In the email to which the document is attached, Stein says he has something to say that he can't include in the report. Something "off the record." Can we meet in the Owl Bar on Thursday at six thirty?

That will be fine, I reply. But then I begin to wonder: What can he have to tell me that he cannot include in the report? Even if it's "off the record," why not just tell me on the phone? Why do we have to meet in person? And why is he so eager to get together when he was so reluctant before, and when he is no longer being paid?

When I have talked to them about this case, with its wide-ranging conspiracy theories, police involvement, scary coverups, and anonymous emails warning me off, friends have sometimes asked me: Aren't you frightened?

The answer has always been no, I've never been frightened—that is, until now. Stein, I keep thinking, is an ex-cop. If the police were involved in a coverup of Rivera's death and Stein has learned about it, I do not believe the private investigator would be on my side. As he admits, Stein, with his half-eaten soul, is a troubled character. As our final meeting draws closer, fear creeps into my life and will not let go.

A few days before our final appointment, I find an abandoned wooden trunk on the Belvedere's loading dock. I take it up to our apartment to restore, and become temporarily obsessed with vintage trunks. The wood of this one is very thick, and it has a flat top, which, I learn, makes it a steamer trunk, intended to fit snugly into the tight space of a ship's passenger cabin. I add brass studs, a decorative brass lock, and rope handles, and I line it with pretty paper and put incense inside to get rid of the moldy smell.

A stiff upholstery fabric, something like calico, would have lined the hat trunks or half-trunks owned by Victorian ladies, whereas gentlemen's trunks were generally lined with leather or hide. In the early years of the twentieth century, there were trunks for all occasions: bevel-top trunks, dome-top trunks, and barrel-top trunks; wardrobe trunks and dresser trunks; stagecoach trunks; Saratoga trunks with complex compartments; and Jenny Lind trunks with hourglass curves like those of the famous Swedish singer.

Eventually, the infinitely cheaper and more portable suitcase replaced the trunk, and although trunks are still made today, mostly as military footlockers, they are generally made of metal or composite wood. For today's commercial travelers, trunks are far too heavy, expensive, and inappropriate to be of any use; they suggest the more measured and deliberate journeys of the past. And the decline of trunk production marked the end of the classic trunk murder.

Bodies will always be found in barrels, boxes, suitcases, and the trunks of cars, but the golden age trunk murder followed a very particular plot. The crime would first come to light when a porter at a railway station smelled a foul odor coming from a locked trunk in the cloakroom. When it was forced open, inside would be found a dead body, usually that of a young girl.

The standard shipping trunk measures from 30 inches to 36 inches long and 16 to 22 inches wide; it comes in a variety of heights. In 1912, the average Western female was around 65 inches high and her hips, the widest point of her body, were, on average, 32 inches wide (compared with 37.5 inches today). If she was short enough, a dead girl could be folded in half like a magician's assistant and stuffed in a trunk intact. Most of the time, however, this is not how trunked bodies were packed.

The best-known trunk murders occurred in France, but it is a different pair of crimes that I find particularly intriguing. The first involved a foul-smelling trunk left in a cloakroom at Brighton railway station in England on June 17, 1934, which, when opened by police, was found to contain the torso of a pregnant woman, aged around twenty-five, wrapped in several layers of blood-soaked paper and cotton wool. The next day a suitcase containing the same woman's legs was found at King's Cross railway station. No one ever learned what her face looked like, because her head was never found; she was known in the press as "the girl with the pretty feet." Neither victim nor murderer was ever identified, though a local abortionist was strongly suspected.

A month later, as part of their investigation into the King's Cross trunk murder, police knocked on the door of a house close to the railway station. The house was being repainted, and the contractor mentioned a disgusting smell coming from the basement apartment. Police traced the offensive stench to a cloth-covered trunk at the foot of the bed. The smell came from the fluid that was leaking from it. Opening the trunk, police discovered a decomposing corpse, this time intact, later identified as a forty-two-year-old former music hall dancer who went by the name of Violet Kaye. At the time of her death, Kaye been working as a prostitute, drinking heavily, and living as the common-law wife of a violent petty criminal and boxer named Tony Mancini, who claimed he had accidentally killed Violet during a domestic fight two months earlier. He had been living with her decomposing body in his small basement apartment ever since. Surprisingly, Mancini was acquitted.

The Violet Kaye trunk murder, discovered in the investigation of the King's Cross trunk murder, turned out to be completely unrelated to it.

On Thursday, I get to the Owl Bar on time, knowing that Stein will be early, as usual. The place is crowded, which is a relief, as it means I can get help if he forces me to leave at gunpoint. I look for him at the corner table; he is not there. It takes me a while to find him sitting at the bar, his briefcase on a barstool by his side—a barstool that he is saving for me. His two drinks are already lined up. This time, he is dressed casually; in fact, as I squeeze onto the barstool beside him, I realize he looks shabby, unshaven, and a little unkempt. He must have noticed my glance, because as I am trying to get the bartender's attention, he apologizes for his appearance. He tells me he been staking out the wife of a well-known football player.

"This guy thinks his wife is cheating," says Stein. "And as I told you before, if you think someone's cheating, they probably are."

"Is he right?" I ask.

"He is right," says Stein. "Boy, is he right."

After a few minutes of conversation about the football player's wife and her lovers, Stein says he has something for me.

"I'm not supposed to be giving this to you because it's against the rules," he says, with a wink, "but I trust you'll keep it confidential."

He holds up a medium-sized manila envelope. My heart lifts. No longer afraid, I become excited, my mind racing. My first assumption is that he's managed to get hold of the homicide file. When I realize the envelope isn't big enough for that, I think it must be the police photographs from the death scene. But when I take the envelope from Stein, I discover it's empty. I turn it over, and there's something written on the back: his name and phone number.

Obviously, I already have Stein's name and phone number.

I take a sip of my drink, give myself time to think about it, but I still don't get it. I look at Stein, waiting for him to explain, but he acts as though nothing has happened. He starts talking about the football player again.

"Maryland has no-fault divorce laws," he says, "but this guy was smart. He has a prenup with an infidelity clause. If you ask me, prenups are the best thing the legal system ever invented. I should have got one myself. My wife left me two weeks ago." He takes a swig from his beer.

"Really?" I don't know what to say.

"It's been a long time coming." Stein wipes the froth from his mustache. "We tried marriage counseling, therapy, everything. There was infidelity on both sides. Yesterday, she told me she's filed for divorce."

I look at him. He smiles. I think it is the first time I have seen him smile.

"My wife's left me," he says. "You're not a client anymore. I'm just saying."

Suddenly, I get it. I look away. The weight of the letdown is enormous. I am so disappointed I think I might cry.

"I'm sorry, I have to leave," I tell Stein, without looking at him. "Thank you for the drink."

Our meeting lasted twenty minutes, at most.

In the elevator, I blink, and two fat tears roll down my face. I am crying because a man came on to me rather than trying to kill me.

Later, when I look back over my encounters with Stein, I realize we have been at cross-purposes all along. I had pressed him to meet with me. I told him we could get together in the evening. When I asked questions about his job, he must have thought my interest was personal. In fact, it was personal, but not in the way he had imagined. In Stein's world, I realize, a woman who shows an interest in a man must be looking for something more than mere conversation. On my part, I had misunderstood his interest in me as a threat, which seemed deeply personal—unlike a sexual interest, which did not seem personal at all.

If I had been kidnapped, on the other hand, people would have paid attention. They would have made "Missing" posters with my picture on them. Smiling uncharacteristically, with my dog on my lap, I would look like someone who needed urgently to be found.

Missing people are like absent friends at a wedding, or the corpse at a funeral. They are attention-grabbers. Even if they are already dead, they are not excluded, as I often feel myself to be, from the world of the living. But if I were to go missing, I would be the center of attention. For once, I would be mysterious and sensational.

When I was in college, a boyfriend introduced me to his grand-mother. Afterward, with a grin, he told me what the old lady had said about me: "I'd watch out for that girl if I were you. She's trunkable."

His grandmother had a saying, my boyfriend told me: "An innocent girl is never found in a trunk." I do not know what it was about me that had made his grandmother say this. Maybe she had some kind of intuition.

I should not have been flattered, but I was.

A friend, horrified by what I tell her about Stein, arranges for me to meet a colleague of her husband's, a former investigative reporter for the *Village Voice*. "He's golden," she emails me. "I think it will be really great. He's a knowledgeable researcher with years of good relationships with crime and cops and access to a lot more useful stuff." This friend, she insists, is reputable and meticulous and just an all-around good guy. He is also a "brilliant crime reporter" and she knows he will be able to help me. Her husband endorses him, too: "He knows pretty much every criminal inves-tigative research channel around. He's also a genuine good person and the reporter with the most integrity I've ever met."

I arrange to meet this man in the Owl Bar on Tuesday, Decem-ber 13, 2016. "I'll be the 40-something guy in the Orioles shirt," he emails me. "I'll be the person looking anxious and disheveled," I reply. We meet at three o'clock in the afternoon. After my recent letdown with Stein, I am eager to discuss details of the case with someone who shares my interests. But I am taken aback to discover that the investigative reporter has brought his daughter with him, a girl of around eight or nine. He does not apologize. On the contrary, he seems almost proud. He tells me the girl is home from school due to illness, although I notice she has already polished off a bowl of chili and is now playing with the packets of crackers that accompanied it, crumbling them up in her sticky little fist. I stand looking at the pair of them, feeling flat and vacant, reluctant even to sit down. How can I possibly talk about the details of a bizarre and violent death in front of this little girl?

Mustering my strength, I join them, turn my chair to face away from the child and toward the reporter, and begin to tell him the story, lowering my voice when it comes to the gruesome parts. But he is not listening. He is distracted; his daughter is writhing and whimpering, and unable to ignore her, he tries to include her in our conversation, as if this were an educational project.

"You can talk to her," he tells me, speaking to me as to someone who understands nothing about children (he is right about that, at least). "She's really smart. She's old enough to understand. I've already explained to her what this is about."

He smiles at the girl.

"There was this man," he says, as though beginning a fairy tale, "and he lived here in this building, and he jumped out of one of the windows." As he continues, confusing all the details, I wonder why he did not call me when he found his daughter was sick, and postpone our meeting. Why did he agree to it in the first place? He seems to have no interest in the case, or in me. After this brief and useless meeting, he never contacts me again.

I am sure my friends were right—I believe he is a brilliant reporter, and full of integrity. The problem was me. I am invisible.

Stein, for all his problems, said something that stuck with me. In his experience, he told me, the motive for a crime is always one of three things: love, drugs, or money.

Everyone who knew Rivera said he kept away from drugs, and neither Stein nor anyone else found evidence of any extramarital affair, straight or gay. But I have to admit that I have never been able to make much sense of Rey's relationship with money.

Neither Rey's nor Allison's family was in a position to help the couple out financially in any significant way. It is difficult to know how much money Rivera had made in the two years he spent working for Stansbury, but it was enough for Rey and Allison to get married in Puerto Rico, take out a mortgage on a $280,000 home, and buy a wedding ring and $15,000 worth of film production equipment. Later, I learned from Allison that when Rey died, he owed over $90,000, but around $70,000 of this debt was expenses that were to have been reimbursed by Agora. He paid all his own expenses for the Oxford Club conference up front, and would have been given a refund check, along with his pay, when he submitted the tape. Allison handed over the tape to Agora when the police returned it to her, but this was ninety days after Rey's death; by then, the investment advice given at the conference was useless, and the tape could no longer be used.

Fate, then, dealt Allison Rivera a most brutal hand. Not only did she lose her soulmate and her husband of six months in horrifying circumstances, but also she then had to pay off Rey's work expenses as well as other costs that Rey put on the credit card, like the wedding ring and the ceremony in Puerto Rico. It has taken her ten years to clear the debt. All of Rey's family have suffered, but for the first time, I am struck by how merciless the last decade must have been for Allison. In her place, I think I would have collapsed from sheer despair. But she appears to have come through with grace and dignity intact.

I asked some of the people who were close to Rey if they would agree that he was "terrible with money." Rey's mother, Maria, told me that he was very frugal, especially when he was living in Barcelona, where everyone lived cheaply, and Rey had very few needs. Allison agreed. "If he didn't have money," she told me, "he didn't spend money and get into debt." She also told me that Rey never had a credit card until about six months before he died; he always used cash. However, once he began to make money, he enjoyed spending it. "He would buy himself whatever he wanted, and he liked nice things," said Allison. "He would not save for a rainy day."

This does not surprise me. In Baltimore, comparing his own standard of living to that of Stansberry and his friends, who were starting to accumulate significant wealth, Rey may have begun to feel that he was falling behind in life, and decided that he deserved the same perks as his colleagues. I have often been surprised by the importance that even otherwise humble and reasonable men place on their reputation with their male peers, especially when it comes to the amount of money they make.

Almost everyone who hears the facts about Rey Rivera's death comes to the assumption that it was "just" a suicide. They cannot seem to get beyond what they regard as two pieces of unshakable evidence: the cryptic letter and the running jump.

Why "just" a suicide? To me, suicide seems the most mysterious possibility of all. What could make a stable, gregarious, newly married man who had just made plans for the weekend suddenly jump off a building?

The FBI's Behavioral Analysis Unit prepared a report on the "suicide note"; I obtained a highly redacted copy. It is as bland as the note itself is cryptic, consisting of broad generalizations and suggestions for further investigation (for example, "BAU recommends requesting forensic analysis of the computer printer where the letter was found," although no explanation is given of why anyone would forge such a peculiar document, especially since the report concludes that it is not, in fact, a suicide note). While confirming that Rivera "had no known physical or mental illness," the FBI psychiatrists who were consulted about the note came up with this startlingly unhelpful theory: "In this particular case, the mental illness suffered by the author of the letter may go virtually undetected by family, friends and coworkers." A little later on, the report continues, "The writer of the letter likely suffers from persecutory delusional disorder. This type of disorder involves believing oneself is being malevolently treated in some fashion." Further: "The writing in this letter is also consistent with someone who suffers from a bipolar disorder. This assumption is based on the flight of ideas that could have been written by someone experiencing an untreated manic episode. The writing in this letter is disorganized, and, to a lesser extent, it is consistent with someone who suffers from schizophrenia." Delusional disorder, bipolar disorder, schizophrenia, or an untreated manic episode. All the bases are covered, but we are none the wiser.

Many people write notes, lists, texts, and memos to themselves that might seem equally bizarre if they turned up in sinister circumstances. Looking now at my own phone, I see a note that reads, "Eternal return and its opposite." What if this memo were to be found after my dead body was discovered in bewildering circumstances? What conspiracy theories and psychological diagnoses might it engender? Yet it was just shorthand for a loose train of thought about an article I was reading that I did not want to forget.

———————

And yet.

While others may clearly disagree, I believe the circumstances of Rey Rivera's death make it impossible for anyone else to have been directly involved. Notwithstanding rumors to the contrary, I could find no evidence that any of Agora's principals—not even Porter Stansberry—have ever planned or carried out an assassination.

The physics show that Rivera must have taken a running jump. He was making plans for the future, and nobody who knew him believed him to be suicidal. Using the logic of Sherlock Holmes, "Once you eliminate the impossible, whatever remains, no matter how improbable, must be the truth," I believe I have covered every eventuality, and I have eliminated suicide, murder, and accident. What remains is, I think, the only plausible answer to the puzzle: that Rey was experiencing an episode of psychosis.

It is true that Rivera had no known family history of schizophrenia, which generally manifests itself between the ages of sixteen and twenty-five in men (slightly later for Hispanics), and that Rey was thirty-two. But schizophrenia can develop at any age. Rey's friends and family say he never displayed any outward sign of mental illness, but this does not mean he was not mentally ill, just that he had none of the most familiar symptoms: He was not depressed, forgetful, or socially withdrawn; his personal hygiene did not deteriorate; he did not seem grandiose, or confused, nor did he exhibit extreme changes of mood.

But signs of schizophrenia vary dramatically from person to person, both in pattern and severity. Only one symptom reliably occurs in over 90 percent of cases, and that is delusions of persecution. Often, such delusions are the first sign of the illness. Those who are experiencing the onset of an episode may feel unsafe and afraid.

When a person feels that unspecified others are listening to them, spying on them, or trying to harm them, they will often behave in uncharacteristic ways. During the days leading up to Rivera's death, he appeared to be increasingly anxious and frightened. He believed he was being watched and possibly followed, that someone was trying to break into the house at night. Even as long as a year before his death, he had begun acting differently, which Allison attributed to the stress of his job: he began to have trouble sleeping; he found it difficult to relax, staying up into the early hours of the morning playing video games to wind down; he seemed unusually tense and anxious; he was feeling guilty about *The Rebound Report*. He even began making odd and irrational statements, as in his phone call telling Stansberry he had "got it all figured out."

Our expectations shape our perceptions; we see what we are looking for. Most people who suffer from schizophrenia are not aware that the symptoms have started. Changes in perception are difficult to know without feedback from other people. If Rey believed he had made enemies who were watching him, then Allison, knowing her husband to be rational and suspicious about Agora—remember that Stansberry, at this time, was being actively investigated by the SEC—naturally attributed his fears to external factors. Perhaps Rey and Allison, isolated from everyone they knew, unknowingly reinforced the cycles of each other's paranoia.

Rivera did not manifest any signs of disorganized speech, but in spite of its broad generalizations, the FBI report on the "suicide note" is accurate in its description of the writing as "disorganized" and "a flight of ideas." Although Rey did make a lot of notes and would often jot things down at random, Allison said his notes did not usually take this form or use this style. This particular note contains a series of loosely associated ideas and shifts rapidly from one topic to another with little apparent connection between one thought and the next. Typographically, the note exhibits features that are typical of the writing of schizophrenic patients (although almost all similar examples are handwritten): single spacing, narrow margins, capital letters, small font, and lists.

Since the document was found at Rey's home, taped to his computer screen, he must have written it before he left the house, perhaps even days or weeks before. It would be interesting to find out when he wrote the note, how long it took him, and whether or not it was revised—all of which could easily be ascertained from a forensic analysis of his computer. If this was done, the information was not released, even to Allison. She told me that, when Rey's body was found, homicide detectives came to their house, took everything from the home office, including the computers, and kept it for ninety days. If anything was discovered, she was never told.

The onset of paranoid schizophrenia can be scarily insidious; barely perceptible symptoms can occur so gradually that nobody, including the person experiencing them, knows anything is wrong. It may begin with something ordinary and apparently innocuous—the person may have trouble sleeping, for example, or find himself noticing things they never paid attention to before. They may start making connections between things that seemed previously unrelated—associations they might then forget or ignore for weeks or months, until they come to attention again. If this is what was happening to Rey, he may not have mentioned it; he may not even have realized there was anything unusual going on until a few days before his death, when he became noticeably paranoid. Perhaps his anxiety increased after Allison left town, leading him to experience a psychotic break.

For many people, schizophrenia comes on gradually and then suddenly. After the slow increase in symptoms, there is a sudden psychotic episode, and delusions can no longer be distinguished from reality. Those who have experienced such a break may believe there are people watching them; they may see things out of the corners of their eyes. Many people describe feeling an intense hostile pressure, as if the brain were seized by a sense of panic. Every encounter provokes the fight-or-flight response, as if everyone they met was carrying a concealed weapon and planning a secret attack.

There is an association between the first episode of psychosis and suicide by jumping. One study showed that nearly half the survivors of a suicide attempt by jumping were found to be suffering from a psychotic illness (no doubt the figure is even higher for those who did not survive). If Rivera was experiencing a psychotic break, it is difficult to know what might have been in his mind when he made his way up to the Belvedere. Perhaps he believed he was being chased and this was the only way out; maybe he thought he could escape his pursuers by leaping to the top of the parking garage opposite the Belvedere, or by landing in what he believed was a swimming pool. If so, his running jump would have indicated not a desire to take his own life, but the result of a terrifying delusion.

This is what Rey's colleague Steven King has always believed. He thinks Rey's death was caused not by suicide, but by a "mental break" as a result of which Rivera did not know what he was doing. King told me that he had a friend who, as he put it, "went off the rails" after a traumatic incident. She had to be hospitalized because she thought people were coming after her. "I know that kind of thing can happen," he told me, "and I've always assumed it's what happened to Rey." After all my investigations, I have come to believe he is right.

It is not easy to accept that someone you loved might have taken their own life, especially when there are real motives for murder. The forensic physicist Rod Cross describes being contacted by the family of Father James Chevedden, a fifty-six-year-old Jesuit priest who plunged to his death from a six-story parking garage in San Jose in 2004. Chevedden had conducted a mass that morning at the Sacred Heart chapel in Los Gatos; he had spent the day on jury duty and appeared perfectly normal. Shortly after the jurors were dismissed, people in the building opposite a parking garage saw something fall from the roof. The priest's dead body was found lying faceup on the ground. His death was determined to be a suicide; his family did not agree with the verdict, and asked Professor Cross to conduct an independent investigation.

Father Chevedden had begun experiencing psychiatric problems eleven years before his death, when he was hospitalized for anxiety and paranoia. He recovered with the help of medication, but became increasingly disillusioned with the Catholic Church. In 1998, at age fifty, he attempted suicide by jumping from a window-washing scaffold. He survived with many injuries including two broken feet, and was confined for a time to a wheelchair at Sacred Heart. To Chevedden's great misfortune, the priest who was assigned to push him from place to place in his wheelchair had a history of sexual abuse; he took advantage of Chevedden's immobility. Chevedden complained to the Jesuit fathers, who eventually paid his family $1.6 million in compensation but did not report the offenses to the police, nor did they remove the offender from Sacred Heart.

Chevedden's family found it highly suspicious that the priest appeared to have landed on his back, and that there were no injuries to his head. They believe he was killed, and then dumped from the parking garage to make his death look like a suicide. To investigate further, Cross, who lives in Australia, sent a private investigator to San Jose to take photographs of the scene. From the photographs, Cross deduced that Chevedden neither fell nor jumped, but appeared to have lain down in a horizontal position and rolled off the roof. In the images taken by the private investigator, Chevedden's foot and handprints were still visible, and Cross discerned that the priest had climbed out to a ledge on the top floor of the parking garage, lain down, and rolled over the edge, which had a downward curve. While at first this may seem an odd way to commit suicide, on further reflection it sounds like a practical alternative for those unable to face the plunge.

The launch speed was slow, and the victim landed ten feet out after falling fifty-seven feet. Unfortunately, Chevedden's family was clearly hoping for a different result. "[They] refused to pay both my bill and the bill of the private investigator who travelled to San Jose to take the photographs," Professor Cross reveals. In 2007, three years after Chevedden's death, his family offered a new reward for information related to the case.

All the experts I spoke to about Rey Rivera's death—Rod Press, Charles Tumosa, staff at the Office of the Chief Medical Examiner—emphasized that they were trained to discover the facts, not the motives. "I always explain, when I'm teaching trace evidence," said Dr. Tumosa, "I can tell you who, what, when, where, and how, but never why. You can reconstruct what happened. You can say that Mr. A. shot Mr. B. Now, he might have had a very good reason for doing it, but I don't have a chemical that turns blue if he had a reasonable motive, and green if it was unreasonable."

"Do you like thinking about those kinds of things: motives, why people kill each other?" I asked him.

"I went to a Jesuit school," he said. "We thought about those things a lot. But as a practical concern, I've worked thousands of homicides, and I've learned that people will do inexplicable things. All we can show is what they did. Often there is no 'why.' We look to make sense out of them, but often they make no sense. None whatsover."

Even the psychologists I know do not seem particularly interested in why people act the way they do; they seem interested only in which aspects of behavior can be regarded as symptoms that fit a particular diagnostic category. I suppose this makes sense; professionals want to get paid; they want to produce the facts then file away the case and move on to the next.

You can be an expert in ballistics or forensic psychology, but there are no experts in motiveless suicide, or impossible murder. In the overburdened police station or forensics lab there is nothing to be gained from asking why. It is only the amateur like me, with no one to answer to, who has time to be compelled by ambiguity.

XVI

I AM WALKING the dog one morning in November 2016 when I notice another "Missing" poster—the first I have seen in ten years. This poster, too, has appeared overnight on the utility poles of Charles and Chase Streets. Underneath the words "Missing Person," there are two color photographs of a young man. His name is Michael Bagley; he is twenty-three years old. The photographs are both in color. The one on the left is a close-up of a man dressed in a gray shirt and black overcoat. He's smiling for the camera in a manner that is jaunty and nonchalant. On the right is a long shot of the same young man with shorter hair, wearing a black-and-white-patterned short-sleeved shirt and cargo shorts. Originally, his right arm was around the shoulders of someone in a green T-shirt who has been cropped from the image. In this picture he looks younger, his smile more relaxed and sincere. Underneath the photographs are the words, "Last seen Sunday November 20 at 1230AM in Fells Point. Michael is diabetic and without his medication." When I first see the posters, Michael Bagley has been missing for six days.

Later, a few blocks away, I see a different poster containing

another close-up photograph and some more information. "Michael Bagley graduated from Loyola University in May with a double major in biology and psychology. He is interested in Animal Rights and Civil Rights. He was last seen in the 1700 block of Thames Street leaving the Waterfront Hotel bar with an unknown woman around 1 a.m."

Five days later, Michael Bagley's body is found floating in the harbor. An autopsy is to be conducted, but there are no obvious signs of foul play. Did his glucose level drop too fast, leaving him dizzy and disoriented? The mystery woman in the hotel bar sounds sinister—but it turns out she was just a girl Michael was talking to for a while. He left the bar alone, after his friends had gone home. If he was very drunk and walking in the dark, he could easily have fallen into the water. There are no pedestrian barriers on the wharf. Of all the bodies found floating in the harbor every year, at least two or three are people who have fallen in when drunk. (The rest are either suicides, homicides, or bodies that have floated from elsewhere and have been in the water so long it is impossible to tell.)

Twenty-three-year-old students usually need no reason to get drunk, but Michael Bagley, I discover, had been through some tough times. His mother died when he was fourteen, and he and his sister had been brought up by their father, Paul, a philosophy professor at Baltimore's Loyola University. As a result of injuries sustained in a car accident, Paul Bagley had been paraplegic for the last twelve years. He died in July 2016, four months before his son. This leads me to wonder whether Michael's death may have been a suicide.

Further investigation reveals that Michael Bagley was so drunk on the night he went missing that he was thrown out of the Waterfront Hotel; he was last seen on the hotel's security cameras, stumbling around outside and trying to get back in. He almost certainly drowned after falling off the wharf, not an unusual occurrence in Fells Point.

Drinking so you're barely able to walk, then trying to find your way home on the waterfront in November—couldn't that be considered suicidal behavior? As far as I can tell, no one had any reason to murder Michael Bagley—but what is suicide, after all, but murder of the self?

I am at the George Peabody Library, making notes from a book by a writer named Bernard Hamilton, called *One World—At a Time,* first published in 1927. The book's title refers to the reply made by Henry David Thoreau when asked whether he was ready for the next world. But the person who used the phrase to Hamilton was not Thoreau, but Hamilton's close friend and neighbor Sir Arthur Conan Doyle, with whom he shared an interest in theosophy, spiritualism, telepathy, and belief in the Other Side.

When I turn the page, something slips out of the book and flutters to my feet. I reach down to pick it up. It is a cheap paper greeting card, faded a little with age. On the front is a picture of a couple in old-fashioned costume in a twilit forest. The man is down on one knee before the woman. The illustration would be tacky were the card not so old; as it is, its rough-cut edges and sepia tinge make the bland image seem poignant. I open the card. It is unsigned. The printed verse reads as follows:

> *If I could have*
> > *my wish today*
> *I'd like to hear*
> > *you laugh and say,*
> *"To you my feelings*
> > *now incline.*
> *Yes, I will be*
> > *Your Valentine."*

Unlike modern greeting cards, this is simply a piece of paper folded over twice, to make two pages. Carefully, I unfold it. In the bottom right-hand corner, there is a message written in an unsteady cursive. It looks like a child's hand. It says, "From Alvin & Eva. We hope you will soon get well Miss Cross."

The Valentine's card has fallen out from between pages 234 and 235 of *One World—At a Time*. On this page, Miss Cross—at least, I like to think it was Miss Cross—has drawn a faint pencil line under this passage:

Why should we doubt old thinkers—the old philosophers who have proved themselves as sound as ever, from Solon and Marcus Aurelius? The men of old had time to think. They were not distracted by incessant sensations or by an over-excited existence, induced by newspapers; by motoring; by crowding into "tubes" and omnibuses; by the hundred nerve-wracking hurries of today. They had time to sit down and *think* about another life; they speculate and weigh evidence.

I return the book to the shelves when I leave—the Peabody is not a lending library—and I walk home imagining Miss Cross as a schoolteacher with spiritual leanings, and spectacles on a silver chain. I'm sure Miss Cross spent a great deal of time thinking seriously about the next life. Perhaps she practiced automatic writing, or table-tapping.

I am so enraptured by my fantasy that it does not occur to me until later that after speculating and weighing evidence of another world, Solon and Marcus Aurelius found that evidence wanting.

True stories about people who died or went missing mysteriously used to make me feel there was more to the world than I could ever know. What I loved about them was the way they seemed to slip back the skin of things, as in an autopsy, revealing the strange and terrifying disruptions lying just beneath the surface. Now, after more than ten years trying to find out what happened to Rey Rivera, I realize these stories come to our attention only because others care about these people, and want to find out what happened to them.

I wonder whether I'm drawn to such stories because they keep me caught up in reverie, distracting me from the unremarkable deaths that surround me. According to Freddie Howard, the evening concierge, most of the deaths in the Belvedere these days are not suicides, but the result of natural causes. After a while, he says, you might notice that somebody's mailbox is full or they have not been picking up their newspapers. If they are not on vacation, he will use the spare key and take a look in their apartment. If they are dead, he will just close the door and call the cops.

What makes a death mysterious? What happened to Rey Rivera transpires every day. People die alone; their bodies are undiscovered for days. It happens everywhere. For most people, there are no "Missing" posters on the neighborhood utility poles. Nobody feels compelled to solve the puzzle. There is nothing cryptic about the deaths of those with no job, no friends, no family to speak of. People disappear every day. But you only "go missing" if somebody notices you've gone.

Notes

EPIGRAPH

ix   *Epigraph:* Trans. Charles S. Singleton (Princeton, N.J.: Princeton University Press, 1990).

II

16   *"a large fresh peaceful hostelry"*: Henry James, *The American Scene* (London: Harper & Brothers, 1907), p. 308.

16   *The Belvedere struggled financially:* "Receivers named for the Belvedere," *Baltimore Sun,* August 24, 1933.

17   *the opening of Fort Meade: Baltimore Sun,* December 29, 1935, and December 14, 1953.

18   *the former Blanche Hardy Hecht:* Tom Siebert, "Secrets of the Belvedere," *Baltimore Magazine,* December 1, 2003. Archived at http://www.baltimoremagazine.net/2003/12/1/secrets-of-the-belvedere. Accessed August 13, 2016. "Consolvo Weds Italian Army Major New York," *Daily Southerner* (Tarboro, NC), May 18, 1922.

19   *"Never felt such oven heat"*: Letter to Hildegarde Watson (1933–1964), *University of Rochester Library Bulletin,* vol. xxix, Summer

1976, no. 2, edited by Cyrus Hoy, http://rbscp.lib.rochester.edu /3572.

20   *"an idiotic affair"*: Cited in Elaine Showalter, *Inventing Herself: Claiming a Feminist Intellectual Heritage* (New York: Simon & Schuster, 2001), p. 186.

23   *"hotel for suicides"*: "Hotel for Suicides," *Washington Post,* May 26, 1912.

23   *a department store in Pittsburgh:* "Count Says Pittsburgh Men Have Wrong Shape," *Pittsburgh Gazette Times,* November 2, 1913.

23   *the reanimation of the dead:* "Danish Nobleman Plans Attempt to Resuscitate Capt. Scott with Pulmotor," *Washington Herald,* April 17, 1913.

23   *"have grown heartily sick"*: Robert Louis Stevenson, "The Suicide Club," in *The New Arabian Nights* (London: Chatto & Windus, 1920), p. 10.

24   *According to a 2006 study:* P. Zarkowski and D. Avery, "Hotel Room Suicide," *Suicide and Life-Threatening Behavior,* vol. 36 (2006), pp. 578–81.

25   *"How to Properly Respond"*: William, Frye, PhD, CHE, "How to Properly Respond to a Guest Death in Your Hotel," *The Rooms Chronicle,* vol. 17, no. 1, published by the College of Hospitality and Tourism Management, Niagara University.

25   *hotel and motel chains:* http://www.crimescenecleaners.com/index .html.

26   *After Las Vegas:* Cited in Valerie Neff Newitt, "Taking Steps to Help Prevent Suicides in Hotels," *Lodging Magazine,* July 21, 2004, http://lodgingmagazine.com/taking-steps-to-help-prevent-suicides -in-hotels/. Accessed September 20, 2016.

26   *"Tales from the Front Desk"*: https://www.reddit.com/r/Tales FromTheFrontDesk/comments/2lyawn/hotel_suicide/. Accessed November 29, 2016. Story #1 by Dodkrieg, November 11, 2016; story #2 by Lord Goran, November 20, 2015; story #3 by Khaominer, November 11, 2014; story #4 by cxtx3, November 11, 2014; story #2 by ObviouslyaMasochist, February 23, 2015.

28   *"they stuff up the cracks"*: Edmund Wilson, "The Jumping-Off Place," *New Republic,* December 23, 1931, pp. 156–58.

III

41   *"love of all that is bizarre"*: Arthur Conan Doyle, "The Red Headed League," *54 Great Sherlock Holmes Stories* (Dover Publications, 1992), p. 20.

43   *riots protesting the dissection of human corpses:* See Julia Bess Frank, "Body Snatching—A Grave Medical Problem," *Yale Journal of Biology and Medicine,* vol. 49 (1976), pp. 399–410.

IV

48   *According to NAMI:* Cited in Scott Anderson, "The Urge to End It All," *New York Times Magazine,* July 6, 2008.

49   *large Japanese cities:* Mark Saldaña, "Tokyo's 'Human Accidents': *Jinshin Jiko* and the Social Meaning of Train Suicide" (2011), Anthropology Honors Projects, Paper 10, Macalester College. Online at http://digitalcommons.macalester.edu/anth_honors/10. Accessed May 17, 2017.

50   *A 1947 article:* Orville Richardson and Herbert S. Breyfogle, "Problems of Proof in Distinguishing Suicide from Accident," *Yale Law Journal,* vol. 56, no. 3 (February 1947), pp. 482–508.

50   *suicide rates worldwide:* Jong-Min Woo, Olaoluwa Okusaga, and Teodor T. Postolache, "Seasonality of Suicidal Behavior," *International Journal of Research in Public Health,* vol. 9, no. 2 (February 2012), pp. 531–47.

50   *"The bright day":* William Shakespeare, *Julius Caesar,* act II, scene 1, line 15.

53   *On this particular night:* See Jane Cadzow, "What Happened to Jacky Sutton?" *Sydney Morning Herald,* November 28, 2015.

54   *"An act like this is prepared":* Albert Camus, *The Myth of Sisyphus,* Justin O'Brien, trans. (New York: Knopf, 1955), p. 4.

55   *"The most unlikely people":* Douglas J. A. Kerr, *Forensic Medicine* (Adam & Charles Black, 4th edition, 1946), note 23 at 92.

55   *British "gas suicide study":* See Ronald V. Clarke and Pat Mayhew, "The British Gas Suicide Story and Its Criminological Implications," *Crime and Justice,* vol. 10 (1988), pp. 79–116. *Bryan v. Aetna Life Ins. Co.,* 25 Tenn.A. 469, 160 S.W.(2d) 423 (1941), s.c. 174 Tenn. 602, 130 S.W.(2d) 85 (1939).

56   *"To the mouse":* J.B.S. Haldane, "On Being the Right Size" (1928), archived at http://irl.cs.ucla.edu/papers/right-size.html. Accessed October 17, 2016.

57   *"Very common is the impulse":* G. Stanley Hall, "A Synthetic Genetic Study of Fear," *American Journal of Psychology,* vol. 25, no. 3 (July 1914), p. 323. Ed. Karl M. Dallenbach, Madison Bentley, Edwin Garrigues Boring, and Margaret Floy Washburn.

60   *according to physicist and philosopher:* See http://www.science20 .com/alpha_meme/suicide_life_ends_six_meters_above_ground -78133. Accessed December 4, 2016.

60   *"each victim of suicide":* Emile Durkheim, *Suicide: A Study in Sociology,* trans. by John A. Spaulding and George Simpson (New York: Free Press, 1930, p. 315.

60   *"the proper question":* http://xroads.virginia.edu/~hyper/poe/m _roget.html. Accessed September 30, 2016.

V

66   *An engineering study:* Stephen Janis, "Mystery Still Surrounds Belvedere Death Scene," *Washington Examiner,* May 17, 2007, http://www.washingtonexaminer.com/mystery-still-surrounds -belvedere-death-scene/article/52752. Accessed September 27, 2016.

70   *The verdict in this case:* Obituary, "Lee Miltz Marlow," *Independent Record* (Helena, MT), May 27, 1929.

71   *Of the 4,323 bodies:* 2006 Annual Report of the Chief Medical Officer of the State of Maryland. See http://dhmh.maryland.gov /ocme/docs/2006AnnualReport.pdf.

71   *"The fact that the":* When I interviewed Janis, he worked for the Real News TV Network. When he covered the Rivera case, he worked for the *Baltimore Examiner.* He has also worked for WBFF (Fox 45) and the *Washington Examiner,* and he founded the Investigative Voice website.

71   *"a piece of paper":* Letterhead Memorandum Summary prepared by the FBI Behavioral Analysis Unit on behalf of the FBI National Center for the Analysis of Violent Crime "regarding the suspicious death of Rey Rivera," dated 08/25/2006. Obtained by the author via FOIA, April 19, 2016, p. 3.

75 *"the strangest and most unique things"*: Arthur Conan Doyle, "The Red Headed League," *Six Great Sherlock Holmes Stories* (Dover Thrift Publications, 1992), p. 21.

76 *The word "apophenia"*: Klaus Conrad, *Die beginnende Schizophrenie* (Stuttgart: Thieme Verlag, 1958). Cited in Aaron L. Mishara, "Klaus Conrad (1905–1961): Delusional Mood, Psychosis, and Beginning Schizophrenia," *Schizophrenia Bulletin,* vol. 36, no. 1 (January 2010), pp. 9–13.

VI

81 *In an 1811 lecture:* "On the Pleasures of the Mind" by the famous Philadelphia surgeon Dr. Benjamin Rush.

81 *The retired police detective Vernon Geberth:* Vernon J. Geberth, *Practical Homicide Investigation*, 4th edition (CRC Press, 2006), p. 859.

84 *"I've had the opportunity"*: Bill Buchalter, "Promising Water Polo Players Being Groomed," *Orlando Sentinel,* January 13, 1991.

84 *In only their second year:* Jack Horton, telephone conversation, April 12, 2014.

90 *Poe's Dupin also prefers to remain invisible:* Edgar Allan Poe, "The Murders in the Rue Morgue," in J. Gerald Kennedy, ed., *The Portable Edgar Allan Poe* (New York: Penguin, 2006), p. 241.

VII

94 *After high school:* Porter Stansberry, "Why College Is a Huge Waste of Time and Money," *The Crux,* January 6, 2015, http://thecrux.com/porter-stansberry-why-college-is-a-waste-of-time-and-money/. Accessed February 27, 2018.

94 *At college, he demonstrated:* Adam Liptak, "Email Stock Tip Tests Limits of Securities Laws," *New York Times,* August 3, 2003.

95 *In 2015, as a guest:* Porter Stansberry, "Self Made Man" (Podcast), interviewed by Mike Dillard, 2015, http://mikedillard.com/episode-1-porter-stansberry-from-the-boston-slums-to-150000000-per-year-here-are-the-values-that-lead-to-lasting-success/. Accessed July 8, 2015.

97   *"a subscription-based publisher"*: http://stansberryresearch.com
       /about-sa/. Accessed December 27, 2016.

98   *"Every murderer"*: Agatha Christie, *The Mysterious Affair at
       Styles* (London: Pan, 1974), p. 95.

98   *"See how this works"*: Footnote 5, United States Securities and
       Exchange Commission VS Pirate Investor, LLC; Frank Porter
       Stansberry. Opinion Part 1, page 6. Argued December 2, 2008,
       decided December 15, 2009, No. 08-1037 (1:03-cv-01042-MJG),
       United States Court of Appeals for the Fourth Circuit.

99   *"frequently found themselves"*: Diana B. Henriques, "An Oasis
       Rich in Shady Operators," *New York Times*, October 4, 1992.

99   *"If I do not receive your application"*: William Gruber, "'Royal
       Society' Draws State Probe," *Chicago Tribune*, December 4, 1987.
       The tape can be heard on SoundCloud, at https://soundcloud.com
       /zachary-leven/the-royal. Accessed July 17, 2017.

100   *One of the businesses*: See the website of Bill Bonner's coauthor
       turned enemy, Lila Rajivo: http://mindbodypolitic.com/2009/04
       /10/turning-beach-sand-into-gold-the-goldcor-swindle.

100   *"The sands that are removed"*: Ibid.

100   *It was, of course*: Rick Tonyan, "Daytona Police Say Goldcor
       Executive's Death Looks Like Murder," *Orlando Sentinel*, August 21,
       1991.

100   *His death was*: Ibid.

102   *Rey's friend B. tells me that*: Phone interview, April 12, 2014.

VIII

106   *If you were not looking carefully*: Name changed on January 1,
       2017 to "The Agora."

107   *"Cancer risks are statistically zero"*: See http://www.theagora.com.
       Accessed January 5, 2017.

108   *"The infinite energy secret"*: See http://www.drmicozzi.com and
       http://www.drpescatore.com, both accessed October 5, 2016.

108   *in a 2014 interview*: Stansberry Radio: *Independent Financial Advice
       with Porter Stansberry,* Episode 172, "Bill Bonner: The Most Valuable
       Secret You'll Ever Hear," July 31, 2014. Available at https://itunes
       .apple.com/us/podcast/stansberry-radio-edgy-source/id481026239
       ?mt=2. Accessed October 8, 2016.

110 *"Essentially critics of the":* Judgment of Appeal, http://www.ca4
.uscourts.gov/opinions/published/081037.pdf, pp. 1212, 1215–16.

111 *B. remembers visiting him in Baltimore:* Personal communication,
April 13, 2010.

IX

117 *Rey "made a big difference":* "Water Polo Preps for ECACS,"
Johns Hopkins Newsletter, September 22, 2005, http://www
.jhunewsletter.com/2005/09/22/water-polo-preps-for-ecacs
-49824/. Accessed October 7, 2016.

122 *"He was a big Latin guy":* See Stephen Janis, "Land of the
Unsolved—The Last Days of Rey Rivera," August 10, 2009, https://
www.facebook.com/BaltimoreTrueCrime/posts/516703798389176.
Accessed July 9, 2016.

125 *"He's a happy guy":* Nicole Fuller, "Family, Police Seek Man Missing for a Week," *Baltimore Sun,* May 23, 2006.

125 *In a podcast interview:* Stansberry Radio Podcast, Episode 172,
"Bill Bonner—The Most Valuable Secret You'll Ever Hear," at
21:12–21:25.

126 *"It happened at a time":* "Fake News? It's All Fake!" Bill Bonner's
Diary, https://bonnerandpartners.com/fake-news-its-all-fake/.
Accessed October 4, 2017.

X

130 *The Court of Appeals disagrees:* Associated Press, "Supreme Court
Won't Hear Appeal of Financial Newsletter Prosecution on Securities Fraud." Fox News, http://www.foxnews.com/us/2010/06/28
/supreme-court-wont-hear-appeal-finacial-newsletter-prosecution
-securities.html. Accessed October 21, 2014.

131 *various amicus briefs: Brief Amici Curiae of the Reporters Committee for Freedom of the Press and Media Organizations in Support
of Petitioners* (U.S., April 29, 2010), Pirate Investor LLC v. United
States SEC; *Brief of Society of Professional Journalists as Amicus
Curiae in Support of Petitioners* (U.S., April 29, 2010), Pirate Investor LLC v. United States Securities and Exchange Commission;
Brief of Investorplace Media, LLC; ALM Media, LLC; CNBC,

Inc.; The E.W. Scripps Company; Eagle Publishing, Inc.; The Financial Publishers Association; Forbes LLC; Gannett Company, Inc.; The Hearst Corporation; Landmark Media Enterprises, LLC; Lee Ent erprises, Inc.; The McClatchy Company; Media General, Inc.; The New York Times Company; The Newspaper Association of America; and WP Company LLC as Amici Curiae in Support of Petitioners (U.S., April 29, 2010), Pirate Investor LLC v. United States Securities and Exchange Commission. All documents accessed at https://stansberrysecfraud.com/legal-documents/index .html, December 23, 2017.

131   *"The Right to Be Wrong":* "The Right to Be Wrong," Editorial, *New York Times,* July 3, 2010.

131   *But the Fourth Circuit:* All legal documents in the case are archived at http://stansberrysecfraud.com/legal-documents/index.html. Accessed October 12, 2016.

136   *the SEC's own website:* See https://www.sec.gov/litigation/complaints /comp18090.htm.

142   *Whatever pseudonym he chooses:* September 10, 2012, http:// politicalandsciencerhymes.blogspot.com/2012/09/marketsmobs -and-messiahsny-times.html. Accessed June 18, 2016.

143   *"Truth is not always in a well":* Edgar Allan Poe, "The Murders in the Rue Morgue," in J. Gerald Kennedy, ed., *The Portable Edgar Allan Poe* (New York: Penguin, 2006), p. 260.

147   *On April 27, 1996:* "His death was ruled an accident—a stroke or a heart attack—but I think he was done. He didn't have a lot left to live for. And he never wanted to grow old. He always refused the "senior discount." Carl Colby, quoted in Maureen Orth, "The Man Nobody Knew," *Vanity Fair,* September 2011. See also Zalin Grant, "William E. Colby: A Highly Suspicious Death," *Zalin Grant's War Tales,* http://www.pythiapress.com/wartales/colby.htm. Accessed April 5, 2017.

147   *Mrs. Ann Rieman Duval:* "Mrs. H. Rieman Duval Dead," *Brooklyn Daily Eagle,* February 18, 1914. See also "Mrs. Duval Is Mourned: Sister of Douglas H. Thomas Died at Belvedere," *Baltimore Sun,* February 19, 1914.

XI

156   *Aleister Crowley in the Hotel Café Royale:* Fiona Ross, *Dining
       with the Famous and Infamous* (Lanham, MD: Rowman and Little-
       field, 2016), p. 216.

156   *"My annual investment goal":* Porter Stansberry, "How I'm Invest-
       ing This Year," *The Crux,* January 2, 2015, http://thecrux.com/porter
       -stansberry-how-im-investing-in-2015/. Accessed July 16, 2016.

156   *"a successful businessman":* Mark Ford, "This Man Went from
       $100,000 in Debt to a $50 Million Net Worth. Here's How He Did
       It," *The Crux,* August 21, 2014, http://thecrux.com/this-is-one-of-the
       -biggest-wealth-building-myths-in-the-world/. Accessed July 16, 2015.

156   *Stansberry Analyst Brian Hunt:* Brian Hunt, "A HUGE Bull
       Market Is Starting Here. Are You on Board?" *Stansberry Digest,*
       April 10, 2015, http://thecrux.com/must-read-the-greatest-deal-in
       -all-of-financial-research/. Accessed July 16, 2016.

156   *"normally, someone like Steve":* Ibid.

157   *The BBB lists:* See http://www.bbb.org/greater-maryland/business
       -reviews/publishers-periodical/stansberry-and-associates-investment
       -research-in-baltimore-md-18012257/complaints. Accessed Octo-
       ber 15, 2016, at which time all the complaints had been resolved.

159   *"Good old bait and switch":* See http://www.bbb.org/greater
       -maryland/business-reviews/publishers-periodical/stansberry-and
       -associates-investment-research-in-baltimore-md-18012257
       /complaints, complaint of September 24, 2015. Accessed Octo-
       ber 15, 2016.

163   *"to the mouse":* J.B.S. Haldane, "On Being the Right Size" (1928),
       https://irl.cs.ucla.edu/papers/right-size.html. Accessed December 18,
       2016.

XII

169   *even under the beds themselves:* See David Mikkelson, "The
       Bawdy Under the Bed," http://www.snopes.com/horrors/gruesome
       /bodybed.asp. Accessed December 28, 2016.

169   *"A feet-first jump":* Email from Rod Cross, April 29, 2017.

169   *"the two-hand push":* K.-P. Shaw and S. Y. Hsu, "Horizontal Dis-
       tance and Height Determining Falling Pattern," *Journal of Foren-
       sic Science,* vol. 43, no. 4 (1998), pp. 765–71.

169   *"an initial velocity"*: Ibid., p. 765.

172   *Out of the 966 "undetermined" deaths:* 2006 Annual Report of the Chief Medical Officer of the State of Maryland. See http://dhmh.maryland.gov/ocme/docs/2006AnnualReport.pdf.

172   *High-profile murders are solved:* See Jess Bidgood, "The Numbers Behind Baltimore's Record Year in Homicides," *New York Times*, January 15, 2016.

173   *"Rey was a very inquisitive man":* Indexed at https://webindexnet.wordpress.com/2009/11/10/rey-rivera/. Accessed July 9, 2016. Many of the conspiracy theories and connections to Agora are contained on this site.

174   *for those who enjoy conspiracy theories:* See http://www.occurrences foreigndomestic.com/wp-content/uploads/2015/09/Madsen-on -911-put-options-2015.pdf for the 9/11 theory; http://www.avaresearch .com/articles/1877/Another-Charlatan-From-Faux-Hero-Syndicate -Joins-Porter-Stansberrys-Boiler-Room—.html for Wall Street; and http://theinfounderground.com/smf/index.php?topic=7962.0 for the CIA, the Rothschilds, George Soros, and the Triads. For Lumumba's murder, see https://www.indymedia.org.uk/en/2008/11/412470.html.

174   *The case went to the Court of Appeals:* See http://mdcourts.gov /opinions/coa/2005/128a03.pdf.

179   *"Remember that onlookers":* Serafettin Demirci and Kamil Hakan Dogan, "Death Scene Investigation from the Viewpoint of Forensic Medicine Expert," in Duarte Nuno Vieira, ed., *Forensic Medicine— From Old Problems to New Challenges,* Intech, September 12, 2011, http://www.intechopen.com/books/forensic-medicine-from-old -problems-to-new-challenges/death-scene-investigation-from-the -viewpoint-of-forensic-medicine-expert. Accessed July 22, 2016.

179   *"It has been my experience":* Vernon J. Geberth, *Practical Homicide Investigation*, 4th edition (CRC Press, 2006). See http://www .practicalhomicide.com/Research/7mistakes.htm. Accessed October 27, 2016.

182   *"Up to this time":* E. V. Frederick, "Bichloride of Mercury Poisoning by Vaginal Application," *Canadian Medical Association Journal,* vol. 10, no. 8 (August 1920), p. 751.

182   *Death of Mrs. Winifred Tredwell:* "Dies at Baltimore," *Cincinnati Enquirer*, April 25, 1921, p. 14, and "Woman Kills Herself with Poison Tablets," *Baltimore Sun*, April 28, 1921, p. 18.

186   *"gay young friskers"*: Robert Browning, "The Pied Piper of Hamelin" (1842), ll. 113–15. Of course, the fate of the rats of Hamelin is also death, but death in a kinder style.

XIII

191   *"When we want to"*: George Bernard Shaw, *Three Plays for Puritans* (New York: Brentano's, 1906), p. xxvii.

194   *"Judging by appearances"*: Details taken from "Wife Slayer Is Better," *Baltimore Sun*, October 30, 1918.

195   *At the trial*: "Webster Hereditary Lunatic, Say Witnesses," *Washington (D.C.) Times,* March 29, 1919.

199   *Suite Ultralounge*: "'Bottle Club' at Center of Violence at Belvedere," *Baltimore Sun*, October 14, 2008, http://articles.baltimoresun.com/2008-10-14/news/0810130089_1_belvedere-bottle-club-paik.

201   *"a drifter from the city's south side"*: "Baltimore Drifter Pleads Guilty to Murder of Deputy Prosecutor," *Washington Post,* October 5, 1982.

201   *"fond of enigmas"*: Edgar Allan Poe, "The Murders in the Rue Morgue," in J. Gerald Kennedy, ed., *The Portable Edgar Allan Poe* (New York: Penguin, 2006), p. 232.

204   *Jayne Miller's WBAL-TV 11 news clip*: See http://www.wbaltv.com/article/suicide-or-murder-evidence-reviewed/7054411. The transcript is still on the site (as of December 25, 2017); the video has been removed, but can be seen here: http://invanddis.proboards.com/thread/5923. Accessed December 21, 2016.

XIV

211   *There are degrees of intention*: See Richard Reichbart, "Western Law and Parapsychology," *Parapsychological Review,* vol. 12, no. 2 (March–April 1981), pp. 9–11.

211   *An article in* Forensic Science International: M. S. Domènech, H. M. Alcázar, A. A. Pallarès, I. G. Vicente, J. C. García, C. V. Gutiérrez, and J. M. Muñiz, "The Murderer Is the Bed: An Unusual Case of Death by Traumatic Asphyxia in a Hotel Folding Bunk Bed," *Forensic Science International,* vol. 220, (July 2012), pp. 1–3. Accessed July 28, 2016.

212   *a sewer worker was overtaken by fumes:* N. Barbera, A. Montana, F. Indorato, N. Arbouche, and G. Romano, "Domino Effect: An Unusual Case of Six Fatal Hydrogen Sulfide Poisonings in Quick Succession," *Forensic Science International,* vol. 260, published online January 29, 2016, e7–e10.

212   *"death may come on":* L. Oesterhelweg and K. Püschel, "'Death May Come On Like a Stroke of Lightning'": Phenomenological and Morphological Aspects of Fatalities Caused by Manure Gas," *International Journal of Legal Medicine,* vol. 122, (March 2008), pp. 101–7.

215   *"the jump speed is almost the same":* For those interested in a more detailed analysis: according to Professor Cross (email, October 19, 2016), the time T to fall through a height H is given by T = square root of (2H/g), where T is measured in seconds, H in meters, and g = acceleration due to gravity = 9.8 m/sec^2 (assuming the fall was straight down from rest or from a horizontal jump— that is, Rivera was not already moving up or down at the top). During that time, Rivera was moving horizontally at speed V if he jumped outward at speed V. The horizontal distance traveled before landing is therefore X = VT. From the top of the Belvedere, H = 36 m, X = 13 m, so T = 2.71 seconds and V = 4.80 m/sec. From top of the Belvedere parking lot, H = 6.93 m, and X = 5.89 m, so T = 1.189 seconds and V = 4.95 m/sec.

217   *I have read numerous articles:* See, for example, T. C. Atanasijevic, S. N. Savic, S. D. Nikolic, and V. M. Djoki, "Frequency and Severity of Injuries in Correlation with the Height of Fall," *Journal of Forensic Science,* vol. 50, no. 3 (May 2005), pp. 608–12; G. Lau, P. L. Ooi, and B. Phoon, "Fatal Falls from a Height: The Use of Mathematical Models to Estimate the Height of Fall from the Injuries Sustained," *Forensic Science International,* vol. 93, no. 1 (April 22, 1998), pp. 33–44.

217   *One such study conducted in Denmark:* Pete Kines, "Construction Workers' Falls Through Roofs: Fatal Versus Serious Injuries," *Journal of Safety Research,* February 2002, p. 10.

219   *At the time of his death:* "Norfolk Man Found Dead in Baltimore," *Washington Post,* February 3, 1929, p. M18.

227   *"The bourgeois interior":* Walter Benjamin, "Reflections and Aphorisms," *Commentary,* vol. 65, no. 6 (June 1978), p. 59.

230   *"And because our reason":* Edgar Allan Poe, "The Imp of the Perverse," in J. Gerald Kennedy, ed., *The Portable Edgar Allan Poe* (New York: Penguin, 2006), p. 74.

XV

243   *It is true that Rivera:* See, for example, J. I. Escobar, E. T. Randolph, and M. Hill, "Symptoms of Schizophrenia in Hispanic and Anglo Veterans," *Culture, Medicine, and Psychiatry,* vol. 10, no. 3 (September 1986), pp. 259–76.

248   *"[They] refused to pay":* http://www.physics.usyd.edu.au/~cross/FORENSIC-PHYSICS/SanJose.htm.

XVI

252   *Hamilton's close friend and neighbor:* These are kept track of at http://chamspage.blogspot.com/2012/01/baltimore-harbor-floaters-baltimore.html. Accessed December 25, 2016.

Illustration Credits

Illustrations on pp. 39, 63, and 127, by Caroline Harwood.

Photographs on pp. 2, 7, 86, 104, 158, 228, and 229, courtesy of Allison Rivera.

Photograph on p. 17, Library of Congress, Prints and Photographs Division, LC-B2-2488-12.

Photograph on p. 112, Library of Congress, Prints and Photographs Division, LC-D4-19121-12.

Photographs on pp. 16, 19, 57, 144, and 149 courtesy of the Maryland Historical Society, photographers unknown.

Photograph on p. 33 © WBAL-TV Channel 11 News, broadcast, May 21, 2007.

Photograph on p. 178 © WhiteMarlinOpen.com, reproduced with permission.

Photograph on p. 193 © *Washington Times*. It appeared on October 29, 1918.

Image on p. 220 © *St. Louis Post-Dispatch*. It appeared on February 2, 1929.

Image on p. 221 © *Who's Who in Delaware County*, ed. John T. Donahue (Chester, PA: Press of Chester Times, 1925).

Photographs on pp. 66, 207, and 216 taken by the author.

Photograph on p. 116 © MLS listings, photographer unknown.

Image on p. 251, photographer unknown.

Acknowledgments

I am grateful to all my interview subjects and correspondents, both anonymous and pseudonymous, and I owe an extra thanks to those people who were prepared to speak to me on the record: Megan Raney Aarons, Cynthia Alcala, Carlos, Jack Horton, Freddie Howard, Stephen Janis, Steven King, Lisa O'Reilly, Maria Rivera, and especially Allison Rivera. Thanks also to Beverly Bambury, John Barry, Rod Cross, Caroline Harwood, Paul Jaskunas, Oliver Munday, Saul Myers, Dereck Mangus, Ruth Toulson, Eglute Trinkauskaite, and Charles Tumosa. Thanks to the team at Henry Holt: Serena Jones, Madeline Jones, Kenn Russell, and Declan Taintor, and thanks to David Sterritt, for everything.